CONSUMER GUIDE®

NEW CAR PRICE GUIDE

CONTENTS

INTRODUCTION

The 1994 edition of the *New Car Price Guide* contains the latest prices and specifications for more than 150 passenger cars, minivans, and sport-utility vehicles. To save space, similar vehicles have been combined into a single entry with one specifications chart, such as Ford Taurus/Mercury Sable. There are separate price lists for each model, except where the same vehicle is sold at identical prices under different brand names.

In most cases, the editors were able to provide dealer invoice prices and our estimated fair prices. In some cases, only the suggested retail prices were available. In all cases, the prices are subject to change by the manufacturers.

The invoice prices in this issue are what the dealer pays to buy the car from the factory. On domestic cars, the invoice price includes the cost of preparing the car for delivery. Import dealers may have to pay an additional preparation or handling fee not included in the invoice. The invoice prices do not include advertising fees charged to dealers (see below).

Cash rebates and dealer incentives are not included because they change so frequently.

The fair price listed for most vehicles is an estimate of what you should expect to pay for a particular model based on national market conditions. The actual selling price for any vehicle depends on market conditions for that car in a particular area.

Supply, demand, and competition determine the selling price, so the fair price should be used only as a guide. Market conditions vary greatly for different cars in different parts of the country. You will have to determine the best price in your area by shopping for the same car at two or more dealers.

Many dealers tell our readers that the prices we publish are incorrect. This often is an attempt by dealers to regain the upper hand in price negotiations. If they can eliminate dealer-invoice price from consideration, then they're back in the driver's seat on price.

If a dealer claims that our prices are incorrect or the information in this issue doesn't match what you see in showrooms, then contact us and we'll do our best to help you out.

The address is listed below.

Destination Charges

The destination charge—the cost of shipping the car to the dealer—is not included in the base prices of the cars unless noted otherwise. This charge must be added to the total price of the car and optional equipment. Dealers do not receive a discount on the destination charge. If the manufacturer's price sticker lists a $500 destination charge, that is what the dealer had to pay—and you will, too.

Advertising Fees

Most dealers try to charge consumers for their advertising costs, claiming they are assessed an advertising fee by the manufacturer or a regional dealer association. Advertising fees are usually expressed by dealers as a flat amount, such as $200. However, most car companies base advertising fees on a percentage of invoice price (usually one percent), which would probably not turn out to be a round figure such as $200.

Are these advertising fees legitimate? In some cases they are and in some they aren't. Unfortunately, it's hard to tell.

Not all manufacturers levy an advertising fee on all cars. In some cases, participation is voluntary, not mandatory. In others, dealers get part of the advertising fee back later.

In any event, the purpose of advertising is to bring in customers. Do you know of other businesses that charge their customers an additional fee for advertising costs?

If a salesman agrees to sell you a new car for $15,000 but later adds a $200 advertising fee, he's actually charging you $15,200. Maybe another dealer can beat that price, so you now have a good reason to keep shopping. Maybe another dealer won't charge an advertising fee.

Instead of arguing over individual charges such as advertising fees, we suggest you take the "bottom line" approach. Ask for a final price showing how much you're going to pay for the car you want. That's what really counts, the amount on the bottom line of the sales contract.

Compare that figure to what other dealers are charging for the same car and you'll know who's giving you the best deal.

The editors invite your questions and comments. Address them to:

Consumer Guide®
7373 N. Cicero Ave.
Lincolnwood, IL 60646

Key to Specifications

Dimensions and capacities are supplied by the manufacturers. **Body styles: notchback** = coupe or sedan with a separate trunk; **hatchback** = coupe or sedan with a rear liftgate. **Wheelbase** = distance between the front and rear wheels. **Curb weight** = weight of base models, not including optional equipment. **Engines: ohv** = overhead valve; **ohc** = overhead camshaft; **dohc** = dual overhead camshafts; **I** = inline cylinders; **V** = cylinders in V configuration; **flat** = horizontally opposed cylinders; **rpm** = revolutions per minute. **S** = standard; **O** = optional; **NA** = not available; **NC** = no charge.

ACURA INTEGRA

Acura Integra GS-R 3-door

Specifications	3-door hatchback	4-door notchback
Wheelbase, in.	101.2	103.1
Overall length, in.	172.4	178.1
Overall width, in.	67.3	67.3
Overall height, in.	52.6	53.9
Curb weight, lbs.	2529	2628
Cargo vol., cu. ft.	13.3	11.0
Fuel capacity, gals.	13.2	13.2
Seating capacity	4	5
Front head room, in.	38.6	38.9
Max. front leg room, in.	42.7	42.2
Rear head room, in.	35.0	36.0
Min. rear leg room, in.	28.1	32.7

Powertrain layout: transverse front engine/front-wheel drive.

Engines	dohc I-4	dohc I-4
Size, liters/cu. in.	1.8/112	1.8/109
Horsepower @ rpm	142 @ 6300	170 @ 7600
Torque (lbs./ft.) @ rpm	127 @ 5200	128 @ 6200

	dohc I-4	dohc I-4
Availability	S	S[1]
EPA city/highway mpg		
5-speed OD manual	25/31	25/31
4-speed OD automatic	24/31	

1. GS-R.

Built in Japan.

PRICES

Acura Integra	Retail Price	Dealer Invoice	Fair Price
RS 3-door hatchback, 5-speed	$14820	$12723	$14320
RS 3-door hatchback, automatic	15570	13367	15070
LS 3-door hatchback, 5-speed	17450	14981	16950
LS 3-door hatchback, automatic	18200	15625	17700
GS-R 3-door hatchback, 5-speed	19650	16870	19150
RS 4-door notchback, 5-speed	15580	13375	15080
RS 4-door notchback, automatic	16330	14019	15830
LS 4-door notchback, 5-speed	17450	14981	16950
LS 4-door notchback, automatic	18200	15626	17700
GS-R 4-door notchback, 5-speed	19980	17153	19480
Destination charge	365	365	365

Standard Equipment

RS: 1.8-liter DOHC 4-cylinder engine, 5-speed manual or 4-speed automatic transmission, 4-wheel disc brakes, driver- and passenger-side air bags, variable-assist power steering, cloth reclining front bucket seats with driver-side lumbar support adjustment, center console with armrest, 50/50 split folding rear seat (hatchback), one-piece folding rear seat (notchback), power windows and mirrors, power door locks (notchbacks), AM/FM cassette player with four speakers, power antenna, tinted glass, remote fuel door and decklid/hatch releases, fog lamps, rear defogger, rear wiper/washer (hatchback), tachometer, coolant temperature gauge, tilt steering column, intermittent wipers, door pockets, cargo cover (hatchback), 195/60HR14 tires. **LS** adds: anti-lock brakes, air conditioning, power door locks, power moonroof (hatchback), cruise control, map lights (hatchback), 195/60HR14 all-season tires. **GS-R** adds: 1.8-liter DOHC VTEC engine, rear spoiler, AM/FM cassette with six speakers, power moonroof, 195/55VR15 all-season tires, alloy wheels.

Options are available as dealer-installed accessories.

ACURA LEGEND

Acura Legend Sedan GS

Specifications

Specifications	2-door notchback	4-door notchback
Wheelbase, in.	111.4	114.6
Overall length, in.	192.5	194.9
Overall width, in.	71.3	71.3
Overall height, in.	53.5	55.1
Curb weight, lbs.	3516	3516
Cargo vol., cu. ft.	14.1	14.8
Fuel capacity, gals.	18.0	18.0
Seating capacity	5	5
Front head room, in.	37.3	38.5
Max. front leg room, in.	42.9	42.7
Rear head room, in.	35.9	36.5
Min. rear leg room, in.	28.7	33.5

Powertrain layout: longitudinal front engine/front-wheel drive.

Engines

Engines	ohc V-6	ohc V-6
Size, liters/cu. in.	3.2/196	3.2/196
Horsepower @ rpm	200 @ 5500	230 @ 6200
Torque (lbs./ft.) @ rpm	210 @ 4500	206@ 5000
Availability	S[1]	S[2]

EPA city/highway mpg	ohc V-6	ohc V-6
5-speed OD manual	18/25	
6-speed OD manual		18/26
4-speed OD automatic	19/24	18/23

1. L, LS sedans. 2. Coupes, GS sedan.

Built in Japan.

PRICES

Acura Legend	Retail Price	Dealer Invoice	Fair Price
L 4-door notchback, 5-speed	$33800	$28335	$31096
L 4-door notchback, automatic	34600	29005	31832
L 4-door w/leather interior, 5-speed	35300	29592	32476
L 4-door w/leather interior, automatic	36100	30263	33212
LS 4-door notchback, automatic	38600	32358	35512
GS 4-door notchback, 6-speed	40700	34119	37444
GS 4-door notchback, automatic	40700	34119	37444
L 2-door coupe, 6-speed	37700	31604	34684
L 2-door coupe, automatic	37700	31604	34684
LS 2-door coupe, 6-speed	41500	34789	38180
LS 2-door coupe, automatic	41500	34789	38180
Destination charge	385	385	385

Standard Equipment:

L: 3.2-liter V-6, 5-speed manual or 4-speed automatic transmission, anti-lock 4-wheel disc brakes, driver- and passenger-side air bags, variable-assist power steering, air conditioning, front bucket seats, 8-way power driver's seat, 4-way power passenger seat, power windows and locks, cruise control, power/tilt telescopic steering column, steering wheel memory system, power moonroof with sunshade, tinted glass, heated power mirrors, Acura/Bose music system, steering wheel mounted radio controls, theft-deterrent system, intermittent wipers, bodyside moldings, rear defogger, remote fuel door and decklid releases, lighted visor mirrors, front door pockets, center console with armrest, digital clock, 205/60VR15 tires, alloy wheels. **L Coupe** adds: 6-speed manual transmission, leather upholstery, leather-wrapped steering wheel, rear headrests. **LS** adds: leather upholstery and leather-wrapped steering wheel (sedan), walnut interior trim, heated front seats, automatic climate control, AM/FM cassette with diversity antenna and anti-theft feature, illuminated entry system. **LS Coupe** adds: traction control, 215/55VR16 tires. **GS** adds to LS sedan: 6-speed manual or 4-speed automatic transmission, traction control, sport suspension, body-color grille, 215/55VR16 tires.

Options are available as dealer-installed accessories.

Prices are accurate at time of publication; subject to manufacturer's change.

ACURA VIGOR

Acura Vigor GS

Specifications

Specifications	4-door notchback
Wheelbase, in.	110.4
Overall length, in.	190.4
Overall width, in.	70.1
Overall height, in.	53.9
Curb weight, lbs.	3150
Cargo vol., cu. ft.	14.2
Fuel capacity, gals.	17.2
Seating capacity	5
Front head room, in.	38.8
Max. front leg room, in.	43.7
Rear head room, in.	36.2
Min. rear leg room, in.	30.3

Powertrain layout: longitudinal front engine/front-wheel drive.

Engines

Engines	ohc I-5
Size, liters/cu. in.	2.5/152
Horsepower @ rpm	176 @ 6300
Torque (lbs./ft.) @ rpm	170 @ 3900

	ohc I-5
Availability	S
EPA city/highway mpg	
5-speed OD manual	20/27
4-speed OD automatic	20/26

Built in Japan.

PRICES

Acura Vigor	Retail Price	Dealer Invoice	Fair Price
LS 4-door notchback, 5-speed	$26350	$22355	$23155
LS 4-door notchback, automatic	27100	22992	23792
GS 4-door notchback, 5-speed	28350	24052	24852
GS 4-door notchback, automatic	29100	24688	25488
Destination charge	385	385	385

Standard Equipment:

LS: 2.5-liter 5-cylinder engine, 5-speed manual or 4-speed automatic transmission, anti-lock 4-wheel disc brakes, power steering, driver- and passenger-side air bags, air conditioning, tinted glass, power windows, door locks and mirrors, cruise control, theft-deterrent system, leather-wrapped steering wheel, lighted visor mirror, rear reading lights, fog lamps, remote fuel and decklid releases, variable intermittent wipers, tachometer, digital clock, cloth upholstery, tilt steering column, rear window defogger, 8-speaker AM/FM cassette, power antenna, alloy wheels, 205/60HR15 all-season tires. **GS** adds: leather upholstery, CD player, power moonroof, rear map pockets, 4-way power driver's seat.

Options are available as dealer-installed accessories.

AUDI 90/CABRIOLET

Specifications	4-door notchback	2-door conv.
Wheelbase, in.	102.8	100.6
Overall length, in.	180.3	176.0
Overall width, in.	66.7	67.6
Overall height, in.	54.3	54.3
Curb weight, lbs.	3197	3494

Audi Cabriolet

	4-door notchback	2-door conv.
Cargo vol., cu. ft.	14.0	6.6
Fuel capacity, gals.	17.4	17.4
Seating capacity	5	4
Front head room, in.	37.8	38.3
Max. front leg room, in.	42.2	40.7
Rear head room, in.	37.2	36.4
Min. rear leg room, in.	32.5	26.5

Powertrain layout: longitudinal front engine/front- or permanent 4WD.

Engines

	ohc V-6
Size, liters/cu. in.	2.8/169
Horsepower @ rpm	172 @ 5500
Torque (lbs./ft.) @ rpm	184 @ 3000
Availability	S

EPA city/highway mpg

5-speed OD manual	20/26
4-speed OD automatic	18/26

Built in Germany.

PRICES

Audi 90	Retail Price	Dealer Invoice	Fair Price
S 4-door notchback	$27820	—	—
CS 4-door notchback	30770	—	—
CS Quattro Sport 4-door notchback	34420	29158	29958
Destination charge	445	445	445

S and CS dealer invoice and fair price not available at time of publication.

Standard Equipment:

S: 2.8-liter V-6 engine, 5-speed manual transmission, driver- and passenger-side air bags, anti-lock 4-wheel disc brakes, air conditioning, power steering, leather-wrapped steering wheel, AM/FM cassette, dual diversity antenna, reclining front seats with height adjustment, split folding rear seat, velour upholstery, power windows and door locks, cruise control, tinted glass, headlight washers, retained accessory power, alarm system, front fog lamps, rear fog lamp, rear window defroster, front and rear fold-down armrests, digital clock, center console, remote trunk and fuel door releases, heated power mirrors, front seatback map pockets, bodyside moldings, intermittent wipers, tachometer, carpeted floor mats, 195/65HR15 all-season tires, 10-spoke alloy wheels. **CS** adds: automatic climate control, wood trim, remote locking system, power sunroof, 8-way power driver's seat, leather upholstery. **CS Quattro Sport** adds: all-wheel drive, sport bucket seats, rear spoiler, sport suspension, 205/60VR15 performance tires, 5-spoke alloy wheels.

Optional Equipment:

	Retail Price	Dealer Invoice	Fair Price
4-speed automatic transmission (NA Quattro)	800	750	770
All-Weather Package, S	430	344	387
CS, CS Quattro	330	264	297
Includes heated front door locks (S), heated front seats, heated windshield washer nozzles.			
Pearlescent paint	510	408	459
Power sunroof, S	930	744	837
Expandable ski/storage sack, CS Quattro	155	124	140

Audi Cabriolet	Retail Price	Dealer Invoice	Fair Price
2-door convertible	$38950	$33041	—
Destination charge	445	445	445

Prices are accurate at time of publication; subject to manufacturer's change.

AUDI

Fair price not available at time of publication.

Standard Equipment:

2.8-liter V-6 engine, 4-speed automatic transmission, anti-lock 4-wheel disc brakes, driver- and passenger-side air bags, air conditioning, cruise control, intermittent wipers, reclining front seats with height adjustment, leather upholstery, power windows, mirrors and door locks, anti-theft system, rear defogger, AM/FM cassettte, digital clock, power antenna, headlight washers, front fog lights, rear fog light, leather-wrapped steering wheel, tachometer, coolant temperature gauge, trip odometer, lighted visor mirrors, power top and boot system, front and rear floormats, 195/65HR15 all-season tires, 5-spoke alloy wheels.

Optional Equipment:	Retail Price	Dealer Invoice	Fair Price
All Weather Pkg.	$430	$344	—
Heated front seats, door locks and windshield washer nozzles.			
Windscreen	370	296	—
Pearlescent paint	510	408	—

AUDI 100

Audi 100 S

Specifications	4-door notchback	5-door wagon
Wheelbase, in.	105.8	105.8
Overall length, in.	192.6	192.6

	4-door notchback	5-door wagon
Overall width, in.	70.0	70.0
Overall height, in.	56.3	56.3
Curb weight, lbs.	3363	3628
Cargo vol., cu. ft.	16.8	65.5
Fuel capacity, gals.	21.1	21.1
Seating capacity	5	7
Front head room, in.	38.3	38.4
Max. front leg room, in.	42.2	42.4
Rear head room, in.	37.6	39.1
Min. rear leg room, in.	34.8	34.2

Powertrain layout: longitudinal front engine/front- or permanent 4WD.

Engines	ohc V-6	Turbo dohc I-5
Size, liters/cu. in.	2.8/169	2.2/136
Horsepower @ rpm	172 @ 5500	227 @ 5900
Torque (lbs./ft.) @ rpm	184 @ 3000	258 @ 1950
Availability	S	S[1]
EPA city/highway mpg		
5-speed OD manual	19/24	18/23
4-speed OD automatic	18/24	

1. S4

Built in Germany.

PRICES

Audi 100	Retail Price	Dealer Invoice	Fair Price
S 4-door notchback	$35120	—	—
S 5-door wagon	38070	31929	32729
CS 4-door notchback	40570	—	—
CS Quattro 4-door notchback	43020	35952	36752
CS Quattro 5-door wagon	47020	39358	40158
S4 4-door notchback	49070	40973	41773
Destination charge	450	450	450

Some dealer invoice and fair prices not available at time of publication.

Standard Equipment:

S: 2.8-liter V-6 engine, 5-speed manual transmission (notchback), 4-

speed automatic transmission (wagon), anti-lock 4-wheel disc brakes, driver- and passenger-side air bags, speed-sensitive power steering, driver- and passenger-side air bags, tilt and telescoping steering column, velour reclining front bucket seats with height and lumbar adjustments, 8-way power driver's seat, 60/40 split folding seat (wagon), 2-place rear seat (wagon), front folding armrest, rear folding armrests with ski-sack (notchback), center storage console with cup holders, air conditioning, tachometer, oil temperature and pressure gauges, voltmeter, coolant temperature gauge, trip odometer, Active Auto Check System, power windows and door locks, cruise control, heated power mirrors, power sunroof, remote decklid release (notchback), AM/FM cassette with diversity antenna, wood trim, seatback pockets, leather-wrapped steering wheel, reading lamps, lighted visor mirrors, anti-theft alarm, tinted glass, rear defogger, rear wiper/washer (wagon), intermittent wipers, analog clock, rear fog light, retractable rear window sunshade (wagon), roof rails (wagon), cargo area cover (wagon), floormats, 195/65HR15 all-season tires, 10-spoke alloy wheels. **CS** adds: 4-speed automatic transmission, front fog lights, leather upholstery, power passenger seat, 4-position memory driver's seat, power memory mirrors, automatic climate control, remote illuminated entry system with automatic driver's seat and mirror adjustment, power glass moonroof, Bose music system. **Quattro sedan** has 5-speed manual transmission and adds: permanently-engaged 4-wheel drive, 5-spoke alloy wheels. **Quattro wagon** adds: 4-speed automatic transmission, heated front seats, retractable headlight washers, roof rack. **S4** adds to Quattro sedan: 2.2-liter turbocharged 5-cylinder engine, engine oil cooler, voice-activated cellular telephone, heated front and rear seats, fender flares, 225/50ZR16 performance tires.

Optional Equipment:

	Retail Price	Dealer Invoice	Fair Price
4-speed automatic transmission (std. wagon and CS)	$800	$750	$770
Leather seats, S	1420	1179	1278
Pearlescent metallic paint	510	408	459
All-Weather Pkg., S	480	384	432
CS, CS Quattro (std. CS Quattro wagon)	380	304	342
Heated front seats and windshield washer nozzles, heated front door locks (S), headlight washers.			
Cellular telephone, S, CS and CS Quattro	990	792	891
10-disc CD changer	790	632	711
Requires Bose music system.			
Bose music system, S	600	480	540
All-weather 215/60VR15 tires, S4	NC	NC	NC

BMW 3-SERIES

BMW 318is

Specifications	2-door notchback	4-door notchback	2-door conv.
Wheelbase, in.	106.3	106.3	106.3
Overall length, in.	174.5	174.5	174.5
Overall width, in.	67.3	66.8	67.3
Overall height, in.	53.8	54.8	53.1
Curb weight, lbs.	2866	2866	3352
Cargo vol., cu. ft.	14.3	15.4	9.0
Fuel capacity, gals.	17.2	17.2	17.2
Seating capacity	5	5	4
Front head room, in.	36.7	37.8	38.1
Max. front leg room, in.	41.2	40.9	41.2
Rear head room, in.	35.9	37.3	36.3
Min. rear leg room, in.	32.7	34.1	28.1

Powertrain layout: longitudinal front engine/rear-wheel drive.

Engines	dohc I-4	dohc I-6
Size, liters/cu. in.	1.8/110	2.5/152
Horsepower @ rpm	138 @ 6000	189 @ 5900
Torque (lbs./ft.) @ rpm	129 @ 4500	181 @ 4200
Availability	S[1]	S[2]

Prices are accurate at time of publication; subject to manufacturer's change.

BMW

EPA city/highway mpg	dohc I-4	dohc I-6
5-speed manual	22/30	19/28
4-speed OD automatic	22/30	20/28

1. 318 models. 2. 325 models.

Built in Germany.

PRICES

BMW 3-Series	Retail Price	Dealer Invoice	Fair Price
318i 4-door notchback	$24675	$20680	$22948
318is 2-door notchback	25800	21625	23994
318iC 2-door convertible	29900	—	—
325i 4-door notchback	30850	25855	28691
325is 2-door notchback	32200	26985	29946
325iC 2-door convertible	38800	32520	36084
M3 2-door notchback	35800	—	—
Destination charge	450	450	450

Standard Equipment:

318i/318is: 1.8-liter DOHC 4-cylinder engine, 5-speed manual transmission, speed-sensitive variable-assist power steering, anti-lock 4-wheel disc brakes, driver- and passenger-side air bags, dual control air conditioning, cloth or leatherette reclining bucket seats with height/tilt adjustments, split folding rear seat (318is), power windows and locks, power mirrors, power sunroof, AM/FM cassette, power diversity antenna, tachometer, trip odometer, digital clock, outside temperature display, tinted glass, intermittent wipers, rear defogger, Service Interval Indicator, Active Check Control system, toolkit, 185/65HR15 tires (318i), 205/60HR15 tires (318is), full-size spare tire. **325 models** add: 2.5-liter DOHC 6-cylinder engine, cruise control, fog lights, 8-way power front seats, premium sound system, 205/60HR15 tires. **325is and 325iC** add: leather upholstery, split folding rear seat (325is).

Optional Equipment:

4-speed automatic transmission	900	740	819
Limited-slip differential	530	430	482
Cruise control, 318i and 318is	695	570	632
Split folding rear seat, 318i and 325i	275	225	250
Leather upholstery, 325i	1150	940	1047
Rollover Protection System, 325iC	1390	1140	1265
All-season traction (ASC+T), 325i, 325is, and 325iC	995	815	905

	Retail Price	Dealer Invoice	Fair Price
Sport Pkg. 1, 325i and 325is	$875	$720	$796
Sport seats, sport suspension, cross-spoke wheels.			
Sport Pkg. 2, 325iC	600	495	546
Sport seats, cross-spoke wheels.			
Heated front seats and heated mirrors	450	370	410
On-board computer, 325i, 325is, and 325iC	430	355	391
Metallic paint	475	390	432

BMW 5-SERIES

BMW 530i

Specifications

	4-door notchback	5-door wagon
Wheelbase, in.	108.7	108.7
Overall length, in.	185.8	185.8
Overall width, in.	68.9	68.9
Overall height, in.	55.6	55.8
Curb weight, lbs.	3484	3760
Cargo vol., cu. ft.	16.2	51.2
Fuel capacity, gals.	21.1	21.1
Seating capacity	5	5
Front head room, in.	38.5	38.5
Max. front leg room, in.	42.0	42.0

	4-door notchback	5-door wagon
Rear head room, in.	37.4	37.7
Min. rear leg room, in.	25.5	34.2

Powertrain layout: longitudinal front engine/rear-wheel drive.

Engines

	dohc I-6	dohc V-8	dohc V-8
Size, liters/cu. in.	2.5/152	3.0/183	4.0/243
Horsepower @ rpm	189 @ 5900	215 @ 5800	282 @ 5800
Torque (lbs./ft.) @ rpm	184 @ 4200	214 @ 4500	295 @ 4500
Availability	S[1]	S[2]	S[3]
EPA city/highway mpg			
5-speed OD manual	19/28	16/23	
4-speed OD automatic	18/25		
5-speed OD automatic		16/25	16/23

1. 525i, 525i Touring. 2. 530i, 530i Touring. 3. 540i.

Built in Germany.

PRICES

BMW 5-Series	Retail Price	Dealer Invoice	Fair Price
525i 4-door notchback	$34900	—	—
525i Touring 5-door wagon	37300	—	—
530i 4-door notchback	40500	33780	38595
530i Touring 5-door wagon	45800	38385	42594
540i 4-door notchback	47500	39805	44175
Destination charge	450	450	450

Standard Equipment:

525i: 2.5-liter DOHC 6-cylinder engine, 5-speed manual transmission, variable-assist power steering, anti-lock 4-wheel disc brakes, driver- and passenger-side air bags, cruise control, air conditioning with dual climate controls, 10-way power front seats, leather-wrapped steering wheel, folding center armrests, anti-theft AM/FM stereo cassette, telescopic steering column, power windows and locks, heated power mirrors, fog lights, tinted glass, tachometer, map lights, intermittent wipers, heated windshield-washer jets, heated driver-side door lock, rear defogger, seatback pockets, trip odometer, power sunroof, Service Interval Indicator, Active Check Control system, fuel economy indicator, lighted visor ger, seatback pockets, trip odometer, power sunroof, Service Interval Indicator, Active Check Control system, fuel economy indicator, lighted visor mirrors, toolkit, 205/60HR15 tires, alloy wheels. **525i Touring** adds: 4-speed automatic transmission, split folding rear seat, cargo area cover, 225/60VR15 tires. **530i** adds to 525i: 3.0-liter DOHC V-8 engine, outside temperature display, 225/60ZR15 tires. **530i Touring** adds to 525i Touring: 3.0-liter DOHC V-8 engine, 5-speed automatic transmission, ASC+T traction control, 225/60ZR15 tires. **540i** adds to 530i: 4.0-liter DOHC V-8 engine, 5-speed automatic transmission, on board computer.

Optional Equipment:	Retail Price	Dealer Invoice	Fair Price
4-speed automatic transmission, 525i	$900	$740	$820
5-speed automatic transmission, 530i	1100	900	1000
ASC+T traction control, 525i and			
525i Touring	995	815	905
530i and 540i	1350	1110	1230
Power sunroof, 530i Touring	1325	1090	1208
Heated front seats	370	305	338
On Board Computer (std. 540i)	430	355	393
Luggage net, Touring	260	215	238

BMW 7-SERIES

BMW 740i

Specifications	4-door notchback	4-door notchback
Wheelbase, in.	111.5	116.0

Prices are accurate at time of publication; subject to manufacturer's change.

	4-door notchback	4-door notchback
Overall length, in.	193.3	197.8
Overall width, in.	72.6	72.6
Overall height, in.	55.6	55.1
Curb weight, lbs.	4002	4090
Cargo vol., cu. ft.	17.6	17.6
Fuel capacity, gals.	21.5	24.0
Seating capacity	5	5
Front head room, in.	38.3	38.3
Max. front leg room, in.	44.3	44.3
Rear head room, in.	37.2	37.2
Min. rear leg room, in.	38.8	42.6

Powertrain layout: longitudinal front engine/rear-wheel drive.

Engines

	dohc V-8	ohc V-12
Size, liters/cu. in.	4.0/243	5.0/304
Horsepower @ rpm	282 @ 5800	296 @ 5200
Torque (lbs./ft.) @ rpm	295 @ 4500	332 @ 4100
Availability	S[1]	S[2]
EPA city/highway mpg		
4-speed OD automatic		12/18
5-speed OD automatic	16/22	

1. 740i, 740iL. 2. 750iL.

Built in Germany.

PRICES

BMW 7-Series	Retail Price	Dealer Invoice	Fair Price
740i 4-door notchback	$55950	$45745	$50745
740iL 4-door notchback	59950	49015	54015
750iL 4-door notchback	83950	68640	73640
Destination charge	450	450	450
Gas Guzzler Tax, 740i, 740iL	1000	1000	1000
750iL	3000	3000	3000

Standard Equipment:

740i/740iL: 4.0-liter DOHC V-8 engine, 5-speed automatic transmission, anti-lock 4-wheel disc brakes, variable-assist power steering, driver- and passenger-side air bags, automatic climate control system with dual controls, 10-way power front seats with driver-side memory system, driver-seat lumbar support adjustment, power tilt/telescopic steering wheel with memory, leather and walnut interior trim, door pockets, power windows and locks, heated power mirrors with 3-position memory, intermittent wipers, heated windshield-washer jets, heated driver-side door lock, cruise control, rear head restraints, rear armrest with storage, automatic dimming mirror, front and rear reading lamps, tinted glass, lighted visor mirrors, Service Interval Indicator, Active Check Control system, on board computer, rear defogger, power sunroof, fog lamps, AM/FM cassette, luggage net, toolkit, 225/60ZR15 tires, alloy wheels, full-size spare tire. **750iL** adds: 5.0-liter V-12 engine, 4-speed automatic transmission, ASC+T traction control, heated front seats, cellular telephone, 6-disc CD changer, power rear sunshade, ski sack.

Optional Equipment:	Retail Price	Dealer Invoice	Fair Price
EDC (Electronic Damping Control)	$1500	$1200	$1395
Heated front seats, 740i, 740iL	370	305	344
Power rear sunshade, 740iL	465	370	432
ASC+T traction control, 740i and 740iL	1350	1110	1256
Ski sack, 740i and 740iL	190	155	177

BUICK LE SABRE/ OLDSMOBILE EIGHTY EIGHT/PONTIAC BONNEVILLE

Specifications	4-door notchback
Wheelbase, in.	110.8
Overall length, in.	199.5
Overall width, in.	74.5
Overall height, in.	55.7
Curb weight, lbs.	3446
Cargo vol., cu. ft.	18.0
Fuel capacity, gals.	18.0
Seating capacity	6

Prices are accurate at time of publication; subject to manufacturer's change.

Buick LeSabre Limited

	4-door notchback
Front head room, in.	39.0
Max. front leg room, in.	43.0
Rear head room, in.	38.3
Min. rear leg room, in.	38.6

Powertrain layout: transverse front engine/front-wheel drive.

Engines	ohv V-6	Supercharged ohv V-6
Size, liters/cu. in.	3.8/231	3.8/231
Horsepower @ rpm	170 @ 4800	225 @ 5000
Torque (lbs./ft.) @ rpm	225 @ 3200	275 @ 3200
Availability	S	O[1]
EPA city/highway mpg		
4-speed OD automatic	19/28	17/25

1. Bonneville SSE.

Built in Flint and Orion, Mich.

PRICES

Buick LeSabre	Retail Price	Dealer Invoice	Fair Price
Custom 4-door notchback	$21080	$18445	$19045

	Retail Price	Dealer Invoice	Fair Price
Custom National Marketing Edition 4-door notchback	$19995	$19063	—
Limited 4-door notchback	24640	21560	22160
Destination charge	575	575	575

National Marketing Edition model's fair price not available at time of publication. National Marketing Edition model includes destination charge and is available with limited optional equipment. Additional "value-priced" models may be available in California.

Standard Equipment:

Custom: 3.8-liter V-6, 4-speed automatic transmission, anti-lock brakes, driver- and passenger-side air bags, power steering, air conditioning, power door locks, power windows with driver-side express down and passenger lockout, AM/FM radio with clock, tilt steering wheel, intermittent wipers, Pass-Key theft-deterrent system, body-color left remote and right manual mirrors, tinted glass, instrument panel courtesy lights, trip odometer, 55/45 cloth seats with armrest, manual front seatback recliners, 205/70R15 all-season tires, wheel covers. **Limited** adds to Custom: variable-assist power steering, cruise control, rear defogger, remote keyless entry, remote decklid release, 6-way power driver's seat, front storage armrest with cup holders, cassette player, power mirrors, power antenna, passenger-side lighted visor mirror, front and rear door courtesy lights, front and rear reading lights, floormats, trunk net, 205/70R15 all-season whitewall tires, alloy wheels.

Optional Equipment:

	Retail Price	Dealer Invoice	Fair Price
Traction control system, Limited	175	151	159
Luxury Pkg. SD, Custom	1106	951	1006
Includes cruise control, rear defogger, cassette player, front seat storage armrest, trunk net, floormats, striping, 205/70R15 all-season whitewall tires, alloy wheels.			
Prestige Pkg. SE, Custom	1852	1593	1685
Pkg. SD plus remote keyless entry system, power mirrors, remote decklid release, 6-way power driver's seat, power antenna, passenger-side lighted visor mirror, door edge guards.			
Prestige Pkg. SE, Limited	670	576	610
Includes 6-way power passenger seat, dual control air conditioning with rear seat climate controls, AM stereo, cornering lamps.			
Gran Touring Pkg., Custom w/Pkg. SE, and Limited	399	343	363
Includes Gran Touring Suspension, 3:06 axle ratio, automatic level control, leather-wrapped steering wheel, 215/60R16 touring tires, alloy wheels.			

	Retail Price	Dealer Invoice	Fair Price
Trailer Towing Pkg., w/o Gran Touring Pkg.	$325	$280	$296
w/Gran Touring Pkg.	150	129	137
Engine and transmission oil coolers, automatic level control.			
Leather/vinyl 55/45 seat, Limited	500	430	455
Gauges and tachometer, Limited	163	140	148
6-way power driver's seat, Custom w/Pkg. SD	305	262	278
Requires Power mirrors.			
Power mirrors, Custom w/Pkg. SD	78	67	71
U1L audio system, Custom w/SE, and Limited w/SD	120	103	109
Includes cassette player, AM stereo, Concert Sound II speakers.			
UM3 audio system, Custom w/Pkg. SE, and Limited	364	313	331
Limited w/Pkg. SE	244	210	222
Includes CD player, AM stereo, Concert Sound II speakers.			
Alloy wheels, Custom	325	280	296
Locking wire wheel covers, Custom w/Pkg. SD/SE, and Limited	NC	NC	NC
205/70R15 whitewall tires, Custom	76	65	69

Oldsmobile Eighty Eight

	Retail Price	Dealer Invoice	Fair Price
4-door notchback	$21120	$18480	$19080
Special Edition 4-door notchback, Pkg. R7B	19995	19121	—
LS 4-door notchback	23220	20918	21518
LS Special Edition 4-door notchback, Pkg. R7C	23295	22273	—
Destination charge	575	575	575

Special Edition fair price not available at time of publication. Special Edition models include destination charge. Additional "value-priced" models may be available in California.

Standard Equipment:

3.8-liter V-6, 4-speed automatic transmission, power steering, driver- and passenger-side air bags, anti-lock brakes, power steering, air conditioning, 55/45 cloth front seat with armrest and reclining seatback, power windows, left remote and right manual mirrors, tinted glass, solar control rear window, rear defogger, intermittent wipers, AM/FM radio, tilt steering wheel, Pass-Key theft-deterrent system, power locks, trip odometer, visor mirrors, 205/70R15 whitewall tires, wheel covers. **Special Edition** adds: Option Pkg. 1SC. **LS** adds to base: cruise control, power mirrors, cassette player, power antenna, power decklid release, front armrest with storage, reading lights, floormats. **LS Special Edition** adds: Option Pkg. 1SB, LSS Pkg., Comfort Pkg., leather seats.

Optional Equipment:	Retail Price	Dealer Invoice	Fair Price
Option Pkg. 1SB, base	$1030	$886	$937
Cruise control, front storage armrest, cassette player, power antenna, floormats, alloy wheels.			
Option Pkg. 1SC, base	1667	1434	1517
Option Pkg. 1SB plus power driver's seat, power mirrors, power decklid release, reading lights, lighted visor mirrors.			
Option Pkg. 1SB, LS	1547	1330	1408
with LSS Pkg., without leather seats	1217	1047	1107
with leather seats, without LSS Pkg.	1497	1287	1362
with LSS Pkg. and leather seats	1167	1004	1062
Dual zone automatic air conditioner, Luxury/Convenience Pkg., Reminder Pkg., steering wheel touch controls, rear storage armrest, overhead console, trunk cargo net, alloy wheels.			
LSS Pkg., LS	845	727	769
Reclining front bucket seats, power driver's seat, center console with floor shifter and storage armrest, full analog gauges, coolant temperature gauge, voltmeter, Driver Information Center, touring suspension, dual auxiliary 12-volt outlets, Reminder Pkg., 225/60R16 tires, alloy wheels. Not available with electronic instrument cluster. Requires Option Pkg. 1SB.			
Remote Accessory Control Pkg., base, Special Edition	225	194	205
Illumination Pkg., programmable power door locks, remote keyless entry system. Base requires Option Pkg. 1SC.			
Luxury/Convenience Pkg., LS	725	624	660
Remote Accessory Control Pkg., programmable power door locks, power driver's seat, lighted visor mirrors, reading lights.			
Comfort Pkg., LS	555	477	505
Power passenger's seat with recliner, cornering lamps, automatic day/night rearview mirror with compass. Requires Option Pkg. 1SB.			
Traction control system	175	151	159
Base requires Option Pkg. 1SC. LS requires Option Pkg. 1SB.			
Power driver's seat, base	350	301	319
Requires Option Pkg. 1SB.			
Leather seats, base, Special Edition	610	525	555
LS	565	486	514
LS with LSS Pkg.	475	409	432
Base requires power driver's seat. LS requires Option Pkg. 1SB.			

Prices are accurate at time of publication; subject to manufacturer's change.

	Retail Price	Dealer Invoice	Fair Price
Striping	$45	$39	$41
Wire wheel covers, base, Special Edition,			
LS with Pkg. 1SB	NC	NC	NC
LS without Pkg. 1SB	316	272	288
Includes 205/70R15 whitewall tires. Base requires Option Pkg. 1SB or 1SC.			
15-inch alloy wheels, LS	330	284	300
205/70R15 whitewall tires	76	65	69
Electronic instrument cluster, LS	345	297	314
Requires Option Pkg. 1SB.			
AM/FM cassette, base	265	228	241
AM/FM cassette and CD	396	341	360
Base requires Option Pkg. 1SB or 1SC.			
Power antenna, base	85	73	77
Engine block heater	18	15	16

Pontiac Bonneville

	Retail Price	Dealer Invoice	Fair Price
SE 4-door notchback sedan	$20424	$17871	$18471
SSE 4-door notchback sedan	25884	22907	23507
Destination charge	575	575	575

Additional "value-priced" models may be available in California.

Standard Equipment:

SE: 3.8-liter V-6, 4-speed automatic transmission, anti-lock brakes, power steering, driver- and passenger-side air bags, air conditioning, cloth 45/55 reclining front seats, front overhead console with reading lights, tilt steering wheel, power windows with driver-side express down, power door locks, AM/FM radio, tinted glass, left remote and right manual mirrors, fog lamps, trip odometer, intermittent wipers, Pass-Key theft-deterrent system, visor mirrors, floormats, 215/65R15 tires, wheel covers. **SSE** adds: variable-assist power steering, rally gauges with tachometer, electronic load leveling suspension, 45/45 cloth bucket seats with center storage console and rear air conditioning vents, overhead console with power outlet, 6-way power driver's seat, rear center armrest with cup holders, rear defogger, heated power mirrors, cruise control, cassette player with equalizer, power antenna, Driver Information Center, remote decklid release, Twilight Sentinel, rear spoiler, accessory emergency road kit (includes spot light, first aid kit, air hose, windshield scraper, gloves), Lamp Group (includes rear courtesy lights, rear assist handles, headlamp-on warning, engine compartment light), lighted visor mirrors, deluxe floormats, 225/60R16 tires, alloy wheels.

Optional Equipment:	Retail Price	Dealer Invoice	Fair Price
Option Group 1SB, SE	$628	$540	$565
Cruise control, rally gauges with tachometer, Lamp Group, illuminated entry, cassette player.			
Option Group 1SC, SE	1281	1102	1153
Group 1SB plus variable-assist steering, 6-way power driver's seat, power mirrors, rear defogger, decklid release.			
Option Group 1SD, SE	1942	1670	1748
Group 1SC plus remote keyless entry system, 45/55 cloth front seat with storage armrest and cup holders, lighted visor mirrors, Twilight Sentinel, leather-wrapped steering wheel, power antenna.			
Sport Luxury Edition (SLE) Pkg. 1SC/H4U, SE	3009	2603	2708
Group 1SC plus 45/45 leather bucket seats with center storage console and rear air conditioning vents, overhead console with power outlet, leather-wrapped steeing wheel and shift knob, power antenna, rear decklid spoiler, monotone side and rocker moldings, 3.06 axle ratio, lighted visor mirrors, trunk net, deluxe floormats, 225/60R16 tires, gold or silver crosslace alloy wheels.			
Sport Luxury Edition (SLE) Pkg. 1SD/H4U, SE	3204	2770	2884
Group 1SD plus SLE Pkg.			
Option Group 1SB, SSE	1440	1238	1296
6-way power seat, head-up display, automatic climate control, remote keyless entry system, automatic day/night rearview mirror, traction control, 8-speaker sound system, fuel door lock.			
Enhancement Group, SE w/Group 1SC	206	177	185
with cloth bucket seats	110	95	99
with leather bucket seats or SLE 1SC/H4U	60	52	54
with Group 1SD	NC	NC	NC
Lighted visor mirrors, leather-wrapped steering wheel, Twilight Sentinel.			
SE Performance and Handling Pkg.	649	558	584
with SLE Pkg.	225	194	203
225/60R16 touring tires, 5-blade alloy wheels.			
SE Monotone Appearance Pkg.	200	172	180
with SLE Pkg.	NC	NC	NC
Monotone bodyside and rocker moldings.			
Rear decklid spoiler, SE	110	95	99
Rear decklid spoiler delete, SE with Sport Edition Pkg. and SSE (credit)	(110)	(95)	(95)

Prices are accurate at time of publication; subject to manufacturer's change.

	Retail Price	Dealer Invoice	Fair Price
SSEi Supercharger Pkg., SSE	$1242	$1068	$1118
with leather bucket seats	1167	1004	1050

Supercharged 3.8-liter engine, boost gauge, driver-selectable shift controls, 2.97 axle ratio, upgraded carpet, SSEi badging and floormats, 225/60ZR16 tires.

	Retail Price	Dealer Invoice	Fair Price
Traction control, SE and SSE	175	151	158
SE with Performance and Handling Pkg.	NC	NC	NC
Rear window defogger, SE	170	146	153
Power glass sunroof, SE	995	856	896
SSE	981	844	883

Requires lighted visor mirrors.

	Retail Price	Dealer Invoice	Fair Price
B20/E6 custom interior, SE	235	202	212

45/55 reclining front bench seat with storage armrest and cup holders, upgraded cloth upholstery, trunk net, deluxe floormats.

	Retail Price	Dealer Invoice	Fair Price
B20/E7 custom interior, SE	505	434	455
with Group 1SD	174	150	157

45/55 cloth bucket seats with center storage console and rear air conditioning vents, lighted visor mirrors, overhead console with power outlet, trunk net, deluxe floormats.

	Retail Price	Dealer Invoice	Fair Price
B20/27 custom interior, SE	1409	1212	1268
with Group 1SD	1028	884	925

45/55 leather bucket seats, floor console.

	Retail Price	Dealer Invoice	Fair Price
45/45 leather bucket seats, SSE	854	734	769
45/45 articulating leather bucket seats, SSE	1404	1207	1264
with Group 1SB	1099	945	989
6-way power driver's seat	305	262	275
6-way power passenger seat	305	262	275
Remote keyless entry system	135	116	122
AM/FM cassette player, SE	170	146	153
AM/FM cassette with equalizer, SE	460	396	414
with Sport Edition Pkg., Enhancement Group, or leather bucket seats	410	353	369
with Group 1SD	325	280	293
AM/FM CD player with equalizer, SE	686	590	617
with Sport Edition Pkg., Enhancement Group, or leather bucket seats	636	547	470
with Group 1SD	551	474	408
AM/FM CD player with equalizer, SSE	226	194	167
Computer Command Ride, SSE	380	327	281

Requires traction control.

	Retail Price	Dealer Invoice	Fair Price
Power antenna, SE	85	73	77
16-inch 5-blade alloy wheels, SE	340	292	306

	Retail Price	Dealer Invoice	Fair Price
16-inch gold or silver alloy wheels, SE ...	(NC)	(NC)	(NC)
225/60R16 blackwall touring tires, SE	$84	$72	$76
Engine block heater	18	15	16

BUICK PARK AVENUE/ OLDSMOBILE NINETY EIGHT

Buick Park Avenue Ultra

Specifications

	4-door notchback
Wheelbase, in.	110.8
Overall length, in.	205.2
Overall width, in.	73.6
Overall height, in.	55.1
Curb weight, lbs.	3536
Cargo vol., cu. ft.	20.3
Fuel capacity, gals.	18.0
Seating capacity	6
Front head room, in.	38.9
Max. front leg room, in.	42.7
Rear head room, in.	37.9
Min. rear leg room, in.	40.7

BUICK

Powertrain layout: transverse front engine/front-wheel drive.

Engines	ohv V-6	Supercharged ohv V-6
Size, liters/cu. in.	3.8/231	3.8/231
Horsepower @ rpm	170 @ 4800	225 @ 5000
Torque (lbs./ft.) @ rpm	225 @ 3200	275 @ 3200
Availability	S	S[1]
EPA city/highway mpg		
4-speed OD automatic	19/27	17/27

1. Park Avenue Ultra; optional, Ninety Eight Elite.

Built in Orion, Mich.

PRICES

Buick Park Avenue	Retail Price	Dealer Invoice	Fair Price
4-door notchback	$27164	$23497	$24197
National Marketing Edition 4-door notchback	25695	24492	—
Ultra 4-door notchback	31864	27562	28262
Destination charge	625	625	625

National Marketing Edition's fair price not available at time of publication. National Marketing Edition includes destination charge and is available with limited optional equipment. Additional "value-priced" models may be available in California

Standard Equipment:

3.8-liter V-6 engine, 4-speed automatic transmission, anti-lock brakes, variable-assist power steering, driver- and passenger-side air bags, air conditioning, 55/45 cloth reclining front seat with storage armrest and cup holders, 6-way power driver's seat, automatic level control, power windows with driver-side express down and passenger lockout, power door locks, power mirrors, overhead console, cruise control, rear defogger, tilt steering wheel, AM/FM cassette player, solar-control tinted glass, Pass-Key theft-deterrent system, remote decklid and fuel door releases, front and rear reading and courtesy lights, passenger-side lighted visor mirror, intermittent wipers, trip odometer, 205/70R15 tires, alloy wheels. **National Marketing Edition model** adds to base: automatic air conditioning, 6-way power passenger seat with power recliner, remote keyless illuminated entry system, Twilight Sentinel headlamp control, analog gauge cluster with tachometer, trip odometer, coolant temperature and oil pressure gauges, power antenna, power decklid pulldown, automatic power door locks, Reminder Pkg. (includes low washer fluid, low coolant, trunk and door ajar indicators), alarm system, automatic day/night inside rearview mirror, Concert Sound II speakers, lighted driver-side visor mirror, cornering lights, 205/70R15 whitewall tires. **Ultra** adds to base: supercharged 3.8-liter V-6 engine, automatic climate control with dual temperature controls, rear seat climate controls, 6-way power front seats with power recliners, leather upholstery, leather-wrapped steering wheel, rear head restraints, remote keyless entry system, illuminated entry system with retained accessory power, Twilight Sentinel headlamp control, analog gauge cluster with tachometer, trip odometer, coolant temperature and oil pressure gauges, power antenna, power decklid pulldown, automatic programmable power door locks, Reminder Pkg. (includes low washer fluid, low coolant, and door ajar indicators), theft-deterrent system with starter interrupt, trunk net, cornering lamps, automatic day/night inside rearview mirror, Concert Sound II speakers, lighted driver-side visor mirror, 4-note horn, 215/70R15 all-season tires.

Optional Equipment:	Retail Price	Dealer Invoice	Fair Price
Luxury Pkg. SD, base	$1821	$1566	$1657

Includes power passenger seat with power recliner, illuminated entry with retained accessory power, remote keyless entry, dual air conditioning controls, theft-deterrent system with starter interrupt, automatic programmable door locks, power decklid pulldown, power antenna, automatic day/night inside rearview mirror, driver-side visor mirror, analog gauge cluster, lamp monitors, Twilight Sentinel headlamp control, Concert Sound II speakers, cornering lamps, Reminder Pkg. (includes low washer fluid, low coolant, and door ajar indicators), door edge guards, trunk net, 4-note horn, 215/70R15 whitewall tires.

Prestige Pkg. SE, base	2496	2147	2271

Pkg. SD plus AM stereo with music search, steering wheel radio controls, heated outside mirrors with automatic left day/night mirror, memory driver's seat and mirrors, rear seat climate controls, self-sealing tires, trunk mat.

Luxury Pkg. SD, Ultra	730	628	664

Includes automatic ride control, traction control system, AM stereo with music search, steering wheel radio and temperature controls.

Prestige Pkg. SE, Ultra	1245	1071	1133

Pkg. SD plus heated outside mirrors with automatic left day/night mirror, heated driver's seat, memory driver's seat and mirrors, self-sealing tires, trunk mat.

	Retail Price	Dealer Invoice	Fair Price
CD player with AM stereo, base	$364	$313	$331
Base w/SD, and Ultra	294	253	268
Base w/SE, and Ultra w/SD/SE	244	210	222
Delco-Bose music system with AM stereo, Ultra	723	622	658
Ultra w/SD/SE	673	579	612
AM/FM cassette, base w/SD, Ultra	50	43	46
Includes AM stereo with music search and Concert Sound II speakers.			
Astroroof, base w/SE	918	789	835
Ultra w/SD/SE	802	690	730
Deletes lamp monitors and rear vanity mirrors.			
Trailering Pkg.	150	129	137
w/Gran Touring Pkg.	123	106	112
Includes auxiliary transmission oil and engine oil cooling, Gran Touring suspension and 3:06 axle ratio.			
Gran Touring Pkg., base and National Marketing Edition	224	193	204
Includes Gran Touring suspension, 215/60R16 touring tires, 3:06 axle ratio, alloy wheels, leather-wrapped steering wheel.			
Automatic level control, base w/SE	380	327	346
Traction control system, base w/SD/SE	175	151	159
Leather/vinyl 55/45 seat w/storage armrest, base	500	430	455
Heated driver's seat, base w/SE	105	90	96
Ultra w/SD	60	52	55
Self-sealing tires, base and Ultra w/o SE	150	129	137
205/70R15 whitewall tires, base	76	65	69
205/70R15 tires, base w/SD	(76)	(65)	(65)
w/SE	(226)	(194)	(194)
National Marketing Edition	NC	NC	NC
215/70R15 blackwall tires, Ultra w/SD (credit)	(80)	(69)	(69)
Wire wheel covers	NC	NC	NC

Oldsmobile Ninety Eight

	Retail Price	Dealer Invoice	Fair Price
Regency 4-door notchback	$26170	$22899	$23599
Regency Special Edition 4-door notchback	25295	24185	—
Regency Elite 4-door notchback	28270	24738	25438
Destination charge	625	625	625

Special Edition fair price not available at time of publication. Special Edition price includes destination charge. Additional "value-priced" models may be available in California.

Standard Equipment:

Regency: 3.8-liter V-6, 4-speed automatic transmission, anti-lock brakes, driver- and passenger-side air bags, power steering, automatic climate control, cloth 55/45 reclining front seat with storage armrest, power driver's seat, cruise control, power windows and door locks, power mirrors, AM/FM radio, power antenna, remote fuel door and decklid releases, tilt steering wheel, cruise control, automatic leveling suspension, solar control glass, power mirrors, intermittent wipers, rear defogger, Pass-Key theft deterrent system, visor mirrors, reading lights, floormats, 205/70R15 whitewall tires, wire wheel covers. **Regency Special Edition** adds to Regency: Option Pkg. 1SB, leather seats, alloy wheels. **Regency Elite** adds to Regency: dual zone air conditioner, power passenger seat, AM/FM cassette, steering wheel touch controls, programmable power door locks, lighted visor mirrors, Remote Accessory Control Pkg., Reminder Pkg., overhead console storage, trunk cargo net, alloy wheels.

Optional Equipment:

	Retail Price	Dealer Invoice	Fair Price
Supercharged 3.8-liter V-6 Engine Pkg.,			
Elite	$1631	$1403	$1484
Elite with leather seats	1541	1325	1402
Supercharged 3.8-liter V-6 engine, touring car ride and handling suspension, traction control system, tachometer, variable-assist power steering, leather-wrapped steering wheel, 225/60R16 tires, alloy wheels. Not available with electronic instrument cluster or Computer Command Ride System. Requires Option Pkg. 1SB.			
Traction control, Regency,			
Elite	175	151	159
Requires Computer Command Ride System and Option Pkg. 1SB.			
Option Pkg. 1SB, Regency	1448	1245	1318
Dual zone air conditioner, Reminder Pkg., lighted visor mirrors, power passenger seat with power recliner, power front seat lumbar adjusters, steering wheel touch controls, AM/FM cassette, Remote Accessory Control Pkg., trunk cargo net.			
Option Pkg. 1SB, Elite	635	546	578
Power trunk pull-down, Twilight Sentinel, heated electrochromatic driver-side outside mirror, electrochromatic day/night rearview mirror with compass, driver-side power seat memory, cornering lamps.			
Astroroof, Regency, Elite	995	856	905
Requires Option Pkg. 1SB.			
Computer Command Ride System,			
Regency, Elite	470	404	428
with leather seats	380	327	346
Requires traction control and Option Pkg. 1SB.			

Prices are accurate at time of publication; subject to manufacturer's change.

	Retail Price	Dealer Invoice	Fair Price
Wire wheel covers, Special Edition, Elite	NC	NC	NC
Not available with supercharged V-6.			
Alloy wheels, Regency	$131	$113	$119
AM/FM cassette and CD player, Regency, Elite	396	341	360
Requires Option Pkg. 1SB.			
Electronic instrument cluster, Regency, Elite	345	297	314
Includes Driver Information Center. Requires Option Pkg. 1SB. Not available with supercharged V-6.			
Custom leather trim, Regency, Elite	515	443	469
Requires Option Pkg. 1SB.			
Cloth seat trim, Special Edition (credit)	(515)	(443)	(443)
Accent stripe	45	39	41
Engine block heater	18	15	16

1995 BUICK RIVIERA

1995 Buick Riviera

Specifications	2-door notchback
Wheelbase, in.	113.8
Overall length, in.	207.2
Overall width, in.	75.0

	2-door notchback
Overall height, in.	55.2
Curb weight, lbs.	3742
Cargo vol., cu. ft.	17.4
Fuel capacity, gals.	20.0
Seating capacity	6
Front head room, in.	38.2
Max. front leg room, in.	42.6
Rear head room, in.	36.2
Min. rear leg room, in.	37.3

Powertrain layout: transverse front engine/front-wheel drive.

Engines

	ohv V-6	Supercharged ohv V-6
Size, liters/cu. in.	3.8/231	3.8/231
Horsepower @ rpm	205 @ 5200	225 @ 5000
Torque (lbs./ft.) @ rpm	230 @ 4000	275 @ 3200
Availability	S	O
EPA city/highway mpg		
4-speed OD automatic	19/29	17/27

Built in Orion, Mich.

PRICES

1995 Buick Riviera	Retail Price	Dealer Invoice	Fair Price
2-door notchback	$27632	$24454	—
Destination charge	625	625	625

Fair price not available at time of publication.

Standard Equipment:

3.8-liter V-6 engine, 4-speed automatic transmission, anti-lock 4-wheel disc brakes, driver- and passenger-side air bags, variable-assist power steering, automatic air conditioning with dual climate controls, cruise control, cloth 6-way power 55/45 split bench front seat with power recliners, front storage armrest with cup holders, rear seat armrest, power windows and mirrors, automatic power door locks, remote keyless entry system, Pass-Key II theft-deterrent system, automatic level control, tachometer, coolant temperature gauge, trip odometer, lighted passenger-side visor mirror, power

Prices are accurate at time of publication; subject to manufacturer's change.

remote fuel door and decklid releases, solar-control tinted glass, AM/FM cassette player, automatic power antenna, intermittent wipers, rear defogger, tilt steering wheel, leather-wrapped steering wheel, front reading and courtesy lights, rear door courtesy lights, supplemental and extendable sunshades, trunk convenience net, 225/60R16 all-season tires, alloy wheels.

Optional Equipment:	Retail Price	Dealer Invoice	Fair Price
3.8-liter supercharged V-6 engine	$1100	$946	—
Includes 225/60R16 touring tires and specific alloy wheels.			
SD Luxury Pkg.	472	406	—
Twilight Sentinel, driver-side lighted visor mirror, programmable automatic door locks, theft-deterrent system, cornering lights, accent striping.			
SE Prestige Pkg.	992	853	—
SD Luxury Pkg. plus memory heated driver's seat, memory heated outside mirrors, automatic inside rear view mirror, steering wheel mounted radio and climate comtrols, driver's seat power lumbar adjustment, traction control system.			
Power astroroof with sunshade	995	856	—
Memory heated driver's seat and outside mirrors	310	267	—
Power leather front bucket seats with operating console	650	559	—
Leather 55/45 split bench seats	600	516	—
AM/FM CD player	244	210	—
AM/FM cassette and CD player	434	373	—
Requires power front bucket seats.			
Engine block heater	18	15	—

BUICK SKYLARK/ OLDSMOBILE ACHIEVA

Specifications	2-door notchback	4-door notchback
Wheelbase, in.	103.4	103.4
Overall length, in.	187.9	187.9
Overall width, in.	67.5	67.5
Overall height, in.	53.4	53.4
Curb weight, lbs.	2738	2799

Buick Skylark Gran Sport 2-door

	2-door notchback	4-door notchback
Cargo vol., cu. ft.	14.0	14.0
Fuel capacity, gals.	15.2	15.2
Seating capacity	5	5
Front head room, in.	37.8	37.8
Max. front leg room, in.	43.3	43.3
Rear head room, in.	36.5	37.0
Min. rear leg room, in.	34.0	35.0

Powertrain layout: transverse front engine/front-wheel drive.

Engines	ohc I-4	ohc I-4	dohc I-4	ohv V-6
Size, liters/cu. in.	2.3/138	2.3/138	2.3/138	3.1/191
Horsepower @ rpm	115 @ 5200	155 @ 6000	170 @ 6200	160 @ 5200
Torque (lbs./ft.) @ rpm	140 @ 3200	150 @ 4800	150 @ 5200	185 @ 4000
Availability	S[1]	O[2]	S[3]	O[4]
EPA city/highway mpg				
5-speed OD manual	23/35		21/30	
3-speed automatic	22/32			
4-speed OD automatic	22/31	21/30		20/29

1. Skylark Custom, Achieva S. 2. Achieva. 3. Achieva SC and SL. 4. Standard, Skylark GS.

Built in Lansing, Mich.

Prices are accurate at time of publication; subject to manufacturer's change.

Buick Skylark	Retail Price	Dealer Invoice	Fair Price
Custom 2-door notchback	$13734	$12841	$13241
National Marketing Edition Custom 2-door notchback	13995	13374	—
Custom 4-door notchback	13734	12841	13241
National Marketing Edition Custom 4-door notchback	13995	13374	—
Limited 4-door notchback	16334	14782	15182
Gran Sport (GS) 2-door notchback	18434	16683	17083
Gran Sport (GS) 4-door notchback	18434	16683	17083
Destination charge	485	485	485

National Marketing Edition models' fair price not available at time of publication. National Marketing Edition models include destination charge and are available with limited option equipment. Additional "value-priced" models may be available in California.

Standard Equipment:

Custom: 2.3-liter 4-cylinder engine, 3-speed automatic transmission, driver-side air bag, anti-lock brakes, door-mounted automatic front seatbelts, power steering, tilt steering wheel, cloth 55/45 split bench seat with seatback recliners, trip odometer, AM/FM radio, tinted glass, automatic power locks, remote fuel door and decklid releases, left remote and right manual mirrors, overhead console with courtesy lights, rear courtesy/reading lights, bright grille, 185/75R14 tires, wheel covers. **National Marketing Edition models** add to Custom: air conditioning, cruise control, 4-way manual driver's seat adjustment, tilt steering wheel, intermittent wipers, front center storage armrest, rear defogger, front and rear floormats. **Limited** adds to Custom: air conditioning, cruise control, tachometer, oil pressure and coolant temperature gauges, power windows, intermittent wipers, 4-way manual driver's seat, front storage armrest, visor mirrors. **GS** adds: 3.1-liter V-6 engine, 4-speed automatic transmission, Gran Touring suspension, reclining leather/cloth bucket seats, split folding rear seatback, leather-wrapped steering wheel and shift handle, body-color grille, lower accent paint, trunk net, floormats, 205/55R16 tires, alloy wheels.

Optional Equipment:

3.1-liter V-6 engine (std. GS)	410	353	373
4-speed automatic transmission (std. GS)	200	172	182

	Retail Price	Dealer Invoice	Fair Price
Air conditioning, Custom	$830	$714	$755
Luxury Pkg. SD, Custom	1623	1396	1477
Air conditioning, rear defogger, cruise control, tilt steering wheel, intermittent wipers, 4-way driver's seat, front seat storage armrest, floormats.			
Prestige Pkg. SE, Custom 2-door	2087	1795	1899
Custom 4-door	2152	1851	1958
Pkg. SD plus cassette player, power windows, covered visor mirrors.			
Prestige Pkg. SE, Limited	1013	871	922
6-way power driver's seat, rear defogger, power mirrors, cassette player, power antenna, Concert Sound speakers, lighted visor mirrors, reading lights, floormats, trunk net.			
Prestige Pkg. SE, GS	1083	931	986
6-way power driver's seat, rear defogger, power mirrors, remote keyless entry, cassette player, power antenna, Concert Sound speakers, lighted visor mirrors, reading lights.			
6-way power driver's seat, Custom w/SD/SE, Limited w/SD, GS w/SD, National Marketing Edition models	270	232	246
Bucket seats and full console, Custom w/SE and Limted w/SE	160	138	146
Split folding rear seat, Limited w/SE	150	129	137
Analog gauge cluster, Custom w/SD/SE	126	108	115
Includes tachometer, trip odometer, voltmeter, oil pressure and coolant temperature gauges.			
Power mirrors, Custom w/SD/SE, Limited w/SE, GS w/SE, National Marketing Edition models	78	67	71
Power windows, National Marketing Edition Custom 2-door	275	236	250
National Marketing Edition Custom 4-door	340	292	309
Power antenna	85	73	77
Remote keyless entry system, Limited w/SE	135	116	123
Gran Touring suspension, Limited w/SE	27	23	25
Requires 3.1-liter engine.			
Cassette player	165	142	150
CD player, Limited w/SE and Gran Sport w/SE	394	339	359
Concert Sound speakers	45	39	41
Wheel covers, Custom, Limited	28	24	25
Lower accent paint (std. GS)	195	168	177

Prices are accurate at time of publication; subject to manufacturer's change.

BUICK

	Retail Price	Dealer Invoice	Fair Price
Engine block heater	$18	$15	$16
Trunk net, Custom and Limited	20	17	18
Alloy wheels with 205/55R16 touring blackwall tires, Limited w/SE	575	495	523
Styled polycast wheels, Custom and Limited	115	99	105
195/65R15 blackwall touring tires, Custom and Limited	131	113	119
Requires styled steel wheel covers.			
Styled steel wheel covers, Custom and Limited	28	24	25
Requires 195/65R15 blackwall tires.			
185/75R14 whitewall tires, Custom and Limited	68	58	62

Oldsmobile Achieva

	Retail Price	Dealer Invoice	Fair Price
S 2-door notchback	$14210	$12860	$13260
S 4-door notchback	14310	12951	13351
S Special Edition 2-door notchback, Pkg. R7B	13995	13252	—
S Special Edition 4-door notchback, Pkg. R7B	13995	13252	—
S Special Edition 2-door notchback, Pkg. R7C	14995	14197	—
S Special Edition 4-door notchback, Pkg. R7C	14995	14197	—
S Special Edition 2-door notchback, Pkg. R7D	17295	16370	—
S Special Edition 4-door notchback, Pkg. R7D	17295	16370	—
SC 2-door notchback	17710	16028	16428
SL 4-door notchback	17710	16028	16428
Destination charge	485	485	485

S Special Edition fair price not available at time of publication. S Special Edition prices include destination charge. Additional "value-priced" models may be available in California.

Standard Equipment:

S: 2.3-liter OHC 4-cylinder engine, 5-speed manual transmission, anti-lock brakes, driver-side air bag, power steering, cloth reclining front bucket seats, dual outside mirrors, console with storage armrest, tilt steering wheel, intermittent wipers, AM/FM radio, tinted glass, rear defogger, automatic power locks, remote fuel door and decklid releases, reading and map lights, 185/75R14 tires, wheel covers. **S Special Edition Pkg. R7B** adds to S: 3-speed automatic transmission, air conditioning, floormats. **S Special Edition Pkg. R7C** adds to S: 4-speed automatic transmission, power windows, Pkg. 1SB. **S Special Edition Pkg. R7D** adds to S: 3.1-liter V-6 engine, 4-speed automatic transmission, power windows. **SC and SL** add to S: 170-horsepower 2.3-liter Quad 4 engine, air conditioning, cruise control, power mirrors, leather-wrapped steering wheel, analog gauges, tachometer, voltmeter, coolant temperature and oil pressure gauges, trip odometer, 4-way manual driver's seat, split folding rear seat with luggage compartment pass-through, cassette player, lighted visor mirrors, floormats, trunk cargo net, fog lamps, rear spoiler, touring suspension, dual exhausts, 205/55R16 tires, alloy wheels.

Optional Equipment:	Retail Price	Dealer Invoice	Fair Price
155-horsepower 2.3-liter Quad 4 engine, S	$410	$353	$373
Requires 4-speed automatic transmission.			
155-horsepower 2.3-liter Quad 4 engine, SC, SL (credit)	(140)	(121)	(121)
Required with automatic transmission.			
3.1-liter V-6, S and Spec. Ed. w/Pkg. R7C	410	353	373
SC, SL (credit)	(140)	(121)	(121)
Requires 4-speed automatic transmission.			
5-speed manual transmission, S Special Edition with Pkg. R7B (credit)	(555)	(477)	(477)
3-speed automatic transmission, S	555	477	505
4-speed automatic transmission S, SC and SL	755	649	687
4-speed automatic transmission, S Special Edition with Pkg. R7B (Calif., Hawaii, N.Y.)	200	172	182
Air conditioning, S	830	714	755
Option Pkg. 1SB, S	1468	1262	1336
Air conditioning, cruise control, analog gauge cluster, power mirrors, cassette player, floormats.			
Option Pkg. 1SC, S 2-door	1968	1692	1791
S 4-door	2033	1748	1850
Pkg. 1SB plus power windows, Remote Lock Control Pkg., 6-speaker stereo, rear window grid antenna.			
Option Pkg. 1SB, SC	400	344	364
SL	465	400	423
Power windows, Remote Lock Control Pkg.			

	Retail Price	Dealer Invoice	Fair Price
Power sunroof	$595	$512	$541
Power windows, 2-doors	275	237	250
4-doors	340	292	309
Power driver's seat	270	232	246
Leather seats, SC, SL	425	366	387
Split folding rear seat, S	150	129	137
Remote Lock Control Pkg., Special Edition with Pkg. R7D	125	108	114
Cassette player, S	140	120	127
AM/FM w/CD player	256	220	233
S requires Option Pkg. 1SB or 1SC.			
Decklid luggage rack, S	115	99	105
Alloy wheels, S and Spec. Ed. w/Pkg. R7C	391	336	356
Includes 195/65R15 touring tires.			
Floormats, S	45	39	41
Trunk cargo net, S	30	26	27
Engine block heater	18	15	16

CADILLAC DE VILLE/ CONCOURS

Specifications

	4-door notchback
Wheelbase, in.	113.8
Overall length, in.	209.7
Overall width, in.	76.6
Overall height, in.	56.3
Curb weight, lbs.	3758
Cargo vol., cu. ft.	20.0
Fuel capacity, gals.	20.0
Seating capacity	6
Front head room, in.	38.5
Max. front leg room, in.	42.6
Rear head room, in.	38.4
Min. rear leg room, in.	43.3

Powertrain layout: transverse front engine/front-wheel drive.

Cadillac De Ville Concours

Engines

Engines	ohv V-8	dohc V-8
Size, liters/cu. in.	4.9/299	4.6/279
Horsepower @ rpm	200 @ 4100	270 @ 5600
Torque (lbs./ft.) @ rpm	275 @ 3000	300 @ 4000
Availability	S[1]	S[2]
EPA city/highway mpg		
4-speed OD automatic	16/26	16/25

1. Sedan de Ville. 2. Concours.

Built in Hamtramck, Mich.

PRICES

Cadillac De Ville/Concours	Retail Price	Dealer Invoice	Fair Price
Sedan de Ville 4-door notchback	$32990	$30186	—
Concours 4-door notchback	37990	34761	—
Destination charge	625	625	625

Fair price not available at time of publication.

Standard Equipment:

Sedan de Ville: 4.9-liter V-8, 4-speed automatic transmission, anti-lock 4-wheel disc brakes, driver- and passenger-side air bags, variable-assist power steering, reclining power front seats with storage armrest, automatic climate control, outside temperature readout, power windows, automatic power locks, remote keyless entry system, heated power mirrors, cruise control, AM/FM cassette with equalizer, power antenna, power decklid pulldown, automatic parking brake release, Twilight Sentinel, tinted glass, automatic level control, intermittent wipers, Driver Information Center, trip odometer, tilt steering wheel, leather-wrapped steering wheel, power decklid release, remote fuel door release, rear defogger, Pass-Key II theft-deterrent system, automatic day/night inside rear view mirror, Speed Sensitive Suspension, cornering lamps, floormats, 215/70R15 whitewall tires, alloy wheels. **Concours** adds: 4.6-liter DOHC V-8 engine, traction control, Road-Sensing Suspension, leather seats, Zebrano wood trim, power front seat recliners, driver's seat power lumbar support with memory, Active Audio System with cassette and 11 speakers, automatic day/night driver side mirror, power decklid pull-down, trunk mat and cargo net, front and rear lighted visor mirrors and map lights, 225/60HR16 blackwall tires.

Optional Equipment:	Retail Price	Dealer Invoice	Fair Price
Traction control,			
De Ville	$175	$149	$158
Option Pkg. 1SB,			
De Ville	428	364	385
Automatic day/night driver side mirror, lighted visor mirror, trunk mat and cargo net.			
Heated windshield			
system	309	263	275
De Ville requires Option Pkg. 1SB.			
Heated front seats,			
De Ville	310	264	276
Concours	120	102	107
De Ville requires Option Pkg. 1SB and leather seats and includes power recliners.			
Astroroof	1550	1318	1380
Theft-deterrent system	295	251	263
Active Audio System with cassette player,			
De Ville	274	233	244
with cassette and CD player,			
De Ville	670	570	596
with cassette and CD player,			
Concours	396	337	352
Chrome wheels	1195	1016	1064
3000-lb. Trailer Towing Pkg.	110	93	98
White diamond paint	500	425	445
Accent striping	75	64	67

CADILLAC FLEETWOOD

Cadillac Fleetwood

Specifications	4-door notchback
Wheelbase, in.	121.5
Overall length, in.	225.0
Overall width, in.	78.0
Overall height, in.	57.1
Curb weight, lbs.	4477
Cargo vol., cu. ft.	21.1
Fuel capacity, gals.	23.0
Seating capacity	6
Front head room, in.	38.7
Max. front leg room, in.	42.5
Rear head room, in.	39.1
Min. rear leg room, in.	43.9

Powertrain layout: longitudinal front engine/rear-wheel drive.

Engines	ohv V-8
Size, liters/cu. in.	5.7/350
Horsepower @ rpm	260 @ 5000
Torque (lbs./ft.) @ rpm	335 @ 2400
Availability	S
EPA city/highway mpg	
4-speed OD automatic	17/25

Built in Arlington, Tex.

PRICES

Cadillac Fleetwood	Retail Price	Dealer Invoice	Fair Price
4-door notchback	$33990	$31101	$31901
Destination charge	625	625	625

Standard Equipment:

5.7-liter V-8, 4-speed automatic transmission, anti-lock brakes, driver- and passenger-side air bags, variable-assist power steering, traction control, power 55/45 front seat with power recliners and storage armrest, automatic climate control, outside temperature readout, power windows and locks, illuminated entry, cruise control, heated power mirrors, lighted vanity mirrors, Pass-Key II theft-deterrent system, AM/FM cassette with equalizer, power antenna, automatic level control, leather-wrapped tilt steering wheel, trip odometer, cornering lamps, automatic parking brake release, tinted glass, intermittent wipers, rear defogger, floormats, door edge guards, Twilight Sentinel, power decklid pulldown and release, trunk mat and cargo net, 235/70R15 whitewall tires, alloy wheels.

Optional Equipment:

	Retail Price	Dealer Invoice	Fair Price
Security Pkg.	545	463	491
Automatic power door locks, remote keyless entry system, remote fuel door release, theft-deterrent system.			
7000-lb. Trailer Towing Pkg.	215	183	193
Performance axle ratio, base	NC	NC	NC
Astroroof	1550	1318	1395
Fleetwood Brougham Pkg. with cloth trim	1680	1428	1512
with leather trim	2250	1913	2025
Heated front seats, 2-position driver's seat memory feature, power lumbar adjustment, articulating front headrests, rear seat storage armrest with cup holders, rear lighted vanity mirrors, full padded roof, unique trim and alloy wheels, 2.93:1 rear axle ratio.			
Leather upholstery, base	570	485	513
Automatic day/night rearview mirror	110	93	99
Compact disc and cassette players	396	337	356
Full padded vinyl roof delete, Brougham	NC	NC	NC
Full padded vinyl roof, base	925	787	833

	Retail Price	Dealer Invoice	Fair Price
Chrome wheels	$1195	$1016	$1076
Full size spare tire	95	80	85

CADILLAC SEVILLE/ ELDORADO

Cadillac Seville STS

Specifications	2-door notchback	4-door notchback
Wheelbase, in.	108.0	111.0
Overall length, in.	202.2	204.4
Overall width, in.	75.5	74.2
Overall height, in.	54.0	54.5
Curb weight, lbs.	3774	3830
Cargo vol., cu. ft.	15.3	14.4
Fuel capacity, gals.	20.0	20.0
Seating capacity	5	5
Front head room, in.	37.4	38.0
Max. front leg room, in.	42.6	43.0
Rear head room, in.	38.3	38.3
Min. rear leg room, in.	36.0	39.1

Powertrain layout: transverse front engine/front-wheel drive.

CADILLAC

Engines

	dohc V-8	dohc V-8
Size, liters/cu. in.	4.6/279	4.6/279
Horsepower @ rpm	270 @ 5600	295 @ 6000
Torque (lbs./ft.) @ rpm	300 @ 4000	290 @ 4400
Availability	S[1]	S[2]
EPA city/highway mpg		
4-speed OD automatic	16/25	16/25

1. Seville SLS, base Eldorado. 2. Seville STS, Eldorado Touring Coupe.

Built in Hamtramck, Mich.

PRICES

Cadillac Seville	Retail Price	Dealer Invoice	Fair Price
SLS 4-door notchback	$41430	$35837	$36837
STS 4-door notchback	45330	39210	40210
Destination charge	625	625	625

Standard Equipment:

SLS: 4.6-liter DOHC V-8, 4-speed automatic transmission, anti-lock 4-wheel disc brakes, driver- and passenger-side air bags, speed-sensitive power steering, Road-Sensing Suspension, traction control, automatic level control, cloth power front seats with power recliners, center console with armrest and storage bins, overhead console, dual zone automatic climate control with outside temperature display, Zebrano wood trim, power windows, automatic power door locks, cruise control, heated power mirrors, automatic day/night rearview mirror, AM/FM cassette, power antenna, remote fuel door and decklid releases, power decklid pull-down, Driver Information Center, Pass-Key II theft-deterrent system, remote keyless entry, leather-wrapped tilt steering wheel, intermittent wipers, rear defogger, solar-control tinted glass, floormats, decklid liner, trunk mat and cargo net, Twilight Sentinel, cornering lamps, reading lights, lighted visor mirrors, trip odometer, automatic parking brake release, 225/60R16 tires, alloy wheels. **STS** adds: High-output 4.6-liter DOHC V-8 engine, touring suspension, leather upholstery, front seat power lumbar adjustment, analog instruments with tachometer, anti-theft alarm, full console, driver-side automatic day/night outside mirror, fog lamps, 225/60ZR16 tires.

Optional Equipment:

Astroroof	$1550	$1318	$1395

	Retail Price	Dealer Invoice	Fair Price
Sport Interior Pkg., SLS	$146	$124	$131
Analog instruments, full center console, leather-wrapped shift knob.			
Anti-theft alarm, SLS	295	251	266
Heated windshield	309	263	278
Leather upholstery, SLS	650	553	585
Heated front seats	120	102	108
Base requires leather upholstery.			
Power lumbar adjustment, SLS	292	248	263
Requires leather upholstery.			
Driver-side automatic day/night outside mirror, SLS	110	94	99
Delco/Bose audio system w/cassette and CD players	972	826	875
White diamond paint	500	425	450
Chrome wheels	1195	1016	1076

Cadillac Eldorado

	Retail Price	Dealer Invoice	Fair Price
2-door notchback	$37690	$32602	$33402
Touring Coupe 2-door notchback	40990	35456	36256
Destination charge	625	625	625

Standard Equipment:

4.6-liter DOHC V-8 engine, 4-speed automatic transmission, anti-lock 4-wheel disc brakes, driver- and passenger-side air bags, speed-sensitive power steering, automatic parking brake release, Road-Sensing Suspension, automatic level control, traction control, automatic climate control, cloth power front bucket seats with power recliners, center console with armrest and storage bins, overhead console, power windows, automatic power locks, remote keyless entry system, cruise control, heated power mirrors, rear defogger, solar-control tinted glass, automatic day/night rearview mirror, Active Audio AM/FM cassette, power antenna, remote fuel door release, power decklid release and pull-down, trip odometer, Driver Information Center, Zebrano wood trim, intermittent wipers, leather-wrapped steering wheel, tilt steering wheel, Pass-Key II theft-deterrent system, Twilight Sentinel, cornering lamps, reading lights, lighted visor mirrors, floormats, trunk mat and cargo net, 225/60R16 tires, alloy wheels. **Touring Coupe** adds: high-output 4.6-liter V-8 engine, power lumbar adjusters, leather seats, automatic day/night driver-side mirror, theft-deterrent system, fog lamps, 225/60ZR16 tires.

Optional Equipment:

Astroroof	$1550	$1318	$1395

Prices are accurate at time of publication; subject to manufacturer's change.

	Retail Price	Dealer Invoice	Fair Price
Sport Appearance Pkg., base	$146	$124	$131
Analog instrumentation, floor console with leather-wrapped shift knob, Touring Coupe alloy wheels.			
Heated windshield system	309	263	278
Leather upholstery, base	650	553	585
Heated front seats	120	102	108
Base requires leather upholstery.			
Power lumbar support, base	292	248	263
Requires leather upholstery.			
Automatic day/night rearview mirror, base	110	94	99
Theft-deterrent system, base	295	251	266
Delco/Bose audio system with cassette and CD player	972	826	875
White diamond paint	500	425	450
225/60R16 whitewall tires, base	76	65	68
Chrome wheels	1195	1016	1076

CHEVROLET BERETTA/ CORSICA

Specifications

Specifications	2-door notchback	4-door notchback
Wheelbase, in.	103.4	103.4
Overall length, in.	183.4	183.4
Overall width, in.	68.2	68.2
Overall height, in.	56.2	56.2
Curb weight, lbs.	2649	2665
Cargo vol., cu. ft.	13.4	13.5
Fuel capacity, gals.	15.6	15.6
Seating capacity	5	5
Front head room, in.	38.1	38.1
Max. front leg room, in.	43.4	43.4
Rear head room, in.	37.4	37.4
Min. rear leg room, in.	35.0	35.0

Powertrain layout: transverse front engine/front-wheel drive.

Engines

Engines	ohv I-4	ohv V-6	dohc I-4
Size, liters/cu. in.	2.2/133	3.1/191	2.3/138

Chevrolet Beretta Z26

	ohv I-4	ohv V-6	dohc I-4
Horsepower @ rpm	120 @ 5200	155 @ 5200	170 @ 6200
Torque (lbs./ft.) @ rpm	130 @ 4000	185 @ 4000	150 @ 5200
Availability	S[1]	O	S[2]
EPA city/highway mpg			
5-speed OD manual	25/34		21/30
3-speed automatic	25/31		
4-speed OD automatic		21/29	

1. Base Beretta, Corsica. 2. Beretta Z26.

Built in Wilmington, Del.

PRICES

Chevrolet Beretta	Retail Price	Dealer Invoice	Fair Price
2-door notchback	$12585	$11389	$11589
National Marketing 2-door notchback	12795	—	—
National Marketing 2-door notchback	13295	—	—
National Marketing 2-door notchback	13995	—	—
Z26 2-door notchback	15310	13856	14056
Z26 National Marketing 2-door notchback	16995	—	—
Destination charge	485	485	485

Dealer invoice, fair price, and standard equipment for National Marketing models not available at time of publication. National Marketing models include destination charge. Additional "value-priced" models may be available in California.

Standard Equipment:

2.2-liter 4-cylinder engine, 5-speed manual transmission, anti-lock brakes, driver-side air bag, power steering, air conditioning, automatic door locks, cloth reclining front bucket seats with 4-way manual driver's seat, center shift console with armrest and storage compartment, cup holders, dual remote mirrors, door map pockets, passenger-side visor mirror, tinted glass, AM/FM radio, door pockets, 185/75R14 tires, wheel covers. **Z26** adds: 2.3-liter DOHC 4-cylinder engine, Level II Sport suspension, 4-way manual passenger seat, front seat lumbar supports, body-color grille and mirrors, front lower and rear spoilers, fog lamps, intermittent wipers, Gauge Pkg. with tachometer and trip odometer, cassette player, day/night rearview mirror with reading lamps, trunk net, 205/60R15 tires.

Optional Equipment:	Retail Price	Dealer Invoice	Fair Price
3.1-liter V-6 engine, base	$1275	$1097	$1122
Z26	525	452	462
Includes 4-speed automatic transmission.			
3-speed automatic transmission, base	555	477	488
Preferred Equipment Group 1, base	165	142	145
w/cassette player, add	140	120	123
w/AM stereo and CD player, add	396	341	348
Intermittent wipers, day/night rearview mirror with reading lamps, visor mirrors, trunk net, floormats.			
Preferred Group 2, base	745	641	656
w/cassette player, add	140	120	123
w/AM stereo and CD player, add	396	341	348
Group 1 plus cruise control, tilt-steering wheel, power decklid release, split-folding rear seat.			
Preferred Equipment Group 1, Z26	463	398	407
w/AM stereo and CD player, add	256	220	225
Cruise control, tilt steering wheel, power decklid release, floormats.			
Cassette player (std. Z26)	140	120	123
CD player, base	396	341	348
Z26	256	220	225
Rear defogger	170	146	150
Gauge Pkg., base	111	95	98
Includes tachometer, coolant temperature and oil pressure gauges, voltmeter, trip odometer.			
Rear spoiler, base	110	95	97
Removable sunroof	350	301	308
Power windows	275	237	242
Engine block heater	20	17	18

	Retail Price	Dealer Invoice	Fair Price
195/70R14 tires, base	$93	$80	$82
205/60R15 tires (std. Z26)	175	151	154
205/55R16 tires	372	320	327

Chevrolet Corsica

	Retail Price	Dealer Invoice	Fair Price
4-door notchback	$13315	$12050	$12350
National Marketing Edition 4-door notchback	13495	—	—
National Marketing Edition 4-door notchback	14495	—	—
Destination charge	485	485	485

Dealer invoice, fair price, and standard equipment for National Marketing models not available at time of publication. National Marketing models include destination charge. Additional "value-priced" models may be available in California.

Standard Equipment:

2.2-liter 4-cylinder engine, 3-speed automatic transmission, anti-lock brakes, driver-side air bag, door-mounted automatic front seatbelts, power steering, air conditioning, automatic power door locks, cloth reclining front bucket seats, 4-way manual driver's seat, center console with cup holders and storage, AM/FM radio, remote manual mirrors, tinted glass, passenger-side visor mirror, front door pockets, 185/75R14 tires, full wheel covers.

Optional Equipment:

	Retail Price	Dealer Invoice	Fair Price
3.1-liter V-6	720	619	634
Includes 4-speed automatic transmission.			
Preferred Equipment Group 1	165	142	145
Intermittent wipers, day/night rearview mirror with reading lights, driver- and passenger-side covered visor mirrors, trunk net, floormats.			
Preferred Equipment Group 2	745	641	656
Group 1 plus cruise control, tilt steering wheel, power decklid release, split-folding rear seat with armrest.			
Power windows	340	292	299
Rear defogger	170	146	150
AM/FM cassette player	140	120	123
AM/FM CD player	396	341	348
Styled steel wheels	56	48	49
185/75R14 whitewall tires	68	58	60
Engine block heater	20	17	18

CHEVROLET CAMARO/ PONTIAC FIREBIRD

Chevrolet Camaro Z28 Convertible

Specifications

Specifications	3-door hatchback	2-door convertible
Wheelbase, in.	101.1	101.1
Overall length, in.	193.2	193.2
Overall width, in.	74.1	74.1
Overall height, in.	51.3	52.0
Curb weight, lbs.	3247	3342
Cargo vol., cu. ft.	12.9	7.6
Fuel capacity, gals.	15.5	15.5
Seating capacity	4	4
Front head room, in.	37.2	38.0
Max. front leg room, in.	43.0	43.0
Rear head room, in.	35.3	39.0
Min. rear leg room, in.	26.8	26.8

Powertrain layout: longitudinal front engine/rear-wheel drive.

Engines

Engines	ohv V-6	ohv V-8
Size, liters/cu. in.	3.4/207	5.7/350
Horsepower @ rpm	160 @ 4600	275 @ 5000
Torque (lbs./ft.) @ rpm	200 @	325 @

	ohv V-6	ohv V-8
	3600	2400
Availability	S[1]	S[2]
EPA city/highway mpg		
5-speed OD manual	19/28	
6-speed OD manual		17/26
4-speed OD automatic	19/28	17/24

1. Base models. 2. Camaro Z28, Firebird Formula, Trans Am, GT.

Built in Canada.

PRICES

Chevrolet Camaro	Retail Price	Dealer Invoice	Fair Price
3-door hatchback	$13499	$12352	—
2-door convertible	18745	17152	—
Z28 3-door hatchback	16999	15554	—
Z28 convertible	22075	20199	—
Destination charge	490	490	490

Fair price not available at time of publication.

Standard Equipment:

3.4-liter V-6 engine, 5-speed manual transmission, anti-lock brakes, driver- and passenger-side air bags, power steering, reclining front bucket seats with 4-way adjustable driver's seat, center console with cup holders and lighted storage compartment, folding rear seatback, solar-control tinted glass, left remote and right manual black sport mirrors, tilt steering wheel, intermittent wipers, AM/FM cassette, day/night rearview mirror with dual reading lights, Pass-Key theft-deterrent system, tachometer, voltmeter, oil pressure and temperature gauges, trip odometer, low oil level indicator system, covered visor mirrors, door map pockets, rear spoiler, front floor mats, 215/60R16 all-season tires. **Z28** adds: 5.7-liter V-8 engine, 6-speed manual transmission, 4-wheel disc brakes, limited-slip differential, performance ride and handling suspension, low coolant indicator system, 235/55R16 all-season tires, alloy wheels.

Optional Equipment:

4-speed automatic transmission	750	645	—
Air conditioning	895	770	—
Base Preferred Equipment Group 1			
hatchback and convertible	1240	1066	—

Air conditioning, cruise control, remote hatch release, fog lamps.

	Retail Price	Dealer Invoice	Fair Price
Base Preferred Equipment Group 2, hatchback and convertible	$2036	$1751	—
Group 1 plus power windows with driver-side express down, power locks and mirrors, remote illuminated entry and hatch release, leather-wrapped steering wheel, transmission shifter and parking brake release.			
Z28 Preferred Equipment Group 1, hatchback and convertible	1350	1161	—
w/4-speed automatic transmission	1240	1066	—
Air conditioning, cruise control, remote hatch release, fog lamps, engine oil cooler (6-speed manual transmission).			
Z28 Preferred Equipment Group 2, hatchback and convertible	2146	1846	—
w/4-speed automatic transmission	2036	1751	—
Group 1 plus power windows with driver-side express down, power locks and mirrors, remote illuminated entry and hatch release, leather-wrapped steering wheel, transmission shifter and parking brake release.			
Performance Pkg., Z28 hatchback	310	267	—
Engine oil cooler, Special Handling Suspension System (includes larger stabilizer bars, stiffer shock absorbers and bushings). Requires 6-speed manual transmission and 245/50ZR tires. Not available with Groups 1 and 2, power driver's seat or removable roof panels.			
6-way power driver's seat	270	232	—
Performance axle ratio, Z28 hatchback	175	151	—
w/Performance Pkg.	65	56	—
Includes engine oil cooler. Requires 6-speed manual transmission and 245/50ZR16 tires.			
Rear defogger	170	146	—
Power locks	220	189	—
Requires Preferred Group 1.			
Removable roof panels	895	770	—
Includes locks and storage provisions.			
Delco/Bose AM/FM cassette player	275	237	—
Delco/Bose AM/FM CD player	531	457	—
Color-keyed bodyside moldings	60	52	—
235/55R16 tires, base	132	114	—
Requires alloy wheels.			
245/50ZR16 tires, Z28	225	194	—
Alloy wheels, base	275	237	—

Pontiac Firebird

	Retail Price	Dealer Invoice	Fair Price
3-door hatchback	$14099	$12901	—
2-door convertible	21179	19379	—
Formula 3-door hatchback	18249	16698	—
Formula 2-door convertible	24279	22215	—
Trans Am 3-door hatchback	20009	18308	—
Trans Am GT 3-door hatchback	21509	19681	—
Trans Am GT 2-door convertible	26479	24228	—
Destination charge	490	490	490

Fair price not available at time of publication.

Standard Equipment:

3.4-liter V-6, 5-speed manual transmission, anti-lock brakes, power steering, driver- and passenger-side air bags, cloth reclining front bucket seats, folding rear bench seat, tilt steering wheel, center console with storage, lamp and cup holder, remote hatch release, AM/FM cassette, intermittent wipers, solar-control tinted glass, front air dam, rear decklid spoiler, left remote and right manual mirrors, coolant temperature and oil pressure gauges, tachometer, trip odometer, Pass-Key theft-deterrent system, day/night rearview mirror with dual reading lamps, covered visor mirrors, front floormats, 215/60R16 tires, alloy wheels. **Convertible** adds: air conditioning, cruise control, automatic power locks, power windows, power mirrors, power top with glass rear window and defogger, 3-piece tonneau cover. **Formula** adds to base hatchback: 5.7-liter V-8, 6-speed manual transmission, anti-lock 4-wheel disc brakes, air conditioning, performance suspension, 3.42 axle ratio, limited-slip differential, 235/50ZR16 touring tires, bright silver alloy wheels. **Formula convertible** adds: 235/55R16 touring tires. **Trans Am** adds: cruise control, power windows with driver-side express down, power mirrors, automatic door locks, fog lamps. **Trans Am GT** adds: articulating cloth bucket seats, 4-way manually adjustable driver's seat, leather-wrapped steering wheel and shift knob, cassette with equalizer and 10-speaker sound system, steering wheel radio controls, rear defogger, remote keyless entry system, body-color bodyside molding, rear floormats, 245/50ZR16 tires.

Optional Equipment:

	Retail Price	Dealer Invoice	Fair Price
4-speed automatic transmission	775	667	—
Air conditioning, base	895	770	—
Air conditioning delete, Formula (credit)	(895)	(770)	(770)
Removable locking hatch roof	895	770	—

	Retail Price	Dealer Invoice	Fair Price
Option Group 1SB, base	$1005	$864	—
Air conditioning, manual 4-way adjustable driver's seat, bodyside moldings, rear floor mats.			
Option Group 1SC, base	2421	2082	—
Group 1SB plus power windows with driver-side express down, automatic power door locks, cruise control, remote keyless illuminated entry, cassette player with equalizer and 10-speaker sound system, leather-wrapped steering wheel with radio controls.			
Option Group 1SB, Formula	906	779	—
Cruise control, power windows with driver-side express down, automatic power door locks, mirrors, bodyside moldings, rear floormats.			
Option Group 1SC, Formula	1491	1282	—
Group 1SB plus remote keyless illuminated entry system, cassette player with equalizer and 10-speaker sound system, leather-wrapped steering wheel with radio controls.			
25th Anniversary Trans Am Pkg., Trans Am GT	995	856	—
White leather upholstery with blue embroidery, bright white alloy wheels, white paint with blue center stripes, anniversary logos and door badges, 25th Anniversary portfolio.			
Cruise control (std. Trans Am and Trans Am GT)	225	194	—
Rear defogger, (std. Trans Am GT)	170	146	—
Hatch roof sunshades	25	22	—
Rear performance axle, Formula	175	151	—
Includes 3.23 axle ratio, engine oil cooler, 245/50ZR16 tires.			
Body-color bodyside moldings, (std. Trans Am GT)	60	52	—
Power mirrors (std. Trans Am and Trans Am GT)	96	83	—
Automatic power door locks (std. Trans Am and Trans Am GT)	220	189	—
Power windows (std. Trans Am and Trans Am GT)	290	249	—
Includes driver-side express down.			
Cassette player with equalizer (std. Trans Am GT)	450	387	—
CD player, (NA Trans Am GT)	226	194	—
CD player with equalizer, base, Formula and Trans Am	676	581	—
Base and Formula with Group 1SC, Trans Am GT	226	194	—
Leather articulating bucket seats, base, Formula and Trans Am	780	671	—

	Retail Price	Dealer Invoice	Fair Price
Trans Am GT	$475	$409	—
4-way manual driver's seat (NA Formula, Trans Am; std. Trans Am GT)	35	30	—
6-way power driver's seat, base, Formula and Trans Am	305	262	—
Base with Group 1SB or 1SC	270	232	—
Remote keyless entry system, (std. Trans Am GT)	135	116	—
235/55R16 touring tires, base	132	114	—
245/50ZR16 tires, Formula	225	194	—
Bright white alloy wheels, (NA base)	(NC)	(NC)	(NC)
Rear floormats, (std. Trans Am GT)	15	13	—

CHEVROLET CAPRICE/ BUICK ROADMASTER

Chevrolet Caprice Classic

Specifications	4-door notchback	5-door wagon
Wheelbase, in.	115.9	115.9
Overall length, in.	214.1	217.3
Overall width, in.	77.0	79.6
Overall height, in.	55.7	60.9
Curb weight, lbs.	4036	4541

Prices are accurate at time of publication; subject to manufacturer's change.

	4-door notchback	5-door wagon
Cargo vol., cu. ft.	20.4	92.7
Fuel capacity, gals.	23.0	22.0
Seating capacity	6	8
Front head room, in.	39.2	39.6
Max. front leg room, in.	42.2	42.2
Rear head room, in.	37.9	39.4
Min. rear leg room, in.	39.5	38.0

Powertrain layout: longitudinal front engine/rear-wheel drive.

Engines

	ohv V-8	ohv V-8
Size, liters/cu. in.	4.3/265	5.7/350
Horsepower @ rpm	200 @ 5200	260 @ 5000
Torque (lbs./ft.) @ rpm	245 @ 2400	330 @ 3200
Availability	S[1]	S[2]
EPA city/highway mpg		
4-speed OD automatic	18/26	17/25

1. Caprice. 2. Roadmaster; optional, Caprice.

Built in Arlington, Tex.

PRICES

Chevrolet Caprice	Retail Price	Dealer Invoice	Fair Price
Classic 4-door notchback	$19153	$16759	$17359
Classic National Marketing 4-door	18995	—	—
Classic LS 4-door notchback	21593	18894	19494
Classic LS National Marketing 4-door	20995	—	—
Impala SS 4-door notchback	22495	—	—
5-door wagon	21338	18671	19271
Destination charge	575	575	575

Dealer invoice, fair price, and standard equipment for Impala SS and National Marketing models not available at time of publication. Impala SS and National Marketing models include destination charge. Additional "value-priced" models may be available in California.

Standard Equipment:

Classic: 4.3-liter V-8 engine, 4-speed automatic transmission, anti-lock brakes, driver-side air bag, power steering, air conditioning, cloth bench seat with center armrest, tilt steering wheel, AM/FM radio, Pass-Key theft-deterrent system, tinted glass, trip odometer, oil change monitor, intermittent wipers, door pockets, left remote and right manual mirrors, passenger-side visor mirror, cup holders, floormats, 215/75R15 tires, full wheel covers. **Wagon** has third rear seat, cassette player, luggage rack, 2-way tailgate, rear wiper/washer, power tailgate window release, 225/75R15 whitewall tires. **Classic LS** adds: cruise control, power door locks and decklid release, power windows with driver-side express down, power mirrors, power driver's seat, custom 55/45 cloth seats with recliners and seatback pockets, front and rear armrests, front and rear reading/courtesy lights, cassette player, driver-side visor mirror, lighted passenger-side visor mirror, trunk net, low fluid level warning lights, cornering lamps, gold grille and striping, alloy wheels.

Optional Equipment:	Retail Price	Dealer Invoice	Fair Price
5.7-liter V-8 engine, Classic w/Group 1 or 2, Classic LS, and wagon	$325	$280	$289
Classic and Classic LS require Sport suspension.			
Preferred Equipment Group 1, Classic	953	820	848
Cruise control, power windows with driver-side express down, power door locks, mirrors, and decklid release.			
w/cassette player, add	175	151	154
w/CD player, add	431	371	379
Preferred Equipment Group 2, Classic	1607	1382	1430
Group 1 plus 6-way power driver's seat, cassette player, power antenna, passenger-side lighted visor mirror, front and rear reading lamps.			
w/CD player, add	256	220	225
Preferred Equipment Group 1, Classic LS	860	740	765
6-way power passenger's seat, remote keyless entry, remote decklid release, rear defogger, heated mirrors, power antenna, automatic day/night rearview mirror.			
w/CD player, add	256	220	225
Preferred Equipment Group 1, wagon	1273	1095	1133
Cruise control, power windows with driver-side express down, power door/tailgate locks, power mirrors.			
w/CD player, add	256	220	225
Preferred Equipment Group 2, wagon	2146	1846	1910
6-way power passenger's seat, rear defogger, heated mirrors, power antenna, automatic day/night rearview mirror, passenger-side lighted visor mirror, rear reading lights, deluxe rear compartment decor, rear compartment security cover.			
w/CD player, add	256	220	225

Prices are accurate at time of publication; subject to manufacturer's change.

	Retail Price	Dealer Invoice	Fair Price
Cruise control	$225	$194	$198
Power door locks, Classic	250	215	223
Wagon	325	280	289
Wagon includes tailgate lock.			
Rear defogger	170	146	151
w/heated mirrors	205	176	182
Cloth 55/45 seat, Classic and wagon	223	192	198
NA wagon Group 2.			
Custom cloth 55/45 seat, wagon w/Group 2	342	294	304
Leather 55/45 seat, Classic LS w/Group 1	645	555	574
Limited-slip differential, notchbacks	250	215	223
wagon	100	86	89
Sport suspension, notchbacks	508	437	452
Automatic leveling suspension, wagon	175	151	156
Ride/Handling suspension, notchbacks	49	42	44
Trailering Pkg., notchbacks	21	18	19
Includes heavy duty cooling.			
Cassette player	175	151	156
Includes AM/FM radio with seek and scan, auto reverse, digital clock.			
CD player, Classic	431	371	384
Classic LS and wagon	256	220	228
Includes AM/FM radio with seek and scan.			
Woodgrain exterior appliqué, wagon	595	512	530
2-tone paint	141	121	125
Pinstriping, Classic and wagon	61	52	54
Cargo net	30	26	27
Wire wheel covers, Classic and wagon	215	185	191
Deluxe wheel covers, Classic and wagon	70	60	62
225/75R15 all-season whitewall tires (std. wagon)	(NC)	(NC)	(NC)
215/70R15 all-season whitewall tires	176	151	157
215/75R15 all-season whitewall tires	80	69	71
235/70R15 all-season whitewall tires	90	77	80
Above tires with full-size spare tire	115	99	102
with full-size spare tire and wire wheel covers	65	56	58
235/70R15 all-season tires	(NC)	(NC)	(NC)
with full-size spare tire	110	95	98
with full-size spare tire and wire wheel covers	60	52	53

Buick Roadmaster

	Retail Price	Dealer Invoice	Fair Price
4-door notchback	$24184	$21161	$21761
National Marketing Edition 4-door	23145	22084	—
Estate 5-door wagon	26584	23261	23861
Limited 4-door notchback	25784	22561	23161
Destination charge	575	575	575

National Marketing Edition model's fair price not available at time of publication. National Marketing Edition model includes destination charge and is available with limited optional equipment. Additional "value-priced" models may be available in California.

Standard Equipment:

5.7-liter V-8 engine, 4-speed automatic transmission, anti-lock brakes, driver- and passenger-side air bags, power steering, air conditioning, power windows with driver-side express down and passenger lockout, power door locks, Pass-Key theft-deterrent system with starter interrupt, AM/FM radio, cloth 55/45 seats with storage armrest and manual seatback recliners, front seatback map pockets, tilt steering wheel, remote decklid release, inside day/night mirror with reading lights, left remote and right manual mirrors, delayed illuminated entry, tinted glass, rear defogger, intermittent wipers, analog gauge cluster with coolant temperature and oil pressure gauges, trip odometer, low fuel warning light, windshield washer fluid, oil, voltage, and coolant level indicators, oil life monitor, visor mirrors, 4-note horn, trunk net, floormats, 235/70R15 all-season whitewall tires, wheel covers. **Estate Wagon** adds: variable-assist steering, luggage rack, solar-control windshield, rear window wiper/washer, vista roof, woodgrain exterior trim, 225/75R15 tires, alloy wheels. **Limited** adds to base: variable-assist steering, automatic climate control, power antenna, remote keyless entry, automatic door locks, front door courtesy and warning lights, automatic day/night rearview mirror, lighted visor mirrors, cassette player, 6-way power front seats with power recliners.

Optional Equipment:

Luxury Pkg. SD, base sedan	858	738	755

6-way power driver's seat, power heated mirrrors, automatic climate control, power antenna, cassette player, Concert Sound speakers.

Luxury Pkg. SD, wagon	1467	1262	1291

6-way power driver's seat, cruise control, automatic climate control, automatic day/night rearview mirror, power heated mirrors, power antenna, storage armrest, front door courtesy and warning lights, cassette player, cargo area security cover, vista shade, floormats.

Prices are accurate at time of publication; subject to manufacturer's change.

	Retail Price	Dealer Invoice	Fair Price
Prestige Pkg. SE, base sedan	$1565	$1346	$1377
Pkg. SD plus power passenger seat, automatic power door locks, remote keyless entry, door courtesy and warning lights, automatic day/night rearview mirror, lighted visor mirrors.			
Prestige Pkg. SE, Limited	350	301	308
Power decklid pull-down, Twilight Sentinel headlamp control, cornering lamps, self-sealing tires.			
Prestige Pkg. SE, wagon	2144	1844	1887
Pkg. SD plus 6-way power passenger seat, remote keyless entry, automatic door locks, Twilight Sentinel headlamp control, lighted visor mirrors, cornering lamps.			
Trailer Towing Pkg., wagon	325	280	286
Base sedan, Limited w/SD	375	323	330
Limited w/SE	225	194	198
2.93 axle ratio, heavy duty engine and transmission cooling, automatic level control, engine oil cooler; sedans add heavy duty suspension and solar-control windshield.			
Limited-slip differential	100	86	88
Heavy-duty cooling, wagon	150	129	132
Base sedan w/SD/SE, Limited	200	172	176
Sedans include solar-control windshield.			
Automatic level control	175	151	154
Requires SD or SE Pkg.			
Leather 55/45 seats, base 4-door, Limited	760	654	669
wagon	540	464	475
AM/FM cassette player, wagon w/SD/SE	185	159	163
Base sedan w/SD/ SE, Limited	150	129	132
Includes equalizer, AM stereo, clock and premium speakers.			
AM/FM CD player, wagon w/SD/SE	429	369	378
Base sedan w/SD/SE, Limited	394	339	347
Includes equalizer, AM stereo, clock and premium speakers.			
Remote keyless entry	135	116	119
Requires SD Pkg. and automatic door locks.			
Lower accent paint, sedans w/SD/SE	150	129	132
Vinyl landau roof, sedans w/SD/SE	695	598	612
Alloy wheels, sedans	325	280	286
Self-sealing 235/70R15 tires, base sedan, wagon, Limited w/SD	150	129	132

CHEVROLET CAVALIER/ PONTIAC SUNBIRD

Chevrolet Cavalier VL 2-door

Specifications	2-door notchback	2-door conv.	4-door notchback	5-door wagon
Wheelbase, in.	101.3	101.3	101.3	101.3
Overall length, in.	182.3	182.3	182.3	181.1
Overall width, in.	66.3	66.3	66.3	66.3
Overall height, in.	52.0	52.0	53.6	52.8
Curb weight, lbs.	2509	2678	2520	2623
Cargo vol., cu. ft.	13.2	10.7	13.0	64.4
Fuel capacity, gals.	15.2	15.2	15.2	15.2
Seating capacity	5	4	5	5
Front head room, in.	37.8	37.8	39.1	38.9
Max. front leg room, in.	42.6	42.2	42.1	42.1
Rear head room, in.	36.1	37.3	37.4	38.5
Min. rear leg room, in.	31.2	32.0	33.3	32.5

Powertrain layout: transverse front engine/front-wheel drive.

Engines	ohc I-4	ohv I-4	ohv V-6
Size, liters/cu. in.	2.0/121	2.2/133	3.1/191
Horsepower @ rpm	110 @ 5200	120 @ 5200	140 @ 4200
Torque (lbs./ft.) @ rpm	124 @ 3600	130 @ 4000	185 @ 3200
Availability	S[1]	S[2]	S[3]

CHEVROLET

EPA city/highway mpg	ohc I-4	ohv I-4	ohv V-6
5-speed OD manual	25/35	25/36	19/28
3-speed automatic	23/31	23/33	20/28

1. Sunbird LE. 2. Cavalier VL, RS. 3. Cavalier Z24, Sunbird SE; optional, Cavalier RS, wagon, and Sunbird LE.

Built in Lordstown, Ohio.

PRICES

Chevrolet Cavalier	Retail Price	Dealer Invoice	Fair Price
VL 2-door notchback	$8970	$8476	$8676
VL 4-door notchback	9120	8618	8818
RS 2-door notchback	10840	10135	10335
RS 4-door notchback	11440	10696	10896
RS 2-door convertible	16995	15890	16390
5-door wagon	11590	10837	11037
Z24 2-door notchback	13995	12665	12865
Z24 2-door convertible	19995	18095	18595
Destination charge	475	475	475

Additional "value-priced" models may be available in California.

Standard Equipment:

VL: 2.2-liter 4-cylinder engine, 5-speed manual transmission, anti-lock brakes, door-mounted automatic front seatbelts, power steering, tinted glass, cloth reclining front bucket seats, automatic power locks, floor console with armrest, left remote and right manual mirrors, 185/75R14 tires, wheel covers. **RS** adds: 3-speed automatic transmission (4-door and convertible), air conditioning, AM/FM radio, intermittent wipers, dome/reading light, visor mirrors, easy entry passenger seat (2-door), mechanical decklid release, bodyside moldings, striping; convertible has power windows with driver-side express down, map light, trunk net, power top. **Wagon** adds to RS notchback: 3-speed automatic transmission, power tailgate release, split-folding rear seat. **Z24** adds: 3.1-liter V-6, 5-speed manual transmission, Level III sport suspension, 4-way driver's seat, cassette player, Gauge Package with tachometer, trip odometer, tilt steering wheel, body-color fascias, rear spoiler, 205/60R15 tires, alloy wheels; convertible also has power windows with driver-side express down, map light, trunk net, power top.

Optional Equipment:

3.1-liter V-6 (RS, wagon)	834	717	734

Includes Performance Handling Pkg., Level III sport suspension, Gauge Pkg., 195/70R14 tires.

	Retail Price	Dealer Invoice	Fair Price
3-speed automatic transmission (VL, RS 2-door, Z24)	$495	$426	$436
Air conditioning	785	675	691
Preferred Equipment Group 1, VL	173	149	152
Mechanical decklid release, intermittent wipers, visor mirrors, bodyside moldings, floormats.			
Preferred Equipment Group 2, VL	543	467	478
Group 1 plus cruise control, tilt steering wheel.			
Preferred Equipment Group 1, wagon	435	374	383
Cruise control, intermittent wipers, tilt steering wheel.			
Preferred Equipment Group 1, RS 2- and 4-door, RS convertible	370	318	326
Cruise control, tilt steering wheel.			
Preferred Equipment Group 1, Z24 2-door	670	576	590
Cruise control, power windows with driver-side express down, split-folding rear seat, trunk net.			
Roof luggage carrier, wagon w/ Group 1	115	99	101
Rear spoiler, RS 2-door	110	95	97
Rear defogger	170	146	150
Split folding rear seat, RS 2- and 4-door	180	155	158
Includes trunk net.			
Vinyl bucket seats, convertibles	75	65	66
Removable sunroof, Z24 2-door	350	301	308
Power windows (NA VL), 2-doors	265	228	233
4-doors and wagons	330	284	290
AM/FM radio, VL	332	286	292
AM/FM cassette, VL	472	406	415
Wagon and RS	140	120	123
AM/FM CD player, VL	728	626	641
Wagon and RS	396	341	348
Z24	256	220	225
Engine block heater	20	17	18
205/60R15 white outline letter tires, Z24	98	84	86

Pontiac Sunbird

	Retail Price	Dealer Invoice	Fair Price
LE 2-door notchback	$9904	$9260	$9460
LE 4-door notchback	9904	9260	9460
LE 2-door convertible	15524	14515	15015

Prices are accurate at time of publication; subject to manufacturer's change.

	Retail Price	Dealer Invoice	Fair Price
SE 2-door notchback	$12524	$11334	$11534
Destination charge	475	475	475

Additional "value-priced" models may be available in California.

Standard Equipment:

LE: 2.0-liter 4-cylinder engine, 5-speed manual transmission, anti-lock brakes, power steering, door-mounted automatic front seat-belts, cloth reclining front bucket seats, center storage console, automatic power locks, tinted glass, trip odometer, left remote and right manual mirrors, illuminated entry, rear courtesy lights, day/night rearview mirror, AM/FM radio, 185/75R14 tires, wheel covers. **Convertible** has power top, power windows with driver-side express down, rear decklid spoiler, intermittent wipers, front storage armrest, visor mirrors, 195/65R15 touring tires, crosslace wheel covers. **SE** adds: 3.1-liter V-6 engine, ride and handling suspension, rally gauges (includes tachometer, coolant temperature and oil pressure gauges, trip odometer), rear decklid spoiler, front and rear fascias, visor mirrors, front and rear floormats, 195/65R15 touring tires, crosslace wheel covers.

Optional Equipment:

	Retail Price	Dealer Invoice	Fair Price
3.1-liter V-6 (std. SE)	712	612	627
Includes rally gauges.			
3-speed automatic transmission	495	426	436
Air conditioning	785	675	691
Option Group 1SB, LE and SE	1234	1061	1086
Air conditioning, cassette player, tilt steering wheel, intermittent wipers, front storage armrest, remote decklid release.			
Option Group 1SC, LE 2-door	1974	1698	1738
LE 4-door	1969	1693	1733
SE 2-door	1904	1637	1676
Group 1SB plus cruise control, power windows with driver-side express down, split folding rear seat, trunk net, rear decklid spoiler (LE 2-door).			
Option Group 1SB, LE convertible	1366	1175	1202
Air conditioning, cruise control, cassette player, tilt steering wheel, remote decklid release, trunk net.			
Special Appearance Pkg., LE convertible	316	272	278
Includes white convertible top, white vinyl interior, color-keyed bodyside moldings, door decals, front and rear fascias, white alloy wheels. Requires Group 1SB.			
Cruise control	225	194	198

	Retail Price	Dealer Invoice	Fair Price
Rear defogger	$170	$146	$150
Power windows, 2-door	265	228	233
4-door	330	284	290
Cassette player	170	146	150
CD player, LE, LE convertible and SE	396	341	349
with Group 1SB or 1SC	226	194	199
White vinyl bucket seats and interior trim, LE convertible	75	65	66
Split folding rear seat (NA convertible)	150	129	132
Decklid spoiler, LE 2-door	70	60	62
Tilt steering wheel	145	125	128
Removable glass sunroof, LE 2-door and SE	350	301	308
195/70R14 touring tires, LE	141	121	124
LE convertible (credit)	(17)	(15)	(15)
195/65R15 touring tires (std. LE convertible and SE)	158	136	139
15-inch crosslace wheelcovers (std. LE convertible and SE)	55	47	48
14-inch alloy wheels, LE	275	237	242
LE convertible and SE	220	189	194

CHEVROLET CORVETTE

Specifications	3-door hatchback	2-door conv.
Wheelbase, in.	96.2	96.2
Overall length, in.	178.5	178.5
Overall width, in.	70.7[1]	70.7
Overall height, in.	46.3	47.3
Curb weight, lbs.	3309	3361
Cargo vol., cu. ft.	12.6	6.6
Fuel capacity, gals.	20.0	20.0
Seating capacity	2	2
Front head room, in.	36.5	36.5
Max. front leg room, in.	42.0	42.0
Rear head room, in.	—	—
Min. rear leg room, in.	—	—

1. 73.1, ZR-1.

Powertrain layout: longitudinal front engine/rear-wheel drive.

Prices are accurate at time of publication; subject to manufacturer's change.

Chevrolet Corvette 3-door

Engines

	ohv V-8	dohc V-8
Size, liters/cu. in.	5.7/350	5.7/350
Horsepower @ rpm	300 @ 5000	405 @ 5800
Torque (lbs./ft.) @ rpm	340 @ 3600	385 @ 5200
Availability	S	S[1]
EPA city/highway mpg		
6-speed OD manual	17/27	17/25
4-speed OD automatic	17/24	

1. ZR-1

Built in Bowling Green, Ky.

PRICES

Chevrolet Corvette	Retail Price	Dealer Invoice	Fair Price
3-door hatchback	$36285	$31024	$32024
2-door convertible	43060	36816	38316
Destination charge	550	550	550

Standard Equipment:

5.7-liter V-8, 6-speed manual or 4-speed automatic transmission, anti-lock 4-wheel disc brakes, driver- and passenger-side air bags, power steering, Acceleration Slip Regulation, Pass-Key theft-deterrent system, automatic keyless entry with remote hatch release, air conditioning, liquid-crystal gauges with analog and digital display,

AM/FM cassette, power antenna, cruise control, rear defogger, reclining leather bucket seats, center console with coin tray and cassette/CD storage, armrest with lockable storage compartment, leather-wrapped tilt steering wheel, solar-control tinted glass, heated power mirrors, power windows with driver-side express down, power door locks, intermittent wipers, removable roof panel (hatchback), day/night rearview mirror with reading lights, fog lamps, lighted visor mirrors, Goodyear Eagle GS-C tires (255/45ZR17 front, 285/40ZR17 rear), alloy wheels. **Convertible** adds: manual folding top.

Optional Equipment:	Retail Price	Dealer Invoice	Fair Price
ZR-1 Special Performance Pkg.	$31258	$26257	—
5.7-liter DOHC V-8, Selective Ride and Handling Pkg., heavy-duty brake system, 6-way power driver's and passenger's seats, leather adjustable sport bucket seats, automatic climate control, low-tire-pressure warning, Delco/Bose Gold audio system with CD and cassette players, 275/40ZR17 front and 315/35ZR17 rear tires, 5-spoke alloy wheels.			
Preferred Equipment Group 1	1333	1120	1186
Automatic climate control, Delco/Bose audio system, 6-way power driver's seat.			
ZO7 Adjustable Performance Handling Pkg.	2045	1718	1820
Selective Ride and Handling Pkg., Bilstein Adjustable Ride Control System, stiffer springs, stabilizer bars, and bushings, heavy-duty brakes, 275/40ZR17 tires. Requires power seats; 4-speed automatic transmission requires performance axle ratio.			
FX3 Selective Ride and Handling Pkg.	1695	1424	1509
Bilstein Adjustable Ride Control System. Requires power seats.			
Leather adjustable sport bucket seats	625	525	556
Requires driver's and passenger's 6-way power seats.			
6-way power seats, each	305	256	271
Delco/Bose system with cassette and CD player with Group 1	396	333	352
Performance axle ratio	50	42	45
Low tire pressure warning indicator	325	273	289
Transparent blue or bronze tint single removable roof panel	650	546	579
Dual transparent blue or bronze tint removable roof panels	950	798	846
Removable hardtop, convertible	1995	1676	1776

Prices are accurate at time of publication; subject to manufacturer's change.

CHEVROLET LUMINA/ PONTIAC GRAND PRIX

Chevrolet Lumina Euro 4-door

Specifications

Specifications	2-door notchback	4-door notchback
Wheelbase, in.	107.5	107.5
Overall length, in.	198.3	198.3
Overall width, in.	71.7	71.0
Overall height, in.	53.3	53.6
Curb weight, lbs.	3269	3333
Cargo vol., cu. ft.	15.7	15.7
Fuel capacity, gals.	16.5	16.5
Seating capacity	6	6
Front head room, in.	37.5	38.7
Max. front leg room, in.	42.4	42.4
Rear head room, in.	37.1	38.0
Min. rear leg room, in.	34.8	36.9

Powertrain layout: transverse front engine/front-wheel drive.

Engines

Engines	ohv V-6	dohc V-6
Size, liters/cu. in.	3.1/191	3.4/207
Horsepower @ rpm	140 @ 4400	210 @ 5200
Torque (lbs./ft.) @ rpm	185 @ 3200	215 @ 4000
Availability	S[1]	S[2]

EPA city/highway mpg	ohv V-6	dohc V-6
4-speed OD automatic	19/29	17/26

1. Base Lumina, Euro and Grand Prix. 2. Lumina Z34; optional, Lumina Euro 4-door, Grand Prix.

Built in Canada.

PRICES

Chevrolet Lumina	Retail Price	Dealer Invoice	Fair Price
4-door notchback	$15305	$13392	$13642
Euro 2-door notchback	16875	14766	15016
Euro 4-door notchback	16515	14451	14701
Z34 2-door notchback	19310	16896	17146
Destination charge	525	525	525

Additional "value-priced" models may be available in California.

Standard Equipment:

3.1-liter V-6 engine, 4-speed automatic transmission, 4-wheel disc brakes, power steering, door-mounted automatic front seatbelts, air conditioning, automatic power locks, 60/40 cloth reclining front seat with center armrest and 4-way manual driver-side adjustment, tilt-steering wheel, AM/FM radio, visor mirrors, tinted glass, left remote and right manual mirrors, day/night rearview mirror with reading lights, intermittent wipers, floormats, 195/75R14 tires, wheel covers. **Euro** adds: anti-lock brakes, firmer suspension, cassette player, power windows (2-door), rear spoiler, upgraded upholstery, front storage armrest, 205/70R15 tires, alloy wheels. **Z34** adds: 3.4-liter DOHC V-6 engine, cruise control, power windows, reclining cloth bucket seats with 4-way driver-side manual seat adjustment, full floor console, remote mirrors, rear spoiler, Gauge Package with tachometer, power decklid release, trunk net, 225/60R16 tires, alloy wheels.

Optional Equipment:

Anti-lock brakes, base	450	387	398
Cruise control	225	194	199
Preferred Equipment Group 1, base	790	679	699
Cruise control, power windows and decklid release, remote mirrors, trunk net, decklid luggage rack.			
Group 1 w/o decklid luggage rack	675	581	597
Preferred Equipment Group 1,			
Euro 2-door	445	383	394
Euro 4-door	775	667	686
Cruise control, power windows (std. 2-door), power decklid release, remote mirrors, Gauge Pkg. with tachometer, trunk net.			

Prices are accurate at time of publication; subject to manufacturer's change.

	Retail Price	Dealer Invoice	Fair Price
Preferred Equipment Group 1, with Euro 3.4 Sedan Pkg.	$775	$667	$686
Cruise control, power windows and decklid release, remote mirrors, Gauge Pkg. with tachometer, trunk net.			
Euro 3.4 Sedan Pkg.	1376	1183	1218
3.4-liter V-6 engine, dual exhaust outlets, sport suspension, reclining cloth bucket seats with full floor console, 4-way manual driver-side seat adjustment, Gauge Pkg. with tachometer, monochromatic color body treatment (includes door handles, tail lamp surround, side and fascia moldings, valance), 225/60R16 tires, alloy wheels.			
Cloth 60/40 front seat with storage armrest	90	77	80
Cloth bucket seats with console, Euro	50	43	44
6-way power driver's seat (NA 2-doors)	270	232	239
Cassette player	140	120	124
Delco/Bose audio system, base	475	409	420
Euro and Z34	335	288	296
CD player, base	396	341	350
Euro and Z34	256	220	227
Rear defogger	170	146	150
Rear spoiler delete, Euro (credit)	(128)	(110)	(110)
Decklid luggage rack	115	99	102
Cellular telephone provision	45	39	40
195/75R14 whitewall tires, base	72	62	64
215/60R16 tires, Euro	112	96	99

Pontiac Grand Prix

	Retail Price	Dealer Invoice	Fair Price
SE 4-door notchback	$16254	$14710	$15210
SE 2-door notchback	16770	15345	15845
Destination charge	525	525	525

Additional "value-priced" models may be available in California.

Standard Equipment:

4-door: 3.1-liter V-6 engine, 4-speed automatic transmission, 4-wheel disc brakes, driver- and passenger-side air bags, power steering, air conditioning, power windows with driver-side express down, automatic power door locks, 45/55 cloth reclining front seat with folding armrest, AM/FM radio, Pass-Key theft-deterrent system, tachometer, trip odometer, coolant temperature gauge, tilt steering wheel, left remote and right manual mirrors, tinted glass, intermittent wipers, fog lamps, day/night rearview mirror, door map pockets, 205/70R15 tires, wheel covers. **2-door** adds: cruise control, cloth reclining bucket seats with storage console, AM/FM cassette player, leather-wrapped steering wheel with radio controls, power mirrors, rear defogger, remote decklid release, covered visor mirrors, front and rear floormats, 215/60R16 tires, alloy wheels.

Optional Equipment:	Retail Price	Dealer Invoice	Fair Price
3.4-liter DOHC V-6, SE 2-door	$1125	$968	$1011
Includes sport suspension and dual exhaust. Requires 225/60R16 tires, alloy wheels.			
Anti-lock brakes	450	387	404
Option Group 1SB, SE 4-door	717	617	644
Cruise control, rear defogger, power mirrors, AM/FM cassette player, remote decklid release, covered visor mirrors.			
Option Group 1SC, SE 4-door	1912	1644	1718
Group 1SC plus anti-lock brakes, 6-way power driver's seat, leather-wrapped steering wheel with radio controls, remote keyless entry, power antenna, front and rear floormats.			
B4U Special Edition Coupe Pkg., SE 2-door	600	516	539
Front and rear fascias, lower aero skirting, wheel flairs, 16x8-inch alloy wheels, dual exhaust, sport suspension, 225/60R16 performance tires.			
GT Performance Pkg. with			
Group 1SB, SE 4-door	2198	1890	1975
with Group 1SC	2103	1809	1890
3.4-liter DOHC V-6 engine, sport suspension, dual exhaust, GT nameplates, 225/60R16 tires, alloy wheels.			
GTP Performance Pkg., SE 2-door	1605	1380	1442
B4U Special Edition Coupe Pkg. plus 3.4-liter DOHC V-6 engine, hood louvers, GTP nameplates.			
6-way power driver's seat	305	262	274
Cruise control	225	194	202
Remote decklid release (std. 2-door)	60	52	54
Rear defogger (std. 2-door)	170	146	153
Power glass sunroof	695	598	625
with Custom Interior Trim Group	646	556	581
Trip computer	199	171	179
Head-up display	250	215	225
Remote keyless entry	135	116	121
B20/C3 Custom Interior Trim			
with Group 1SB, 4-door	628	540	565
with Group 1SC	533	458	480
with GT Performance Pkg.	(NC)	(NC)	(NC)
Replaces 45/55 front bench seat with custom bucket seats.			
B20/C6 Custom Interior Trim with			
Group 1SB, 4-door	488	420	439

Prices are accurate at time of publication; subject to manufacturer's change.

	Retail Price	Dealer Invoice	Fair Price
with Group 1SC	$393	$338	$354
45/55 reclining front bench seat with storage armrest, upgraded cloth upholstery, leather-wrapped steering wheel, front overhead miniconsole with front and rear reading lights, door courtesy lights, rear seat pass through, rear folding armrests, lighted visor mirrors, trunk net, deluxe floormats.			
B20/23 Custom Interior Trim			
with Group 1SB, 4-door	1103	949	993
with Group 1SC	1008	867	907
with GT Performance Pkg.	475	409	428
Adds leather upholstery.			
UN6 AM/FM cassette player, 4-door	170	146	153
UT6 AM and FM stereo cassette player			
with Group 1SB	400	344	359
with 1SB and Custom Interior Trim Group	350	301	315
with Group 1SC	225	194	202
Includes equalizer and steering wheel radio controls.			
U1C AM and FM stereo			
with CD player	396	341	356
with Group 1SB or 1SC	226	194	203
Includes equalizer and steering wheel radio controls.			
UP3 AM and FM stereo with CD player with Group 1SB	626	538	563
with Group 1SB and Custom Interior Group	576	495	518
with Group 1SC	451	388	405
Includes equalizer and steering wheel radio controls.			
Steering wheel radio controls	175	151	157
with Custom Interior Group	125	108	112
Requires UT6, U1C, or UP3 radio.			
Power antenna	85	73	76
Dual exhausts	90	77	81
Alloy wheels	275	237	247
215/60R16 touring tires	112	96	101
225/60R16 performance tires	150	129	135
Cellular phone provisions	35	30	31
Front and rear floormats	45	39	40
Covered visor mirrors (std. 2-door)	14	12	13

CHEVROLET LUMINA MINIVAN/OLDSMOBILE SILHOUETTE/PONTIAC TRANS SPORT

Chevrolet Lumina Minivan LS

Specifications	**4-door van**
Wheelbase, in.	109.8
Overall length, in.	191.5
Overall width, in.	73.9
Overall height, in.	65.7
Curb weight, lbs.	3554
Cargo vol., cu. ft.	112.6
Fuel capacity, gals.	20.0
Seating capacity	7
Front head room, in.	39.2
Max. front leg room, in.	40.0
Rear head room, in.	39.0
Min. rear leg room, in.	36.1

Powertrai\n layout: transverse front engine/front-wheel drive.

Engines	**ohv V-6**	**ohv V-6**
Size, liters/cu. in.	3.1/191	3.8/231

CHEVROLET

	ohv V-6	ohv V-6
Horsepower @ rpm	120 @ 4200	170 @ 4800
Torque (lbs./ft.) @ rpm	175 @ 2200	225 @ 3200
Availability	S	O[1]
EPA city/highway mpg		
3-speed automatic	19/23	
4-speed OD automatic		17/25

1. Standard, Silhouette Spec. Edition.

Built in Tarrytown, N.Y.

PRICES

Chevrolet Lumina Minivan	Retail Price	Dealer Invoice	Fair Price
4-door van	$17015	$15399	$15899
Destination charge	530	530	530

Additional "value-priced" models may be available in California.

Standard Equipment:

3.1-liter V-6, 3-speed automatic transmission, anti-lock brakes, driver-side air bag, power steering, 4-way adjustable driver's seat, reclining front bucket seats, 3-passenger middle seat, tinted glass with solar-control windshield, lockable center console with cup holders, front and rear reading lights, rear auxiliary power outlet, left remote and right manual mirrors, AM/FM radio, intermittent wipers, rear wiper/washer, 205/70R15 tires, wheel covers.

Optional Equipment:

	Retail Price	Dealer Invoice	Fair Price
3.8-liter V-6	619	532	551
Requires 4-speed automatic transmission and air conditioning.			
4-speed automatic transmission	200	172	178
Requires 3.8-liter V-6 engine.			
Front and rear air conditioning	1280	1101	1139
Requires 3.8-liter V-6 engine and Preferred Equipment Group 2 or 3.			
Preferred Equipment Group 1	778	669	692
Air conditioning, cruise control, tilt steering wheel, power door/tailgate locks with side door delay, power mirrors.			
Preferred Equipment Group 2	2323	1998	2067
Group 1 plus cassette player, power windows with driver-side express down, rear defogger, remote keyless entry, deep-tinted glass, 7-passenger seating, cargo area net.			

	Retail Price	Dealer Invoice	Fair Price
Preferred Equipment Group 3	$2843	$2445	$2530
Group 2 plus LS Trim Pkg. (includes body-color bumpers and rocker panels, upgraded cloth upholstery) and 6-way power driver's seat.			
Air conditioning	830	714	739
7-passenger seating	660	568	587
Two front bucket seats and five modular rear seats.			
Trailering Pkg.	320	275	285
Includes load leveling suspension. Requires 3.8-liter V-6 engine and Preferred Equipment Group 2 or 3.			
Traction Control	350	301	312
Requires Group 3.			
Manual sunroof (NA base or with Group 1)	300	258	267
Luggage rack (NA base)	145	125	129
Rear defogger	170	146	151
Deep-tinted glass	245	211	218
Power door/tailgate locks	300	258	267
Power windows (NA base)	275	237	245
Includes driver-side express down.			
Power mirrors	78	67	69
6-way power driver's seat (NA base or with Group 1)	270	232	240
Child safety seats	225	194	200
Requires 7-passenger seating.			
Power sliding side door	295	254	263
Requires Group 3.			
Remote keyless entry	125	108	111
Load leveling suspension (NA base or with Group 1)	170	146	151
Requires 205/70R15 tires (3.1-liter); 205/70R15 tires and Trailering Pkg. (3.8-liter).			
Cruise control	225	194	200
Tilt steering wheel	145	125	129
Cassette player	140	120	125
CD player	396	341	352
w/Group 2 and 3	256	220	228
Custom 2-tone paint	148	127	132
Cargo area net	30	26	27
205/70R15 touring tires	35	30	31
205/70R15 self-sealing tires	150	129	134
Alloy wheels	275	237	245
Engine block heater	20	17	18

Oldsmobile Silhouette

	Retail Price	Dealer Invoice	Fair Price
4-door van	$20365	$18430	$18830
Special Edition 4-door van with Pkg. R7B	20195	19310	—
Special Edition 4-door van with Pkg. R7C	21995	21029	—
Destination charge	530	530	530

Special Edition fair price not available at time of publication. Special Edition price includes destination charge. Additional "value-priced" models may be available in California.

Standard Equipment:

Base: 3.1-liter V-6, 3-speed automatic transmission, anti-lock brakes, driver-side air bag, power steering, front air conditioning, 4-way adjustable driver's seat, 7-passenger seating (front bucket seats, three middle and two rear modular seats), center console with locking storage, power mirrors, tachometer, coolant temperature and oil pressure gauges, voltmeter, trip odometer, AM/FM radio, tilt steering wheel, tinted glass, intermittent wipers, rear wiper/washer, rear defogger, fog lamps, visor mirrors, floormats, 205/70R15 tires, alloy wheels. **Special Edition w/Pkg. R7B** adds to base: 3.8-liter V-6 engine, 4-speed automatic transmission, Option Pkg. 1SB. **Special Edition w/Pkg. R7C** adds: Option Pkg. 1SC, custom leather trim.

Optional Equipment:

	Retail Price	Dealer Invoice	Fair Price
3.8-liter V-6 engine, base	800	688	716
Includes 4-speed automatic transmission.			
Traction control system, base	350	301	313
Requires FE3 Touring Suspension and 3.8-liter V-6, or Option Pkg. 1SC.			
Option Pkg. 1SB, base	1660	1428	1486
Convenience Pkg., AM/FM cassette, Remote Lock Control Pkg., deep-tinted glass, roof luggage carrier, overhead console with compass and temperature readout, cargo area net.			
Option Pkg. 1SC, base	3270	2812	2927
Base with sunroof	3095	2662	2770
Option Pkg. 1SB plus 3.8-liter V-6 engine, 4-speed automatic transmission, power driver's seat, power sliding door, steering wheel touch controls, leather-wrapped steering wheel.			
Convenience Pkg., base	800	688	716
Power windows, programmable power door locks with sliding door delay, cruise control.			
Integrated dual child seats, base	225	194	201
Rear air conditioning	450	387	403
Base requires Option Pkg. 1SB plus 3.8-liter V-6 engine, or Option Pkg. 1SC.			

	Retail Price	Dealer Invoice	Fair Price
Deep-tinted glass, base	$245	$211	$219
Power driver's seat	270	232	242
Base requires Option Pkg. 1SB.			
Power sliding door, base	295	254	264
Requires Option Pkg. 1SB.			
FE3 Touring Suspension, base	205	176	183
Includes eletronic level control, air inflation kit, 205/70R15 touring tires. Requires Option Pkg. 1SB or 1SC.			
Towing Pkg., base	355	305	318
Requires 3.8-liter V-6 engine or Option Pkg. 1SC. Includes FE3 Touring Suspension and traction control system.			
Cassette player, base	140	120	125
Base with Option Pkg. 1SB	30	26	27
AM/FM radio and CD player, Base with Option Pkg. 1SB	256	220	230
Base with Option Pkg. 1SC	226	194	202
Roof luggage carrier, base	145	125	130
Sunroof, base	350	301	313
Requires Option Pkg. 1SC.			
Cargo area net, base	30	26	27
Custom leather trim, base and Special Edition	870	748	779
Base with Option Pkg. 1SC	780	671	698
Engine block heater	18	15	16
Black roof delete	NC	NC	NC

Pontiac Trans Sport

	Retail Price	Dealer Invoice	Fair Price
SE 4-door van	$17469	$15809	$16309
Destination charge	530	530	530

Additional "value-priced" models may be available in California.

Standard Equipment:

SE: 3.1-liter V-6 engine, 3-speed automatic transmission, anti-lock brakes, driver-side air bag, power steering, 4-way adjustable driver's seat, front reclining bucket seats, 3-passenger middle seat, cloth upholstery, tinted glass with solar-control windshield, tachometer, coolant temperature and oil pressure gauges, voltmeter, trip odometer, AM/FM radio, Lamp Group (includes overhead console map lights, rear reading lights, cargo area lights, underhood light), left remote and right manual mirrors, door and seatback pockets, intermittent wipers, fog lamps, rear wiper/washer, visor mirrors, front and rear floormats, 205/70R15 tires, wheel covers.

Optional Equipment:

	Retail Price	Dealer Invoice	Fair Price
3.8-liter V-6 engine	$819	$704	$734
Includes 4-speed automatic transmission.			
Front air conditioning	830	714	744
Front and rear air conditioning			
with rear heater	1280	1101	1147
with Group 1SB, 1SC, 1SD, or 1SE	450	387	403
Requires automatic level control and deep-tint glass.			
Automatic level control	200	172	179
Includes rear saddle bags.			
Option Group 1SB	1388	1194	1244
Front air conditioning, cruise control, cassette player, power mirrors, tilt steering wheel.			
Option Group 1SC	2483	2153	2235
Group 1SB plus automatic power door locks, power windows with driver-side express down, rear defogger, 7-passenger seating, deep-tint glass.			
Option Pkg. 1SD	3033	2626	2730
Group 1SC plus 6-way power driver's seat, remote keyless entry system, luggage rack.			
Option Pkg. 1SE	4008	3465	3611
Group 1SD plus automatic level control, cassette player with equalizer, self-sealing touring tires, alloy wheels.			
Rear defogger	170	146	152
Luggage rack	175	151	157
Includes rear saddle bags.			
Power mirrors	48	41	43
Automatic power door locks	300	258	269
Power windows with driver-side			
express down	275	237	246
Requires automatic power door locks.			
Power sliding side door	295	254	264
Requires automatic power door locks. Requires remote keyless entry when ordering Group 1SC.			
Remote keyless entry system	135	116	121
Cassette player	140	120	125
Cassette player with equalizer,			
with Group 1SD	315	271	282
Includes steering wheel radio controls and leather-wrapped steering wheel.			
CD player with equalizer,			
with Group 1SD	541	465	485
with Group 1SE	206	177	185
Includes steering wheel radio controls and leather-wrapped steering wheel.			

	Retail Price	Dealer Invoice	Fair Price
6-way power driver's seat	$270	$232	$242
7-passenger seating	705	606	632
Three second row and two third row modular seats, cargo area net.			
7-passenger seating with leather upholstery, with Group 1SD or 1SE	870	748	780
Integral child seat	125	108	112
Requires 7-passenger seating.			
Two integral child seats	225	194	202
Requires 7-passenger seating.			
Deep-tint glass	245	211	220
Pop-up glass sunroof	300	258	269
Traction control	350	301	314
Trailer towing provisions	150	129	134
205/70R15 touring tires	35	30	31
Self-sealing touring tires	185	159	166
Alloy wheels	275	237	246

CHEVROLET S10 BLAZER/GMC JIMMY/ OLDSMOBILE BRAVADA

Specifications	3-door wagon	5-door wagon
Wheelbase, in.	100.5	107.0
Overall length, in.	170.3	176.8
Overall width, in.	65.4	65.4
Overall height, in.	64.1	64.3
Curb weight, lbs.	3536	3776
Cargo vol., cu. ft.	67.3	74.3
Fuel capacity, gals.	20.0	20.0
Seating capacity	4	6
Front head room, in.	39.1	39.1
Max. front leg room, in.	42.5	42.5
Rear head room, in.	38.7	38.8
Min. rear leg room, in.	35.5	36.5

Powertrain layout: longitudinal front engine/rear-wheel drive or on-demand 4WD (permanent 4WD Bravada).

Chevrolet S10 Blazer Tahoe LT 5-door

Engines

	ohv V-6	ohv V-6
Size, liters/cu. in.	4.3/262	4.3/262
Horsepower @ rpm	165 @ 4000	200 @ 4500
Torque (lbs./ft.) @ rpm	235 @ 2400	260 @ 3600
Availability	S	O[1]
EPA city/highway mpg		
5-speed OD manual	16/21	
4-speed OD automatic		16/22

1. Standard, Bravada.

Built in Pontiac, Mich., and Moraine, Ohio.

PRICES

Chevrolet S10 Blazer	Retail Price	Dealer Invoice	Fair Price
3-door wagon, 2WD	$15641	$14155	$14355
3-door wagon, 4WD	17437	15780	15980
5-door wagon, 2WD	16931	15323	15773
5-door wagon, 4WD	19165	17344	17794
Destination charge	475	475	475

Standard Equipment:

3-door: 4.3-liter V-6, 5-speed manual transmission, anti-lock brakes, power steering, solar-control tinted glass, coolant temperature and oil pressure gauges, voltmeter, AM radio, tow hooks (4WD), dual outside mirrors, front armrests, trip odometer, highback vinyl front reclining bucket seats with folding seatbacks, door map pockets, intermittent wipers, day/night rearview mirror, 205/75R15 tires, full-size spare tire. **5-door** adds: 60/40 reclining cloth front bench seat with storage armrest and cup holders, folding rear bench seat (4WD), Tahoe trim (includes reading lights and illuminated entry, lighted visor mirrors, chrome bumpers and grille, bright bodyside and wheel opening moldings, bright wheel trim rings (4WD), floormats, upgraded interior trim). 4WD models have Insta-Trac part-time 4WD.

Optional Equipment:	Retail Price	Dealer Invoice	Fair Price
RY8 Enhanced Powertrain Pkg.	$1160	$998	$1032
High output 4.3-liter V-6, 4-speed automatic transmission, engine and transmission oil coolers.			
Optional axle ratio	(NC)	(NC)	(NC)
Locking differential	252	217	224
Air conditioning	805	692	716
Tahoe Equipment Group 2,			
2WD 3-door	1378	1185	1226
4WD 3-door	1346	1158	1198
Chrome bumpers and grille, bright bodyside and wheel opening moldings, bright wheel trim rings (4WD), upgraded interior trim, seat separator console, reading lights, lighted visor mirrors, cargo net, tilt steering wheel, cruise control, AM/FM radio, cloth reclining bucket seats with manual lumbar adjustment, folding rear seat, deep-tinted side glass with light-tinted rear window, 205/75R15 white-letter tires.			
Tahoe Equipment Group 2,			
2WD 5-door	651	560	579
4WD 5-door	190	163	169
Cruise control, tilt steering wheel, cloth reclining bucket seats with manual lumbar support, folding rear seat (std. 4WD), AM/FM radio, deep-tinted side glass with light-tinted rear window, 205/75R15 white letter tires.			
Tahoe Equipment Group 3, 2WD 3-door	2943	2531	2619
4WD 3-door	2943	2531	2619
2WD 5-door	2365	2034	2105
4WD 5-door	1962	1687	1746
Group 2 plus air conditioning, cassette player, Driver Convenience Pkg. ZM8 (remote tailgate release and rear defogger), Operating Convenience Pkg. (power door locks and windows), rear wiper/washer, luggage carrier, alloy wheels.			
Tahoe LT Preferred Equipment Group,			
2WD 3-door	4245	3651	3778

Prices are accurate at time of publication; subject to manufacturer's change.

	Retail Price	Dealer Invoice	Fair Price
4WD 3-door	$4410	$3793	$3925
2WD 5-door	3776	3247	3361
4WD 5-door	3538	3043	3149

LT trim adds to Tahoe trim reclining leather bucket seats with power lumbar adjustment, 6-way power driver's seat, overhead console, remote keyless entry system, 205/75R15 white letter tires (2WD), 235/75R15 white letter tires (4WD), 2-tone paint, air conditioning, tilt steering wheel, cruise control, power tailgate release, rear defogger, cassette player, deep-tinted glass with light-tinted rear window, rear wiper/washer.

	Retail Price	Dealer Invoice	Fair Price
Folding cloth rear seat (std. 4WD 5-door)	435	374	387
with vinyl trim	409	352	364
Deluxe cloth 60/40 reclining bench seat, 5-door	(NC)	(NC)	(NC)
5-door with Tahoe Group 2 or 3 (credit)	(237)	(203)	(203)

Credit when 60/40 reclining cloth bench seat replaces standard reclining cloth bucket seats.

	Retail Price	Dealer Invoice	Fair Price
Custom highback vinyl bucket seats (NA 5-doors)	(NC)	(NC)	(NC)
Deluxe cloth highback reclining bucket seats with manual lumbar adjustment, 3-door	221	190	197
5-door	211	181	188
Deluxe cloth highback reclining bucket seats with power lumbar adjustment and 6-way power driver's seat, 3-door	366	315	326
5-door	501	431	446
3- and 5-door with Tahoe Group 2 or 3	290	249	258
3- and 5-door with Tahoe LT Group (credit)	(650)	(559)	(559)

Requires Operating Convenience Pkg.

	Retail Price	Dealer Invoice	Fair Price
Operating Convenience Pkg., 3-door	367	316	327
5-door	542	466	482

Includes power windows with driver-side express down and automatic power door locks.

	Retail Price	Dealer Invoice	Fair Price
Driver Convenience Pkg. ZQ3	383	329	341

Includes cruise control and tilt steering wheel.

	Retail Price	Dealer Invoice	Fair Price
Driver Convenience Pkg. ZM8	197	169	175

Includes rear defogger and remote tailgate release.

	Retail Price	Dealer Invoice	Fair Price
Electronic instrumentation	195	168	174
Air dam with fog lamps	115	99	102
Power mirrors	83	71	74
Heavy duty shock absorbers	40	34	36

	Retail Price	Dealer Invoice	Fair Price
Heavy duty front springs	$63	$54	$56
Includes heavy duty shock absorbers.			
Electronic shift transfer case, 4WD	123	106	109
Heavy duty battery	56	48	50
Heavy duty cooling system, with 5-speed manual transmission	135	116	120
Spare wheel and tire carrier	159	137	142
Cold Climate Pkg., 5-door	109	94	97
3-door	179	154	159
Front console	145	125	129
Overhead console	83	71	74
Luggage carrier, base and Tahoe Group 2	126	108	112
Deep-tinted glass	225	194	200
Tahoe Group 2 and 3, Tahoe LT	81	70	72
with light-tinted rear window (std. Tahoe LT)	144	124	128
Rear wiper/washer	125	108	111
Requires Driver Convenience Pkg. ZM8.			
Sliding side window, 3-door	257	221	229
Requires deep-tint glass.			
Radio delete (credit)	(95)	(82)	(82)
AM/FM radio	131	113	117
AM/FM cassette	253	218	225
with Tahoe Group 2	122	105	109
AM/FM cassette with equalizer	403	347	359
with Tahoe Group 2	272	234	242
with Tahoe Group 3 and Tahoe LT	150	129	134
AM/FM CD player	537	462	478
with Tahoe Group 2	406	349	361
with Tahoe Group 3 and Tahoe LT	284	244	253
Shield Pkg. (NA 2WD)	75	65	67
Includes transfer case, front differential skid plates, fuel tank and steering linkage shield.			
Off-road suspension	182	157	162
with Tahoe Group 2 or 3	122	105	109
Trailering Special Equipment (heavy duty) with Enhanced Powertrain Pkg.	210	181	187
with 5-speed manual transmission	345	297	307
Trailering Special Equipment (light duty), with Enhanced Powertrain Pkg.	109	94	97
with 5-speed manual transmission	300	258	267
Special 2-tone paint	227	195	202
Custom 2-tone (std. Tahoe LT)	275	237	245

	Retail Price	Dealer Invoice	Fair Price
Wheel opening moldings, 3-door	$43	$37	$38
5-door	13	11	12
Rally wheels, 3-door	92	79	82
Alloy wheels	340	292	303
5-door or Tahoe Group 2	248	213	221
Special alloy wheels, 5-door or with Tahoe Group 2	280	241	249
205/75R15 on/off road white letter tires	170	146	151
with Tahoe Group 2 or 3	49	42	44

GMC Jimmy

	Retail Price	Dealer Invoice	Fair Price
3-door wagon, 2WD	$15842	$14337	$14537
3-door wagon, 4WD	17761	16074	16274
5-door wagon, 2WD	17144	15515	15965
5-door wagon, 4WD	19501	17648	18098
Destination charge	475	475	475

Standard Equipment:

3-door: 4.3-liter V-6 engine, 5-speed manual transmission, part-time 4WD with electronic transfer case (4WD), 4-wheel anti-lock brakes, power steering, solar-control tinted glass, coolant temperature and oil pressure gauges, voltmeter, trip odometer, AM/FM radio, dual outside mirrors, front highback reclining buckets seats, door map pockets, 205/75R15 tires, full-size spare tire, front tow hooks, wheel trim rings (4WD). **5-door** adds: cloth 60/40 reclining split bench seat with folding center armrest, folding rear 3-passenger bench seat (4WD), mirrors, illuminated entry, reading lights, lighted visor mirrors, seatback convenience net, cupholders, floormats, bodyside moldings, wheel trim rings.

Option Pkgs., 3-door:

	Retail Price	Dealer Invoice	Fair Price
SL Pkg. 2	684	588	609
AM/FM cassette, cruise control, tilt steering wheel, folding rear 3-passenger bench seat, deep-tinted glass with light-tinted rear window, luggage carrier.			
SLS Pkg. 2, 2WD	1310	1127	1166
4WD	1278	1099	1137
SL Pkg. 2 contents plus SLS Sport Decor Pkg.			
SLE Pkg. 2	1412	1214	1257
SL Pkg. 2 contents plus SLE Comfort Decor Pkg.			
SLE Pkg 3	2662	2289	2369

	Retail Price	Dealer Invoice	Fair Price
SLE Comfort Decor Pkg. plus air conditioning, AM/FM cassette, cruise control, tilt steering wheel, power door locks and windows, rear wiper/washer, alloy wheels, folding rear 3-passenger bench seat, deep-tinted glass, luggage carrier.			
SLS Pkg. 3	$2708	$2329	$2410
SLS Sport Decor Pkg. plus air conditioning, AM/FM cassette, cruise control, tilt steering wheel, power door locks and windows, rear wiper/washer, alloy wheels, folding rear 3-passenger bench seat, deep-tinted glass, luggage carrier.			
SLT Pkg. 4, 2WD	4216	3626	3752
4WD	4441	3819	3952
SLT Touring Decor Pkg. plus air conditioning, cruise control, tilt steering wheel, AM/FM cassette with equalizer, power mirrors, rear defogger, power tailgate release, rear wiper/washer, deep-tinted glass, luggage carrier.			

Option Pkgs., 5-door:

	Retail Price	Dealer Invoice	Fair Price
SLE Pkg. 2, 2WD	410	353	365
4WD (credit)	(25)	(22)	(22)
Cruise control, tilt steering wheel, AM/FM cassette, folding rear 3-passenger bench seat (std. 4WD), deep-tinted glass with light-tinted rear window, luggage carrier.			
SLE Pkg. 3, 2WD	2194	1887	1953
4WD	1791	1540	1594
SLE Pkg. 2 plus air conditioning, power door locks and windows, rear wiper/washer, rear defogger, power tailgate release, cloth reclining bucket seat and floor console (60/40 split bench seat may be substituted at no additional cost), alloy wheels.			
SLS Pkg. 3, 2WD	2248	1933	2001
4WD	1845	1587	1642
SLS Pkg. 2 plus air conditioning, power door locks and windows, rear wiper/washer, rear defogger, power tailgate release, cloth reclining bucket seat and floor console (60/40 split bench seat may be substituted at no additional cost), alloy wheels.			
SLT Pkg. 4, 2WD	3735	3212	3324
4WD	3557	3059	3166
SLT Touring Decor Pkg. plus air conditioning, cruise control, tilt steering wheel, AM/FM cassette with equalizer, power mirrors, rear defogger, power tailgate release, rear wiper/washer, deep-tinted glass, luggage carrier.			

Individual Options:

	Retail Price	Dealer Invoice	Fair Price
Enhanced Powertrain Pkg.	1160	998	1032
Includes high output 4.3-liter V-6, 4-speed automatic transmission, extra capacity cooling.			

	Retail Price	Dealer Invoice	Fair Price
Optional axle ratio	(NC)	(NC)	(NC)
Locking differential	$252	$217	$224
Manual transfer case, 4WD (credit)	(123)	(106)	(106)
Replaces standard electronic push button shift with manual floor mounted shift.			
SLE Comfort Decor Pkg. (std. 5-door),			
3-door 2WD	900	774	801
4WD	868	746	773
Reclining bucket seats, cloth upholstery, upgraded door trim, chrome grille, bodyside and wheel opening moldings, floor console, illuminated entry, lighted visor mirrors, reading lights, floormats, rally wheels (2WD), wheel trim rings (4WD).			
SLS Sport Decor Pkg., 3-door	1202	1034	1070
Reclining bucket seats, floor console, leather-wrapped steering wheel, illuminated entry, lighted visor mirrors, reading lights, convenience net (2-door), body-color bumpers and grille, upgraded door trim, bodyside and wheel opening moldings, floormats, alloy wheels.			
SLS Sport Decor Pkg. 5-door 2WD	302	260	269
5-door 2WD with bucket seats	513	441	457
5-door 4WD	334	287	297
5-door 4WD with bucket seats	545	469	485
Leather-wrapped steering wheel, body-color bumpers, grille, and wheel opening moldings, alloy wheels.			
SLT Touring Decor Pkg., 3-door 2WD	3325	2860	2959
3-door 4WD	3550	3053	3160
5-door 2WD	2844	2446	2531
5-door 4WD	2666	2293	2373
Reclining leather buckets seat with driver- and passenger-side lumbar adjustment, 6-way power driver's seat, folding rear 3-passenger bench seat, floor and overhead consoles, power windows and door locks, remote keyless entry system, illuminated entry, reading lights, lighted visor mirrors, leather-wrapped steering wheel, body-color bumpers, bodyside and wheel opening moldings, upgraded door trim, conventional 2-tone paint, convenience net (3-door), floormats, 205/75R15 all-season tires, alloy wheels. 4WD adds: Bilstein shocks, 235/75R15 all-season tires.			
Air conditioning	780	671	694
Folding rear seat, 3-door	409	352	364
Cloth folding rear seat, 3-door and			
5-door 2WD	435	374	387
Cloth bucket seats, 3-door	76	65	68
5-door	211	181	188
Deep-tinted glass	225	194	200
with light-tinted rear window	144	124	128
Requires Convenience Pkg. ZM8.			

	Retail Price	Dealer Invoice	Fair Price
6-way power driver's seat and driver/ passenger power lumber support	$290	$249	$258
Requires SLE or SLS Decor Pkgs., power windows and locks, reclining bucket seats.			
Floor console	145	125	129
Requires reclining bucket seats.			
Overhead console	83	71	74
Includes reading lights and storage compartments. Requires SLE or SLS decor Pkgs., bucket seats.			
Heavy duty battery	56	48	50
Spare wheel and tire carrier	159	137	142
Cold Climate Pkg., 3-door	179	154	159
SLE, SLS or SLT 3-door, 5-door	109	94	97
Convenience Pkg. ZQ3	383	329	341
Cruise control, tilt steering wheel.			
Convenience Pkg. ZM8	197	169	175
Remote tailgate release, rear defogger.			
Convenience Pkg. ZQ2, 3-door	367	316	327
5-door	542	466	482
Power windows and locks.			
Air deflector with fog lamps, 2WD	115	99	102
Rear wiper/washer	125	108	111
Requires ZM8 Convenience Pkg.			
Sliding side window (2WD only)	257	221	229
Electronic instrumentation	195	168	174
Remote keyless entry	135	116	120
Requires ZQ2 and ZM8 Convenience Pkgs., bucket seats, floor console.			
Luggage carrier	126	108	112
Power mirrors	83	71	74
Wheel opening moldings	43	37	38
Special 2-tone paint	172	148	153
Conventional 2-tone paint (NA SL or SLS decor)	172	148	153
AM/FM cassette	122	105	109
AM/FM cassette with equalizer	272	234	242
AM/FM with CD player	406	349	361
AM/FM radio delete (credit)	(226)	(194)	(194)
AM radio (credit)	(131)	(113)	(113)
Credit when AM radio is substituted for standard AM/FM radio.			
Shield Pkg., 4WD (NA SLT Decor Pkg.)	75	65	67
Heavy duty shock absorbers (NA SLT Decor Pkg.)	40	34	36
Heavy duty front springs, 4WD	63	54	56

Prices are accurate at time of publication; subject to manufacturer's change.

	Retail Price	Dealer Invoice	Fair Price
Softride Suspension, 4WD 5-door	$235	$202	4209
with 235/75R15 WL tires	358	308	319
Off-Road Suspension Pkg., 3-door, 4WD	122	105	109
Bilstein gas shock absorbers, larger torsion bar, jounce bumpers, stabilizer bar, larger body mounted tow hooks. NA SLT.			
Heavy duty trailering equipment	345	297	307
with high output 4.3-liter V-6 engine	210	181	187
Light duty trailering equipment	300	258	267
with high output 4.3-liter V-6 engine	109	94	97
205/75R15 on/off-road OWL tires	170	146	151
205/75R15 all-season OWL tires	121	104	108
235/75R15 all-season tires	153	132	136
235/75R15 all-season OWL tires, 4WD	286	246	255
with SLT	133	114	118
235/75R15 on/off-road WL tires, 4WD	335	288	298
WL denotes white letter; OWL denotes outline white letter.			
Alloy wheels	340	292	303
with SLE	284	244	253
Wheel trim rings, 3-door	60	52	53
Rally wheels, 2WD	92	79	82
Body striping	55	47	49
Cargo area security shade	69	59	61
NA 3-door; requires spare tire carrier.			
Front floormats	25	22	22

Oldsmobile Bravada

	Retail Price	Dealer Invoice	Fair Price
5-door 4WD wagon	$26320	$23819	$24269
Special Edition 5-door 4WD wagon	25295	24178	—
Destination charge	475	475	475

Special Edition fair price not available at time of publication. Special Edition price includes destination charge. Additional "value-priced" models may be available in California.

Standard Equipment:

4.3-liter V-6, 4-speed automatic transmission, permanent 4-wheel drive, anti-lock brakes, power steering, air conditioning, power driver's seat, driver and passenger power lumbar adjustment, center console with cup holders and electrical outlets, overhead console with compass, outside temperature readout and reading lamps, folding rear seat with armrest, solar control tinted windshield and front door glass, deep-tint rear windows, cruise control, power windows, power locks with remote control, power mirrors, rear wiper/

washer, intermittent wipers, rear defogger, coolant temperature and oil pressure gauges, voltmeter, trip odometer, fog lamps, remote tailgate release, roof luggage rack, AM/FM cassette with equalizer, tilt steering wheel, leather-wrapped steering wheel, lighted visor mirrors, map lights, floormats, 235/75R15 tires, alloy wheels, full-size spare tire. **Special Edition** adds: custom leather trim, electronic instruments, exterior spare tire carrier, towing package.

Optional Equipment:	Retail Price	Dealer Invoice	Fair Price
Custom leather trim	$650	$559	$579
CD player	134	115	119
Towing Pkg.	255	219	227
Electronic instruments	195	168	174
235/75R15 white outline letter tires	133	114	118
Special Edition	NC	NC	NC
Exterior spare tire carrier	159	137	142
Engine block heater	33	28	29
Gold Pkg.	60	52	53
Special Edition	NC	NC	NC

Gold-tinted exterior emblems, gold-tinted cast aluminum wheels with black ports.

CHRYSLER LE BARON

Chrysler LeBaron GTC Convertible

Specifications	2-door conv.	4-door notchback
Wheelbase, in.	100.6	103.5
Overall length, in.	184.8	182.7

	2-door conv.	4-door notchback
Overall width, in.	69.2	68.1
Overall height, in.	52.4	55.9
Curb weight, lbs.	3122	2971
Cargo vol., cu. ft.	9.2	14.4
Fuel capacity, gals.	14.0	16.0
Seating capacity	4	6
Front head room, in.	38.3	38.4
Max. front leg room, in.	42.5	41.9
Rear head room, in.	37.0	37.9
Min. rear leg room, in.	33.0	38.3

Powertrain layout: transverse front engine/front-wheel drive.

Engines

	ohc V-6
Size, liters/cu. in.	3.0/181
Horsepower @ rpm	141 @ 5000
Torque (lbs./ft.) @ rpm	171 @ 2400
Availability	S

EPA city/highway mpg

3-speed automatic	21/27
4-speed OD automatic	20/28

Built in Newark, Del., and Mexico.

PRICES

Chrysler LeBaron Convertible	Retail Price	Dealer Invoice	Fair Price
GTC 2-door convertible w/Pkg. 26A	$16999	$15939	$16439
Destination charge	530	530	530

Standard Equipment:

Pkg. 26A: 3.0-liter V-6 engine, 4-speed automatic transmission, driver- and passenger-side air bags, power steering, power convertible top, air conditioning, cloth reclining front bucket seats, center console with armrest, rear defogger, tinted glass, tachometer, coolant temperature and oil pressure gauges, voltmeter, trip odometer, dual remote mirrors, AM/FM cassette radio, power windows, intermittent wipers, reading lights, 205/60R15 tires, wheel covers.

Optional Equipment:

	Retail Price	Dealer Invoice	Fair Price
Pkg. 26T	$1000	$850	$870
Deluxe Convenience Group, Power Convenience Group, power driver's seat, remote decklid release, floormats.			
Pkg. 26W	2000	1700	1740
Pkg. 26T plus leather seats, leather-wrapped steering wheel, Light Group, alloy wheels.			
Anti-lock disc brakes	699	594	608
Deluxe Convenience Group	372	316	324
Cruise control, tilt steering wheel.			
Power Convenience Group	338	287	294
Automatic power locks, heated power mirrors.			
Bright LX Decor Group	50	43	44
Bright grille, decklid and taillamp moldings, bodyside moldings, exterior badges.			
Light Group, w/Pkg. 26T	196	167	171
Includes illuminated entry system and lighted vanity mirrors.			
Vinyl seats, w/Pkg. 26T	102	87	89
Leather seats, w/Pkg. 26T	668	568	581
Includes 6-way power driver's seat.			
Premium leather seats,			
w/Pkg. 26T	1092	928	950
w/Pkg. 26W	424	360	369
Includes 12-way power driver's seat.			
Trip computer, w/Pkg. 26T or 26W	93	79	81
Security alarm, w/Pkg. 26T or 26W	149	127	130
AM/FM cassette with equalizer and Infinity speakers,			
w/Pkg. 26T or 26W	524	445	456
CD player with equalizer and Infinity speakers, w/Pkg. 26T or 26W	694	590	604
Extra cost paint	97	82	84
16-inch Alloy Wheel/Performance Group, w/Pkg. 26T	516	439	449
w/Pkg. 26W	188	160	164
Performance Handling Suspension, 205/55R16 performance tires, alloy wheels.			
15-inch alloy wheels, w/Pkg. 26T	328	279	285

Chrysler LeBaron Sedan

	Retail Price	Dealer Invoice	Fair Price
LE 4-door notchback	$16551	$14869	$15169
Landau 4-door notchback	17933	16072	16372
Destination charge	505	505	505

Prices are accurate at time of publication; subject to manufacturer's change.

CHRYSLER

Standard Equipment:

LE: 3.0-liter V-6 engine, 3-speed automatic transmission, driver-side air bag, motorized front passenger shoulder belt, power steering, air conditioning, cloth 50/50 front seat, split folding rear seat, tachometer, trip odometer, coolant temperature and oil pressure gauges, voltmeter, tilt steering wheel, cruise control, power windows and locks, AM/FM radio, tinted glass, rear defogger, heated power mirrors, intermittent wipers, visor mirrors, map lights, remote decklid release, floormats, striping, 195/70R14 tires, wheel covers. **Landau** adds to base: 4-speed automatic transmission, cassette player, landau vinyl roof, whitewall tires.

Optional Equipment:

	Retail Price	Dealer Invoice	Fair Price
LE Pkg. 28U	$173	$147	$151
4-speed automatic transmission.			
LE Pkg. 28X	639	543	559
Handling Suspension, cassette player, 205/60R15 tires, alloy wheels. Requires 4-speed automatic transmission.			
Landau Pkg. 28L	760	646	665
Interior Illumination Group, overhead console, leather-wrapped steering wheel, wire wheel covers.			
Anti-lock 4-wheel disc brakes	699	594	612
Interior Illumination Group, LE	195	166	171
Illuminated entry, lighted visor mirrors.			
Electronic Display Group, Landau w/Pkg. 28L	317	269	277
Electronic instruments, trip computer.			
Power driver's seat, LE w/Pkg. 28U or 28X, Landau	306	260	268
Cassette player, LE	170	145	149
Cassette with equalizer and Infinity speakers,			
LE w/Pkg. 28U	520	442	455
LE w/Pkg. 28X or Landau	350	298	306
Wire wheel covers, Landau	240	204	210
Leather seats, Landau	974	828	852
Includes power driver's seat, leather-wrapped steering wheel.			
195/70R14 whitewall tires, LE w/Pkg. 26 U or 28U	73	62	64
Conventional spare tire, LE w/Pkg. 26U or 28U, Landau	95	81	83

CHRYSLER NEW YORKER/LHS

Chrysler LHS

Specifications	4-door notchback
Wheelbase, in.	113.0
Overall length, in.	207.4
Overall width, in.	74.4
Overall height, in.	56.3
Curb weight, lbs.	3457
Cargo vol., cu. ft.	17.9
Fuel capacity, gals.	18.0
Seating capacity	6
Front head room, in.	39.3
Front leg room, max., in.	42.3
Rear head room, in.	37.8
Rear leg room, min. , in.	40.6

Powertrain layout: longitudinal front engine/front-wheel drive.

Engines	ohc V-6
Size, liters/cu. in.	3.5/215
Horsepower @ rpm	214 @ 5800
Torque (lbs./ft.) @ rpm	221 @ 2800
Availability	S

Prices are accurate at time of publication; subject to manufacturer's change.

EPA city/highway mpg	ohc V-6
4-speed OD automatic	18/26

Built in Canada.

PRICES

Chrysler New Yorker/LHS	Retail Price	Dealer Invoice	Fair Price
New Yorker 4-door notchback	$25541	$22580	$23541
LHS 4-door notchback	30283	26691	28283
Destination charge	595	595	595

Standard Equipment:

New Yorker: 3.5-liter V-6 engine, 4-speed automatic transmission, anti-lock 4-wheel disc brakes, driver- and passenger-side air bags, variable-assist power steering, air conditioning, 50/50 cloth front seat with center armrests, 8-way power driver's seat with manual lumbar adjustment, tilt steering wheel, cruise control, power windows and locks, heated power mirrors, speed-sensitive intermittent wipers, rear defogger, solar control tinted glass, tachometer, trip odometer, coolant temperature gauge, AM/FM cassette, power decklid release, lighted visor mirrors, reading lights, floormats, trunk cargo net, touring suspension, 225/60R16 touring tires, wheel covers. **LHS** adds: traction control, automatic temperature control, leather upholstery, 8-way power passenger seat, power front seat recliners, center console with cup holders and storage bin, overhead console with compass and thermometer, trip computer, leather-wrapped steering wheel and shift knob, power antenna, automatic day/night rearview mirror, remote keyless illuminated entry system, time-delay headlamp system, power moonroof, Chrysler/Infinity cassette system with equalizer and 11 speakers, theft security alarm, fog lamps, alloy wheels, conventional spare tire.

Optional Equipment:

	Retail Price	Dealer Invoice	Fair Price
New Yorker Pkg. 26B	1338	1137	1271
Automatic temperature control, mini overhead console with compass and outside temperature readout, trip computer, Remote/Illuminated Entry Group, Chrysler/Infinity AM/FM cassette system with equalizer and 11 speakers, power antenna, automatic day/night rearview mirror, time-delay headlamp system, security alarm, lighted visor mirrors.			
New Yorker Pkg. 26C	2633	2238	2501
Pkg. 26B plus 8-way power passenger seat, leather upholstery, leather-wrapped steering wheel, alloy wheels, conventional spare tire.			
Traction control, New Yorker	175	149	166

	Retail Price	Dealer Invoice	Fair Price
8-way power front passenger seat, New Yorker	$377	$320	$358
Leather seats, New Yorker	1075	914	1021
Includes power front passenger seat and leather-wrapped steering wheel.			
Power moonroof, New Yorker w/Pkg. 26B or 26C	792	673	752
Chrysler/Infinity CD System, New Yorker w/Pkg. 26B or 26C, LHS	169	144	161
Includes equalizer, power antenna, and 11 speakers.			
Extra cost paint	97	82	92
Bright platinum metallic paint	200	170	190
Alloy wheels, New Yorker	328	279	312
Conventional spare tire, New Yorker	95	81	90

DODGE CARAVAN/ CHRYSLER TOWN & COUNTRY/PLYMOUTH VOYAGER

Dodge Grand Caravan ES

Specifications	4-door van	4-door van
Wheelbase, in.	112.3	119.3

DODGE

	4-door van	4-door van
Overall length, in.	178.1	192.8
Overall width, in.	72.0	72.0
Overall height, in.	66.0	66.7
Curb weight, lbs.	3306	3574
Cargo vol., cu. ft.	117.0	141.3
Fuel capacity, gals.	20.0	20.0
Seating capacity	7	7
Front head room, in.	39.1	39.1
Max. front leg room, in.	38.3	38.3
Rear head room, in.	38.5	38.7
Min. rear leg room, in.	37.6	37.7

Powertrain layout: transverse front engine/front-wheel drive or permanent 4WD.

Engines	ohc I-4	ohc V-6	ohv V-6	ohc V-6
Size, liters/cu. in.	2.5/153	3.0/181	3.3/201	3.8/204
Horsepower @ rpm	100 @ 4800	142 @ 5000	162 @ 4800	162 @ 4400
Torque (lbs./ft.) @ rpm	135 @ 2800	173 @ 2400	194 @ 3600	213 @ 3600
Availability	S	O	O	O[1]
EPA city/highway mpg				
3-speed automatic	20/24	19/23		
4-speed OD automatic		18/23	18/23	16/22

1. Standard, Town & Country.

Built in St. Louis, Mo., and Canada.

PRICES

Dodge Caravan	Retail Price	Dealer Invoice	Fair Price
Base SWB	$15520	$14158	$14858
Base Grand	18178	16522	17222
SE SWB	18139	16462	17162
Grand SE	19304	17513	18413
Grand SE AWD	21982	19869	20769
LE SWB	21963	19827	20727
Grand LE	22883	20662	21562
Grand LE AWD	25560	23017	23917
ES SWB	22472	20275	21175
Grand ES	23392	21110	22010

	Retail Price	Dealer Invoice	Fair Price
Grand ES AWD	$26069	$23466	$24366
Destination charge	560	560	560

SWB denotes standard wheelbase; AWD denotes All-Wheel Drive.

Standard Equipment:

Base: 2.5-liter 4-cylinder engine, 3-speed automatic transmission, driver- and passenger-side air bags, power steering, cloth front bucket seats, 3-passenger middle bench seat, tinted glass, trip odometer, coolant temperature gauge, dual outside mirrors, visor mirrors, AM/FM radio, intermittent wipers, rear wiper/washer, 195/75R14 tires, wheel covers. **Base Grand** adds: 3.0-liter V-6 engine, 7-passenger seating (front buckets and 2-place middle and 3-place rear bench seats), rear trim panel storage and cup holders, 205/70R15 tires. **SE** adds to Base: 3.0-liter V-6 engine, 3-speed automatic transmission, cruise control, power mirrors, cassette player, power remote tailgate release, tilt steering wheel, front passenger lockable underseat storage drawer, striping, dual note horn. **Grand SE** adds to Base Grand: 3.3-liter V-6 engine, 4-speed automatic transmission, cruise control, power mirrors, cassette player, power remote tailgate release, tilt steering wheel, front passenger lockable underseat storage drawer, striping, dual note horn. **LE** adds to SE: front air conditioning, front storage console, overhead console with trip computer, rear defogger, power rear quarter vent windows, power door locks, remote keyless entry system, tachometer, oil pressure gauge, voltmeter, heated power mirrors, lighted visor mirrors, illuminated entry system, headlamp time delay, floormats, 205/70R15 tires. **Grand LE** adds to Grand SE: front air conditioning, front storage console, overhead console with trip computer, rear defogger, power rear quarter vent windows, power door locks, remote keyless entry system, tachometer, oil pressure gauge, voltmeter, heated power mirrors, lighted visor mirrors, illuminated entry system, headlamp time delay, floormats. **ES** adds to LE and Grand LE: ES Decor Group. **AWD** models have permanently engaged all-wheel drive.

Quick Order Packages:

	Retail Price	Dealer Invoice	Fair Price
Pkgs. 21T, 22T, 24T Base SWB and 26T Base SWB, Base Grand	213	181	196

Front air conditioning, map and cargo lights, power remote liftgate release, front passenger underseat lockable storage drawer, bodyside molding, dual horns. Pkg. 22T requires 3-speed automatic transmission; Pkg. 24T requires 3.0-liter engine and 3-speed automatic transmission; Pkg. 26T requires 3.0-liter engine and 4-speed transmission.

	Retail Price	Dealer Invoice	Fair Price
Pkg. 26B SE SWB and Pkg. 28B SE SWB, Grand SE, Grand SE AWD	$213	$181	$196

Pkgs. 26-28B add to SE standard equipment front air conditioning, map and cargo lights, rear defogger. SE SWB Pkg. 24B requires 4-speed automatic transmission; SE SWB Pkg. 28B requires 3.3-liter engine and 4-speed automatic transmission.

	Retail Price	Dealer Invoice	Fair Price
Pkg. 26D SE SWB, and Pkg. 28D SE SWB, Grand SE, Grand SE AWD	1159	985	1066

Pkgs. 26-28D add to Pkgs. 26-28B forward and overhead consoles, oil pressure and voltage gauges, tachometer, lighted visor mirrors, Light Group, power door locks and rear quarter vent windows, floormats, deluxe insulation. SE SWB Pkg. 26D requires 4-speed automatic transmission; SE SWB Pkg. 28D requires 3.3-liter engine and 4-speed automatic transmission.

	Retail Price	Dealer Invoice	Fair Price
Pkg. 26K LE SWB, and Pkg. 28K LE SWB, Grand LE, Grand LE AWD and Pkg. 29K Grand LE, Grand LE AWD	306	260	282

Pkgs. 26K-29K add to LE standard equipment: power driver's seat, power windows, AM/FM radio with cassette player, equalizer and six Infinity speakers, sunscreen glass. LE SWB Pkg. 26K requires 4-speed automatic transmission; LE SWB Pkg. 28K requires 3.3-liter engine and 4-speed automatic transmission; Grand LE and Grand LE AWD require 3.8-liter engine.

	Retail Price	Dealer Invoice	Fair Price
Pkg. 28L and 29L Grand LE, Grand LE AWD	962	818	885

Pkgs. 28L-29L add to 28K-29K: Woodgrain Decor Group (woodgrain trim and moldings, front and rear body-color fascias, luggage rack, whitewall tires, alloy wheels). Requires 3.8-liter engine.

	Retail Price	Dealer Invoice	Fair Price
Pkg. 26M and ES SWB, and Pkg. 28M ES SWB, Grand ES and Pkg. 29M, Grand ES	431	366	397
Pkg. 28 and 29M, Grand ES AWD	306	260	282

Pkgs. 26M-29M add to 26K-29K, ES SWB, Grand ES SWB: ES Decor Group (body-color fascia, cladding, and grille, fog lamps, alloy wheels), Sport Handling Group (heavy duty brakes, firmer front and rear sway bars, upgraded front struts and rear shocks, 205/70R15 tires, alloy wheels). Pkgs. 28M-29M add to 28K-29K Grand ES AWD: ES Decor Pkg. with Sport Handling Suspension, 205/70R15 tires, alloy wheels. (Sport Handling Group not available with AWD); deletes 2-tone paint. ES SWB Pkg. 26M requires 4-speed automatic transmission; ES SWB Pkg. 28M requires 3.3-liter engine and 4-speed automatic transmission; Grand ES and Grand ES AWD require 3.8-liter engine.

Individual Options:

	Retail Price	Dealer Invoice	Fair Price
3.0-liter V-6, Base SWB	767	652	706

	Retail Price	Dealer Invoice	Fair Price
Requires 3-speed automatic transmission.			
3.3-liter V-6, SE, LE, and ES SWB	$102	$87	$94
Requires 4-speed automatic transmission.			
3.8-liter V-6, Grand LE, ES	302	257	278
Includes 4-speed transmission.			
3-speed automatic transmission, Base SWB	601	511	553
4-speed automatic transmission, SE, LE ES, SWB and Base Grand	198	168	182
Anti-lock brakes: SE SWB with Pkgs. 26-28B or 26-28D	687	584	632
SE SWB with Pkgs. 26-28B or 26-28D and alloy wheels, Trailer Tow, Sport Handling, Gold Special Edition, or Sport Wagon Groups; Grand SE with Pkgs. 28B or 28D	599	509	551
LE SWB with Pkgs. 26-28K or 26-28M; Grand LE with Pkgs. 26-28K, 26-28L, or 26-28M	599	509	551
Front air conditioning, Base SWB and Base Grand	857	728	788
Front air conditioning with sunscreen glass, Base SWB with Pkg. 26T, SE SWB with Pkg. 26-28B and 26-28D, Base Grand with Pkg. 26T and SE Grand with Pkg. 28B and 28D	414	352	381
Not available with Sport Wagon Decor Group.			
Sunscreen glass, Grand SE AWD with Pkg. 28B and 28D	414	352	381
Rear air conditioning with rear heater and sunscreen glass, Base Grand with Pkg. 26T, Grand SE with Pkg. 28B, Grand SE AWD with Pkg. 28B	988	840	909
Grand SE and Grand SE AWD with Pkg. 28B and Sport Wagon Decor Group	574	488	528
with Trailer Towing Group	925	786	851
with Sport Wagon Decor Group and Trailer Towing Group	511	434	470
Grand SE and Grand SE AWD with Pkg. 28D	880	748	810
with Sport Wagon Decor Group	466	396	429
with Trailer Towing Group	818	695	753

Prices are accurate at time of publication; subject to manufacturer's change.

	Retail Price	Dealer Invoice	Fair Price
with Sport Wagon Decor Group and Trailer Towing Group	$404	$343	$372
Grand LE and Grand LE AWD with Pkgs. 28-29K, 28-29L, or 28-29M	466	396	429
with Trailer Towing Group	404	343	372
Requires rear defogger.			
Rear bench seat, Base SWB	346	294	318
7-passenger seating with integrated child seat, Base SWB	570	485	524
SE, LE and ES SWB, Grand, Grand AWD	225	191	207
Quad Command Seating, SE, LE, and ES	597	507	549
Two front and two middle bucket seats, 3-passenger rear bench seat.			
Converta-Bed 7-passenger seating, SE, LE, and ES	553	470	509
Leather trim, ES	865	735	796
Not available with integrated child seat.			
Heavy Duty Trailer Towing Group, SE SWB with Pkgs. 26-28B and 26-28D	556	473	512
with Gold Special Edition Group	442	376	407
LE SWB with Pkgs. 26-28K, Grand SE with Pkgs. 28B and 28D and Grand LE with Pkgs. 28-29K and 28-29L	442	376	407
SE SWB with Pkgs. 26-28B and 26-28D, LE SWB with Pkgs. 26-28K, ES SWB with Pkgs. 26-28M, Grand SE with Pkgs. 28B and 28D, Grand LE with Pkgs. 28-29K and 28-29L, Grand ES with Pkgs. 26-28M	410	349	377
Grand SE AWD with Pkgs. 28B and 28D, Grand LE AWD with Pkgs. 28-29K, 28-29L, and 28-29M	373	317	343
Heavy duty brakes, battery, load suspension and radiator, trailer towing wiring harness, 205/70R15 all-season tires, conventional spare tire.			
Sport Handling Group, SWB SE with Pkg. 26-28B and 26-28D	239	203	220
Grand SE with Pkg. 28B and 28D, Grand LE with Pkg. 28-29L	125	106	115
Heavy duty brakes, front and rear sway bars, 205/70R15 tires. Not available with Sport Wagon Decor Pkg.			
LE SWB with Pkg. 26-28K and Grand LE with Pkg. 28-29K	488	415	449
Heavy duty brakes, front and rear sway bars, 205/70R15 tires, alloy wheels.			

	Retail Price	Dealer Invoice	Fair Price
Convenience Group I, Base SWB and Base Grand	$372	$316	$342
Cruise control, tilt steering wheel.			
Convenience Group II, Base SWB and Base Grand	694	590	638
SE SWB with Pkg. 26-28B and Grand SE with Pkg. 28B	265	225	244
Convenience Group I plus power mirrors and door locks.			
Convenience Group III, SE SWB with Pkg. 26-28B and Grand SE with Pkg. 28B	673	572	619
SE SWB with Pkg. 26-28D and Grand SE with Pkg. 28D	408	347	375
Convenience Group II plus power windows and remote keyless entry system.			
AWD Convenience Group I, Grand SE AWD with Pkg. 28B	265	225	244
Power mirrors and door locks.			
AWD Convenience Group II, Grand SE AWD with Pkg. 28B	673	572	619
with Pkg. 28D	408	347	375
AWD Convenience Group I plus power windows and remote keyless entry system.			
Gold Special Edition Group, SE	250	213	230
Gold striping, moldings and badging, 205/70R15 tires, gold-color alloy wheels.			
Sport Wagon Decor Group, SE	750	638	690
Sunscreen glass, front and rear fascias, leather-wrapped steering wheel, fog lamps, Sport Handling Group, alloy wheels.			
Rear defogger	168	143	155
Power door locks	265	225	244
Luggage rack	143	122	132
Cassette player	170	145	156
AM and FM stereo with CD player, equalizer and six Infinity speakers SE SWB with Pkg. 26-28D, Grand SE with Pkg. 28D, Grand SE AWD with Pkg. 28D	501	426	461
LE SWB with Pkg. 26-28K and 26-28L, Grand LE with Pkg. 28-29K, 28-29L, 28-29M, Grand LE AWD with Pkg. 28-29K, 28-29L, 28-29M	170	145	156
Infinity speaker system, SE	202	172	186
Firm Ride Heavy Load Suspension, 2WD	178	151	163

	Retail Price	Dealer Invoice	Fair Price
with Sport Handling Group	$146	$124	$134
Includes conventional spare tire.			
205/70R14 whitewall tires, Base SWB and SE SWB	143	122	132
205/70R15 whitewall tires, SWB SE, SWB LE, Base Grand, Grand SE, Grand LE, Grand SE AWD, Grand LE AWD	69	59	63
Not available with Sport Handling, Gold Special Edition, Sport Wagon Groups.			
Conventional spare tire	109	93	100
15-inch alloy wheels, LE SWB with Pkg. 26-28K, Grand LE with Pkg. 28-29K, Grand LE AWD with Pkg. 28-29K	363	309	334
Extra-cost paint	97	82	89

Chrysler Town & Country

	Retail Price	Dealer Invoice	Fair Price
4-door van with Pkg. 29X	$27284	$24700	$25600
AWD 4-door van with Pkg. 29X	29380	26544	27444
Destination charge	560	560	560

Standard Equipment:

Pkg. 29X: 3.8-liter V-6, 4-speed automatic transmission, anti-lock brakes, power steering, driver- and passenger-side air bags, front and rear air conditioning, 7-passenger seating (bucket seats in front and middle rows and 3-passenger rear bench seat), power driver's seat, cloth and leather upholstery, power front door and rear quarter vent windows, programmable power locks, forward storage console, overhead console (with compass, outside temperature readout, and front and rear reading lights), rear defogger, intermittent wipers, rear wiper/washer, cruise control, leather-wrapped tilt steering wheel, illuminated remote keyless entry system, remote fuel door and decklid releases, tinted windshield and front door glass, sunscreen glass (other windows), electronic instruments (tachometer, coolant temperature and oil pressure gauges, trip odometer), floormats, luggage rack, heated power mirrors, lighted visor mirrors, AM/FM cassette with six Infinity speakers, imitation woodgrain exterior trim, fog lamps, 205/70R15 tires, alloy wheels. **AWD** has permanent all-wheel drive.

Optional Equipment:

	Retail Price	Dealer Invoice	Fair Price
Trailer Towing Group	$270	$230	$236
AWD	201	171	176

	Retail Price	Dealer Invoice	Fair Price
Leather seat trim	NC	NC	NC
Pkg. 29Y	NC	NC	NC
Substitutes gold stripe and gold painted alloy wheels for woodgrain exterior trim.			
7-passenger bench seating	NC	NC	NC
Front bucket seats, reclining 2-passenger middle and folding 3-passenger rear bench seats. Includes integrated child seats.			
CD player with equalizer and six Infinity speakers	$170	$145	$149
Extra cost paint	97	82	85
Whitewall tires, with Pkg. 29X	69	59	60
Alloy wheels, gold painted, with Pkg. 29X	NC	NC	NC
Alloy wheels, white painted, with Pkg. 29Y	NC	NC	NC

Plymouth Voyager

	Retail Price	Dealer Invoice	Fair Price
Base SWB	$15520	$14158	$14858
Base Grand	18178	16522	17222
SE SWB	18139	16462	17162
Grand SE	19304	17513	18413
Grand SE AWD	21982	19869	20769
LE SWB	21963	19827	20727
Grand LE	22883	20662	21562
Grand LE AWD	25560	23017	23917
LX SWB	22472	20275	21175
Destination charge	560	560	560

SWB denotes standard wheelbase; AWD denotes All-Wheel Drive.

Standard Equipment:

Base: 2.5-liter 4-cylinder engine, 3-speed automatic transmission, driver- and passenger-side air bags, power steering, cloth front bucket seats, 3-passenger middle bench seat, tinted glass, trip odometer, coolant temperature gauge, dual outside mirrors, visor mirrors, AM/FM radio, intermittent wipers, rear wiper/washer, 195/75R14 tires, wheel covers. **Base Grand** adds: 3.0-liter V-6 engine, 7-passenger seating (front buckets and 2-place middle and 3-place rear bench seats), rear trim panel storage and cup holders, 205/70R15 tires. **SE** adds to Base: 3.0-liter V-6 engine, 3-speed automatic transmission, cruise control, power mirrors, cassette player, power remote tailgate release, tilt steering wheel, front passenger lockable underseat storage drawer, striping, dual note horn. **Grand SE** adds to Base Grand: 3.3-

liter V-6 engine, 4-speed automatic transmission, cruise control, power mirrors, cassette player, power remote tailgate release, tilt steering wheel, front passenger lockable underseat storage drawer, striping, dual note horn. **LE** adds to SE: front air conditioning, front storage console, overhead console with trip computer, rear defogger, power rear quarter vent windows, power door locks, remote keyless entry system, tachometer, oil pressure gauge, voltmeter, heated power mirrors, lighted visor mirrors, illuminated entry system, headlamp time delay, floormats, 205/70R15 tires. **Grand LE** adds to Grand SE: front air conditioning, front storage console, overhead console with trip computer, rear defogger, power rear quarter vent windows, power door locks, remote keyless entry system, tachometer, oil pressure gauge, voltmeter, heated power mirrors, lighted visor mirrors, illuminated entry system, headlamp time delay, floormats. **LX** adds to LE SWB: LX Decor Group. **AWD** models have permanently engaged all-wheel drive.

Quick Order Packages:	**Retail Price**	**Dealer Invoice**	**Fair Price**
Pkgs. 21T, 22T, 24T Base SWB and 26T Base SWB, Base Grand	$213	$181	$196
Air conditioning, map and cargo lights, power remote liftgate release, front passenger underseat lockable storage drawer, bodyside molding, dual horns. Pkg. 22T requires 3-speed automatic transmission; Pkg. 24T requires 3.0-liter engine and 3-speed automatic transmission; Pkg. 26T requires 3.0-liter engine and 4-speed transmission.			
Pkg. 26B SE SWB and Pkg. 28B SE SWB, Grand SE, Grand SE AWD	213	181	196
Pkgs. 24-28B add to SE standard equipment: air conditioning, map and cargo lights, rear defogger. SE SWB Pkg. 24B requires 4-speed automatic transmission; SE SWB Pkg. 28B requires 3.3-liter engine and 4-speed automatic transmission.			
Pkg. 26D SE SWB, and Pkg. 28D SE SWB, Grand SE, Grand SE AWD	1159	985	1066
Pkgs. 26-28D add to Pkgs. 26-28B forward and overhead consoles, oil pressure and voltage gauges, tachometer, lighted visor mirrors, Light Group, power door locks and rear quarter vent windows, floormats, deluxe insulation. SE SWB Pkg. 26D requires 4-speed automatic transmission; SE SWB Pkg. 28D requires 3.3-liter engine and 4-speed automatic transmission.			
Pkg. 28L and 29L Grand LE, Grand LE AWD	$962	$818	$885
Pkgs. 28L-29L add to 28K-29K: Woodgrain Decor Group (woodgrain trim and moldings, front and rear body-color fascias, luggage rack, whitewall tires, alloy wheels). Requires 3.8-liter engine.			

	Retail Price	Dealer Invoice	Fair Price
Pkg. 26K LE SWB, and Pkg. 28K LE SWB, Grand LE, Grand LE AWD and Pkg. 29K Grand LE, Grand LE AWD	$306	$260	$282
Pkgs. 26K-29K add to LE standard equipment: power driver's seat, power windows, AM/FM radio with cassette player, equalizer and six Infinity speakers, sunscreen glass. LE SWB Pkg. 26K requires 4-speed automatic transmission; LE SWB Pkg. 28K requires 3.3-liter engine and 4-speed automatic transmission; Grand LE and Grand LE AWD require 3.8-liter engine.			
Pkg. 26M-28M LX SWB	431	366	397
Pkgs. 26M-29M add to 26K-28K LX SWB: LX Decor Group (body-color fascia, cladding, and grille, fog lamps, alloy wheels), Sport Handling Group (heavy duty brakes, firmer front and rear sway bars and front struts and rear shocks, 205/70R15 tires, alloy wheels). LX SWB Pkg. 26M requires 4-speed automatic transmission; LX SWB Pkg. 28M requires 3.3-liter engine and 4-speed automatic transmission.			

Individual Options:

	Retail Price	Dealer Invoice	Fair Price
3.0-liter V-6, Base SWB	767	652	706
Requires 3-speed automatic transmission.			
3.3-liter V-6, SE, LE, and ES SWB	102	87	94
Requires 4-speed automatic transmission.			
3.8-liter V-6, Grand LE, and Grand LE AWD	302	257	278
Includes 4-speed transmission.			
3-speed automatic transmission, Base SWB	601	511	553
4-speed automatic transmission, SE, LE, LX SWB and Base Grand	198	168	182
Anti-lock brakes: SE SWB with Pkgs. 26-28B or 26-28D	687	584	632
SE SWB with Pkgs. 26-28B or 26-28D and alloy wheels, Trailer Tow, Sport Handling, Gold Special Edition, or Sport Wagon Groups; Grand SE with Pkgs. 28B or 28D	599	509	551
LE SWB with Pkgs. 26-28K or 26-28M; Grand LE with Pkgs. 26-28K, 26-28L or 26-28M	599	509	551
Sunscreen glass, Grand SE AWD with Pkg. 28B and 28D	414	352	381
Front air conditioning, Base SWB and Base Grand	857	728	788

Prices are accurate at time of publication; subject to manufacturer's change.

	Retail Price	Dealer Invoice	Fair Price
Front air conditioning with sunscreen glass, Base SWB with Pkg. 26T, SE SWB with Pkg. 26-28B and 26-28D, Base Grand with Pkg. 26T and SE Grand with Pkg. 28B and 28D	$414	$352	$381
Not available with Sport Wagon Decor Group.			
Rear air conditioning with rear heater and sunscreen glass, Base Grand with Pkg. 26T, Grand SE with Pkg. 28B, Grand SE AWD with Pkg. 28B	988	840	909
Grand SE and Grand SE AWD with Pkg. 28B and Sport Wagon Decor Group ...	574	488	528
with Trailer Towing Group	925	786	851
with Sport Wagon Decor Group and Trailer Towing Group	511	434	470
Grand SE and Grand SE AWD with Pkg. 28D	880	748	810
with Sport Wagon Decor Group	466	396	429
with Trailer Towing Group	818	695	753
with Sport Wagon Decor Group and Trailer Towing Group	404	343	372
Grand LE and Grand LE AWD with Pkgs. 28-29K, 28-29L, or 28-29M	466	396	429
with Trailer Towing Group	404	343	372
Requires rear defogger.			
Rear bench seat, Base SWB	346	294	318
7-passenger seating with integrated child seat, Base SWB	570	485	524
SE, LE and LX SWB, Grand, Grand AWD	225	191	207
Quad Command Seating, SE, LE and LX	597	507	549
Two front and two middle bucket seats, 3-passenger rear bench seat.			
Converta-Bed 7-passenger seating, SE, LE and LX	553	470	509
Leather trim, LX	865	735	796
Not available with integrated child seat.			
Sport Handling Group, SWB SE with Pkg. 26-28B and 26-28D	239	203	220
Grand SE with Pkg. 28B and 28D, Grand LE with Pkg. 28-29L	125	106	115
Heavy duty brakes, front and rear sway bars, 205/70R15 tires. Not available with Sport Wagon Decor Pkg.			
LE SWB with Pkg. 26-28K and Grand LE with Pkg. 28-29K	488	415	449

	Retail Price	Dealer Invoice	Fair Price
Heavy duty brakes, front and rear sway bars, 205/70R15 tires, alloy wheels.			
Heavy Duty Trailer Towing Group, SE SWB			
with Pkgs. 26-28B and 26-28D	$556	$473	$512
with Gold Special Edition Group	442	376	407
LE SWB with Pkgs. 26-28K, Grand SE with Pkgs. 28B and 28D and Grand LE with Pkgs. 28-29K and 28-29L	442	376	407
SE SWB with Pkgs. 26-28B and 26-28D, LE SWB with Pkgs. 26-28K, LX SWB with Pkgs. 26-28M, Grand SE with Pkgs. 28B and 28D, Grand LE with Pkgs. 28-29K and 28-29L	410	349	377
Grand SE AWD with Pkgs. 28B and 28D, Grand LE AWD with Pkgs. 28-29K, 28-29L and 28-29M	373	317	343
Heavy duty brakes, battery, load suspension and radiator, trailer towing wiring harness, 205/70R15 all-season tires, conventional spare tire.			
Convenience Group I, Base SWB and Base Grand	372	316	342
Cruise control, tilt steering wheel.			
Convenience Group II, Base SWB and Base Grand	694	590	638
SE SWB with Pkg. 26-28B and Grand SE with 28B	265	225	244
Convenience Group I plus power mirrors and door locks.			
Convenience Group III, SE SWB with Pkg. 26-28B and Grand SE with Pkg. 28B	673	572	619
SE SWB with Pkg. 26-28D and Grand SE with Pkg. 28D	408	347	375
Convenience Group II plus power windows and remote keyless entry system.			
AWD Convenience Group I, Grand SE AWD with Pkg. 28B	265	225	244
Power mirrors and door locks.			
AWD Convenience Group II, Grand SE AWD			
with Pkg. 28B	673	572	619
with Pkg. 28D	408	347	375
AWD Convenience Group I plus power windows and remote keyless entry system.			
Gold Special Edition Group, SE	250	213	230
Gold striping, moldings and badging, 205/70R15 tires, gold-color alloy wheels.			
Power door locks	265	225	244

	Retail Price	Dealer Invoice	Fair Price
Sport Wagon Decor Group, SE	750	638	690
Sunscreen glass, front and rear fascias, leather-wrapped steering wheel, fog lamps, Sport Handling Group, alloy wheels.			
Rear defogger	168	143	155
Luggage rack	143	122	132
Cassette player	170	145	156
AM and FM stereo with CD player, equalizer and six Infinity speakers, SE SWB with Pkg. 26-28D, Grand SE with Pkg. 28D, Grand SE AWD with Pkg. 28D	501	426	461
LE SWB with Pkg. 26-28K and 26-28L, Grand LE with Pkg. 28-29K, 28-29L, 28-29M, Grand LE AWD with Pkg. 28-29K, 28-29L, 28-29M	170	145	156
Infinity speaker system, SE	202	172	186
Firm Ride Heavy Load Suspension, 2WD	178	151	164
with Sport Handling Group	146	124	134
Includes conventional spare tire.			
205/70R14 whitewall tires, Base SWB and SE SWB	143	122	132
205/70R15 whitewall tires, SWB SE, SWB LE, Base Grand, Grand SE, Grand LE, Grand SE AWD, Grand LE AWD	69	59	63
Not available with Sport Handling, Gold Special Edition, Sport Wagon Groups.			
Conventional spare tire	109	93	100
15-inch alloy wheels, LE SWB with Pkg. 26-28K, Grand LE with Pkg. 28-29K, Grand LE AWD with Pkg. 28-29K	363	309	334
Extra-cost paint	97	82	89

DODGE/PLYMOUTH COLT AND EAGLE SUMMIT

Specifications	2-door notchback	4-door notchback
Wheelbase, in.	96.1	98.4
Overall length, in.	171.1	174.0

Dodge Colt ES 2-door

Specifications

	2-door notchback	4-door notchback
Overall width, in.	66.1	66.1
Overall height, in.	51.4	51.4
Curb weight, lbs.	2085	2195
Cargo vol., cu. ft.	10.5	10.5
Fuel capacity, gals.	13.2	13.2
Seating capacity	5	5
Front head room, in.	38.6	38.6
Max. front leg room, in.	42.9	42.9
Rear head room, in.	36.4	36.2
Min. rear leg room, in.	31.1	33.5

Powertrain layout: transverse front engine/front-wheel drive.

Engines

	ohc I-4	ohc I-4
Size, liters/cu. in.	1.5/90	1.8/112
Horsepower @ rpm	92 @ 6000	113 @ 6000
Torque (lbs./ft.) @ rpm	93 @ 3000	116 @ 4500
Availability	S	O[1]
EPA city/highway mpg		
5-speed OD manual	32/39	26/33
3-speed automatic	28/32	
4-speed OD automatic		26/33

1. Standard, 4-door models.

Built in Japan.

PRICES

Dodge/Plymouth Colt	Retail Price	Dealer Invoice	Fair Price
Base 2-door notchback	$9319	$8900	$9100
ES/GL 2-door notchback	10277	9773	9973
Base 4-door notchback	11545	10953	11153
ES/GL 4-door notchback	12298	11581	11781
Destination charge	430	430	430

Dodge and Plymouth Colts are identical. Dodge's higher-priced models are called ES and Plymouth's are called GL.

Standard Equipment:

Base 2-door: 1.5-liter 4-cylinder engine, 5-speed manual transmission, driver-side air bag, motorized front passenger shoulder belt, cloth reclining front bucket seats, front console with armrest, engine temperature gauge, left remote mirror, automatic day/night rearview mirror, 145/80R13 tires. **Base 4-door** adds: 1.8-liter 4-cylinder engine, power steering, split folding rear seat, dual outside mirrors, trip odometer, body-colored bumpers, rear spoiler, 175/70R13 tires, wheel covers. **ES/GL 2-door** adds to base 2-door: dual remote mirrors, trip odometer, body-colored bumpers, 155/80R13 tires, wheel covers. **ES/GL 4-door** adds: upgraded interior trim, tachometer (5-speed), intermittent wipers, remote fuel door and decklid releases, 185/65R14 tires.

Optional Equipment:

	Retail Price	Dealer Invoice	Fair Price
Anti-lock disc brakes, ES/GL 4-door	699	601	615
Pkg. 21C, base 2-door	419	360	369
Rear defogger, tinted glass, AM/FM radio, dual outside mirrors.			
Pkg. 21D, base 2-door	1229	1057	1082
Pkg. 21C plus air conditioning.			
Pkg. 21G/22G, ES/GL 2-door	100	86	88
Rear defogger, tinted glass, AM/FM radio. Pkg. 22G requires 3-speed automatic transmission.			
Pkg. 21H/22H, ES/GL 2-door	1386	1192	1220
Pkg. 21G plus power steering, air conditioning, cassette player, split folding rear seat, intermittent wipers, remote fuel door and decklid releases. Pkg. 22H requires 3-speed automatic transmission.			
Pkg. 23K/24K, ES/GL 2-door	1834	1577	1614
Pkg. 21H plus 1.8-liter engine, touring suspension, tachometer (5-speed), 185/65R14 tires, alloy wheels. Pkg. 24K requires 4-speed automatic transmission.			

	Retail Price	Dealer Invoice	Fair Price
Pkg. 23C/24C, base 4-door	$580	$499	$510
Tinted glass, rear defogger, AM/FM radio, bodyside moldings, floormats, intermittent wipers, dual remote mirrors, remote fuel door and decklid releases. Pkg. 24C requires 4-speed automatic transmission.			
Pkg. 23D/24D, base 4-door	1390	1195	1223
Pkg. 23C plus air conditioning. Pkg. 24D requires 4-speed automatic transmission.			
Pkg. 23K/24K, ES/GL 4-door	1213	1043	1067
Air conditioning, tinted glass, rear defogger, AM/FM cassette, floormats, variable-intermittent wipers, tilt steering column, cruise control, power mirrors. Pkg. 24K requires 4-speed automatic transmission.			
Pkg. 23L/24L, ES/GL 4-door	1996	1717	1756
Pkg. 23L plus power windows and locks, alloy wheels. Pkg. 24L requires 4-speed automatic transmission.			
3-speed automatic transmission	518	445	456
Requires 1.5-liter engine.			
4-speed automatic transmission	641	551	564
Requires 1.8-liter engine.			
Air conditioning	810	697	713
Rear defogger	66	57	58
AM/FM radio with four-speakers, base 4-door	271	233	238
AM/FM cassette w/clock and four-speakers	181	156	159
Requires Option Pkg.			
Bodyside moldings, base with any Option Pkg.	54	46	48

Eagle Summit

	Retail Price	Dealer Invoice	Fair Price
DL 2-door notchback	$9319	$8900	$9100
ES 2-door notchback	10277	9773	9973
LX 4-door	11545	10953	11153
ES 4-door notchback	12298	11581	11781
Destination charge	430	430	430

Standard Equipment:

DL 2-door: 1.5-liter 4-cylinder engine, 5-speed manual transmission, driver-side air bag, motorized front shoulder belts, cloth/vinyl reclining front bucket seats, center console with armrest, engine temperature gauge, left manual mirror, 145/80R13 tires; **ES 2-door** adds: cloth seats, dual remote mirrors, color-keyed bumpers and bodyside moldings, rear spoiler, 155/80R13 tires, wheel covers. **LX 4-door**

Prices are accurate at time of publication; subject to manufacturer's change.

adds to DL 2-door: 1.8-liter 4-cylinder engine, power steering, cloth seats, touring suspension, dual manual mirrors, trip odometer, color-keyed bumpers, 175/70R13 tires, wheel covers. **ES 4-door** adds: split folding rear seat with armrest, tachometer (5-speed), dual remote mirrors, intermittent wipers, remote fuel door release, visor mirrors, color-keyed bodyside moldings, 185/65R14 tires.

Optional Equipment:	Retail Price	Dealer Invoice	Fair Price
Pkg. 21C, DL	$419	$360	$369
Tinted glass, rear defogger, dual manual mirrors, AM/FM radio.			
Pkg. 21D, DL	1229	1057	1082
Pkg. 21C plus air conditioning.			
Pkg. 21G/22G, ES 2-door	100	86	88
Tinted glass, rear defogger, AM/FM radio. Pkg. 22G requires 3-speed automatic transmission.			
Pkg. 21H/22H, ES 2-door	1386	1192	1220
Pkg. 21G plus air conditioning, cassette player, power steering, split folding rear seat, remote fuel door and decklid releases, intermittent wipers. Pkg. 22H requires 3-speed automatic transmission.			
Pkg. 23K/24K, ES 2-door	1834	1577	1614
Pkg. 21H plus 1.8-liter 4-cylinder engine and ESi Pkg. (touring suspension, 185/65R14 tires, alloy wheels). 5-speed adds tachometer. Pkg. 24K requires 4-speed automatic transmission.			
Pkg. 23C/24C, LX	580	499	510
Tinted glass, rear defogger, AM/FM radio, bodyside moldings, floormats, dual remote mirrors, remote fuel door and decklid releases, intermittent wipers, passenger visor mirror. Pkg. 24C requires 4-speed automatic transmission.			
Pkg. 23D/24D, LX	1390	1195	1223
Pkg. 23C plus air conditioning. Pkg. 24D requires 4-speed automatic transmission.			
Pkg. 23K/24K, ES 4-door	1213	1043	1067
Air conditioning, tinted glass, rear defogger, AM/FM cassette, floormats, tilt steering column, cruise control, variable-intermittent wipers, power mirrors. Pkg. 24K requries 4-speed automatic transmission.			
Pkg. 23L/24L, ES 4-door	1996	1717	1756
Pkg. 23K plus power windows and locks, ESi Pkg. (alloy wheels). Pkg. 24L requires 4-speed automatic transmission.			
3-speed automatic transmission, 2-door	518	445	456
4-speed automatic transmission, 2-door w/ESi Pkg., 4-door	641	551	564
Anti-lock disc brakes, ES 4-door	699	601	615
Air conditioning	810	697	713
Rear defogger	66	57	58
AM/FM radio, LX	271	233	238

	Retail Price	Dealer Invoice	Fair Price
AM/FM cassette	$181	$156	$159
Bodyside moldings, DL, LX	54	46	48

DODGE INTREPID/ CHRYSLER CONCORDE/ EAGLE VISION

Dodge Intrepid ES

Specifications	4-door notchback
Wheelbase, in.	113.0
Overall length, in.	201.7
Overall width, in.	74.4
Overall height, in.	56.3
Curb weight, lbs.	3271
Cargo vol., cu. ft.	16.7
Fuel capacity, gals.	18.0
Seating capacity	6
Front head room, in.	38.4
Front leg room, max., in.	42.3
Rear head room, in.	37.2
Rear leg room, min. , in.	38.7

Powertrain layout: longitudinal front engine/front-wheel drive.

Engines

	ohv V-6	ohc V-6
Size, liters/cu. in.	3.3/201	3.5/215
Horsepower @ rpm	161 @ 5300	214 @ 5800
Torque (lbs./ft.) @ rpm	181 @ 3200	221 @ 2800
Availability	S	O[1]
EPA city/highway mpg		
4-speed OD automatic	20/28	18/26

1. Standard, Eagle TSi.

Built in Canada.

PRICES

Dodge Intrepid	Retail Price	Dealer Invoice	Fair Price
4-door notchback	$17690	$15737	$16537
ES 4-door notchback	19630	17386	18186
Destination charge	535	535	535

Standard Equipment:

3.3-liter V-6 engine, 4-speed automatic transmission, driver- and passenger-side air bags, power steering, air conditioning, cloth front bucket seats, console with armrest and cupholders, solar control glass, dual remote mirrors, rear defogger, tilt steering wheel, intermittent wipers, tachometer, coolant temperature gauge, headlamp shut-off delay, trip odometer, AM/FM radio, reading lights, visor mirrors, touring suspension, 205/70R15 tires, wheel covers. ES adds: 4-wheel disc brakes, variable-assist power steering, cruise control, premium cloth front bucket seats with lumbar support adjustment, cassette player, remote decklid release, fog lamps, Message Center, floormats, trunk cargo net, 225/60R16 touring tires, alloy wheels.

Optional Equipment:

Pkg. 22C, base	891	757	846

Power windows and locks, cruise control, cassette player, floormats.

Pkg. 22D/26D, base	1653	1405	1570

Pkg. 22C plus 4-wheel disc brakes, power driver's seat, heated power mirrors, remote decklid release, Message Center, lighted visor mirrors. Pkg. 26D requires 3.5-liter engine.

Pkg. 22L/26L, ES	1268	1078	1205

Power driver's seat, power windows and locks, Remote/Illuminated Entry Group, heated power mirrors, leather-wrapped steering wheel, lighted visor mirrors. Pkg. 26L requires 3.5-liter engine.

	Retail Price	Dealer Invoice	Fair Price
Pkg. 26M, ES	$3016	$2563	$2865
Pkg. 22L plus anti-lock brakes, automatic temperature control, overhead console with compass and thermometer, automatic day/night rearview mirror, Chrysler/Infinity cassette system, security alarm, conventional spare tire. Requires 3.5-liter engine.			
3.5-liter V-6 engine	725	616	689
Anti-lock 4-wheel disc brakes, base	624	530	593
ES, Base w/Pkgs. 22D, 26D	599	509	569
Traction control, ES w/Pkgs. 22L, 26L, 26M	175	149	166
Requires anti-lock brakes.			
Automatic temperature control, ES w/Pkgs. 22L, 26L	152	129	144
Overhead console, base w/Pkgs. 22D, 26D	296	252	281
ES w/Pkgs. 22L, 26L	378	321	359
Compass/temperature/traveler displays, front and rear reading lamps, storage compartment. Base requires bucket seats.			
AM/FM cassette, base	200	170	190
Chrysler/Infinity Spatial Imaging Cassette Sound System, base w/Pkgs. 22D, 26D, ES w/Pkgs. 22L, 26L	708	602	673
AM/FM cassette with equalizer, amplifier, 11 Infinity speakers, power antenna.			
Chrysler/Infinity Spatial Imaging Compact Disc Sound System, base w/Pkgs. 22D, 26D, ES w/Pkgs. 22L, 26L	877	745	833
ES w/Pkg. 26M	169	144	161
AM/FM stereo, compact disc player, equalizer, amplifier, power antenna.			
Power moonroof, base w/Pkgs. 22D, 26D	1012	860	961
ES w/Pkgs. 22L, 26L	1094	930	1039
ES w/Pkg. 26M	716	609	680
Power door locks, base	250	213	238
Power decklid release, base w/Pkg. 22C	61	52	58
Power Convenience Group, ES	684	581	650
Power windows and locks, heated power mirrors.			
Integrated child seat	100	85	95
Not available with leather seats.			
Cloth 50/50 front bench seat, base	NC	NC	NC
Power driver's and passenger's seats, ES w/Pkgs. 22L, 26L	377	320	358
Cruise control, base	224	190	213

Prices are accurate at time of publication; subject to manufacturer's change.

	Retail Price	Dealer Invoice	Fair Price
Leather front bucket seats, ES w/Pkgs. 22L, 22L, 26M	$1009	$858	$959
Includes power front seats, leather-wrapped shift knob.			
Remote/ Illuminated Entry Group, base w/Pkgs. 22D, 26D	221	188	210
Keyless remote and illuminated entry systems.			
Security alarm, ES w/Pkgs. 22L, 26L	149	127	142
Requires automatic temperature control, Power Convenience Group.			
Performance Handling Group, ES w/Pkgs. 22L, 26L	217	184	206
Performance suspension, 225/60R16 performance tires. Requires anti-lock brakes, traction control, conventional spare tire.			
16-inch Wheel and Handling Group, base w/Pkgs. 22C, 22D, 26D	404	343	384
Variable-assist power steering, 16-inch polycast wheels 225/60R16, touring tires.			
Conventional spare tire	95	81	90
Extra cost paint	97	82	92

Chrysler Concorde

	Retail Price	Dealer Invoice	Fair Price
4-door notchback w/Pkg. 22A	$19896	$17627	$18427
Destination charge	535	535	535

Standard Equipment:

Pkg. 22A: 3.3-liter V-6 engine, 4-speed automatic transmission, 4-wheel anti-lock disc brakes, driver- and passenger-side air bags, touring suspension, power steering, air conditioning, tinted glass with solar control front and rear windows, cloth front bucket seats, lumbar adjustment, front console with armrest, tachometer, trip odometer, coolant temperature gauge, AM/FM cassette radio, rear defogger, intermittent wipers, heated power mirrors, tilt steering wheel, cruise control, remote decklid release, visor mirrors, reading lights, trunk cargo net, floormats, 205/70R15 tires.

Optional Equipment:

	Retail Price	Dealer Invoice	Fair Price
Chrysler/Infinity cassette system, w/Pkg. 22C or 26C	708	602	673
Includes equalizer, 11 speakers, amplifier, power antenna.			
Pkg. 22B	596	506	566
Power windows and locks, lighted visor mirrors.			
Pkg. 22C/26C	1226	1042	1165
Pkg. 22B plus automatic temperature control, power driver's seat, illuminated/remote entry systems. Pkg. 26C requires 3.5-liter engine.			

	Retail Price	Dealer Invoice	Fair Price
Pkg. 22D/26D	$2350	$1997	$2233
Pkg. 26C plus speed-sensitive power steering, Infinity cassette system, overhead console, security alarm, automatic day/night rearview mirror. Pkg. 26D requires 3.5-liter engine.			
3.5-liter V-6 engine	725	616	689
Requires Pkg. 26C or 26D.			
Traction control, w/Pkg. 22C, 26C, 22D, or 26D	175	149	166
Integrated child seat	100	85	95
Cloth 50/50 front bench seat	NC	NC	NC
Power driver's seat, w/Pkg. 22B	377	320	358
Power driver's and front passenger's seats,			
w/Pkg. 22B	754	641	716
w/Pkg. 22C, 26C, 22D, or 26D	377	320	358
Leather seats, w/Pkg. 22C, 26C, 26D	1069	909	1016
Includes power front seats, leather-wrapped steering wheel and shift knob. Not available with integrated child seat.			
Power moonroof, w/Pkg. 22C or 26C	1094	930	1039
w/Pkg. 22D or 26D	716	609	680
Remote/Illuminated Entry System, w/Pkg. 22B	221	188	210
Security alarm, w/Pkg. 22C or 26C	149	127	142
Full overhead console, w/Pkg. 22C or 26C	378	321	359
Includes trip computer, compass, outside temperature readout, lighted visor mirrors.			
Chrysler/Infinity CD system,			
w/Pkg. 22C or 26C	877	745	833
w/Pkg. 22D or 26D	169	144	161
Includes equalizer, 11 speakers, amplifier, power antenna.			
16-inch Wheel and Handling Group,			
w/Pkg. 22B, 22C, or 26C	628	534	597
w/Pkg. 22D or 26D	524	445	498
Variable-assist power steering, 225/60R16 touring tires, alloy wheels.			
Conventional spare tire	95	81	90
Extra cost paint	97	82	92

Eagle Vision

	Retail Price	Dealer Invoice	Fair Price
ESi 4-door notchback	$19747	$17500	$18300
TSi 4-door notchback	23212	20480	21280
Destination charge	535	535	535

Standard Equipment:

ESi: 3.3-liter V-6 engine, 4-speed automatic transmission, 4-wheel disc brakes, driver- and passenger-side air bags, variable-assist power steering, air conditioning, reclining front bucket seats with lumbar support adjustment, console with armrest and cup holders, remote decklid release, rear defogger, tinted glass, intermittent wipers, tachometer, trip odometer, coolant temperature gauge, power windows and locks, dual power mirrors, AM/FM cassette, tilt steering wheel, cruise control, touring suspension, dual visor mirrors, reading lights, floormats, 205/70R15 tires, wheel covers. **TSi** adds: 3.5-liter V-6 engine, anti-lock brakes, automatic temperature control, power driver's seat, overhead console with compass and thermometer, illuminated/remote keyless entry system, trip computer, leather-wrapped steering wheel, lighted visor mirrors, trunk cargo net, 2-tone front and rear fascias, fog lamps, 225/60R16 tires, alloy wheels.

Optional Equipment:	Retail Price	Dealer Invoice	Fair Price
Pkg. 22C, ESi	$601	$511	$571
Power driver's seat, illuminated/remote keyless entry sytem, lighted visor mirrors.			
Pkg. 22D, ESi	1767	1502	1679
Pkg. 22C plus automatic temperature control, automatic day/night rearview mirror, Chrysler/Infinity cassette system, security alarm, overhead console with compass and thermometer, trip computer.			
Pkg. 26L, TSi	980	833	931
Power front passenger's seat, automatic day/night rearview mirror, Chrysler/Infinity cassette system.			
Pkg. 26M, TSi	1706	1450	1621
Pkg. 26L plus leather seats, security alarm, conventional spare tire.			
Anti-lock brakes, ESi	599	509	569
Traction control, TSi w/Pkg. 26L	175	149	166
Power passenger seat, TSi	377	320	358
Power driver's seat, ESi	377	320	358
Leather seats, TSi w/Pkg. 26L	620	527	589
Performance Handling Group, TSi w/Pkgs. 26L, 26M	217	184	206
Performance suspension, 225/60VR16 tires. Requires traction control and conventional spare tire.			
Chrysler/Infinity cassette system	708	602	673
Includes equalizer, 11 speakers, power antenna.			
Chrysler/Infinity CD system, ESi w/Pkg. 22D, TSi w/Pkgs. 26L, 26M	169	144	161
Includes equalizer, 11 speakers, power antenna.			

	Retail Price	Dealer Invoice	Fair Price
Integrated child seat	$100	$85	$95
Not available with leather seats.			
Security alarm, TSi w/Pkg. 26L	149	127	142
Alloy wheel group	374	318	355
225/60R16 tires, alloy wheels.			
Conventional spare tire	95	81	90

1995 DODGE/ PLYMOUTH NEON

1995 Dodge Neon Sport

Specifications	4-door notchback
Wheelbase, in.	104.0
Overall length, in.	171.8
Overall width, in.	67.4
Overall height, in.	54.8
Curb weight, lbs.	2338
Cargo vol., cu. ft.	11.8
Fuel capacity, gals.	11.2
Seating capacity	5
Front head room, in.	39.6
Front leg room, max., in.	42.5
Rear head room, in.	36.5
Rear leg room, min. , in.	35.1

Powertrain layout: transverse front engine/front-wheel drive.

Engines

	ohc I-4
Size, liters/cu. in.	2.0/121
Horsepower @ rpm	132 @ 6000
Torque (lbs./ft.) @ rpm	129 @ 5000
Availability	S
EPA city/highway mpg	
5-speed OD manual	29/38
3-speed automatic	27/33

Built in Belvidere, Ill.

PRICES

1995 Dodge/Plymouth Neon	Retail Price	Dealer Invoice	Fair Price
Base 4-door notchback	$8975	$8332	—
Highline 4-door notchback	10690	9909	—
Sport 4-door notchback	12215	11069	—
Destination charge	500	500	500

Fair price not available at time of publication.

Standard Equipment:

Base: 2.0-liter 4-cylinder engine, 5-speed manual transmission, driver- and passenger-side air bags, cloth reclining bucket seats, floor storage console with dual cup holders and coin holder, left remote outside rearview mirror, passenger-side visor mirror, 165/80R13 all-season tires. **Highline** adds to Base: power steering, 60/40 split folding rear seat, tinted glass, intermittent wipers, dual manual remote mirrors, driver-side visor mirror, AM/FM radio with four speakers, touring suspension, bodyside moldings, 185/70R13 all-season tires, wheel covers. **Sport** adds to Highline: anti-lock brakes, power mirrors and door locks, padded covered floor storage console with tissue pack holder, dual cup holders, and cassette/CD holders, rear defogger, remote decklid release, tilt steering wheel, tachometer, low fuel light, 185/65R14 all-season touring tires, deluxe wheel covers.

Optional Equipment:

3-speed automatic transmission	557	496	—
Anti-lock brakes, Base and Highline	565	503	—
AM/FM radio with four speakers, Base	334	297	—
AM/FM cassette player	170	151	—

	Retail Price	Dealer Invoice	Fair Price
Base Pkg. 21B/22B	$1861	$1712	—
Air conditioning, power steering, rear defogger, intermittent wipers, AM/FM radio, dual manual remote mirrors, touring suspension, bodyside moldings, tinted glass. Pkg. 22B requires 3-speed automatic transmission.			
Highline Pkg. 21D/22D	753	670	—
Air conditioning, rear defogger, floor storage console, remote decklid release. Pkg. 22D requires 3-speed automatic transmission.			
Highline Pkg. 21F/22F	1252	1114	—
Pkg 21D/22D plus power mirrors and door locks, tilt steering wheel, tachometer with low fuel light, 14-inch Wheel Dress-Up Pkg., Light Pkg. (lighted visor mirrors, lighted ignition key cylinder, ashtray and glove box lights, trunk and underhood lamps), and rear floormats. Pkg. 22F requires 3-speed automatic transmission.			
Sport Pkg. 21K/22K	527	469	—
Air conditioning, Light Pkg., AM/FM cassette player, front and rear floormats. Pkg. 22K requires 3-speed automatic transmission.			
Convenience Group, Highline	297	264	—
Power mirrors and door locks.			
Rear defogger, Base and Highline	173	154	—
Bodyside moldings, Base	30	27	—
14-inch Wheel Dress-Up Pkg., Highline	80	71	—
185/65R14 all-season touring tires, wheel covers.			
Dual manual remote mirrors, Base	70	62	—
Roof rack	100	89	—
Integrated child seat	—	—	—
Cruise control, Highline and Sport	224	199	—
Tilt steering wheel, Highline and Sport	148	132	—
Tachometer with low fuel light, Highline	93	83	—
Intermittent wipers, Base	66	59	—
Front and rear floormats	46	40	—
Extra-cost paint, Base and Highline	97	86	—
Sport	NC	NC	NC

FORD AEROSTAR

Specifications	4-door van	Ext. 4-door van
Wheelbase, in.	118.9	118.9
Overall length, in.	174.9	190.3
Overall width, in.	71.7	72.0

Ford Aerostar XLT extended

	4-door van	Ext. 4-door van
Overall height, in.	72.2	72.3
Curb weight, lbs.	3481	3558
Cargo vol., cu. ft.	140.0	170.0
Fuel capacity, gals.	21.0	21.0
Seating capacity	7	7
Front head room, in.	39.5	39.5
Max. front leg room, in.	41.4	41.4
Rear head room, in.	38.8	38.8
Min. rear leg room, in.	39.5	40.5

Powertrain layout: longitudinal front engine/rear-wheel drive or permanent 4WD.

Engines	ohv V-6	ohv V-6
Size, liters/cu. in.	3.0/182	4.0/245
Horsepower @ rpm	135 @ 4600	155 @ 4000
Torque (lbs./ft.) @ rpm	160 @ 2800	230 @ 2400
Availability	S	S[1]
EPA city/highway mpg		
5-speed OD manual	17/24	
4-speed OD automatic	17/23	16/20

1. *Aerostar 4WD; optional extended length 2WD.*

Built in St. Louis, Mo.

PRICES

Ford Aerostar Wagon	Retail Price	Dealer Invoice	Fair Price
XL regular length, 2WD	$15150	$13493	$13793

	Retail Price	Dealer Invoice	Fair Price
XL extended, 2WD	$16595	$14764	$15064
XL regular length, 4WD	18620	16546	16846
XL extended, 4WD	19515	17333	17633
XL Plus regular, 2WD	16685	14844	15144
XL Plus extended, 2WD	17725	15759	16059
XL Plus regular, 4WD	19695	17492	17792
XL Plus extended, 4WD	20520	18218	18518
XLT regular length, 2WD	20590	18280	18580
XLT extended, 2WD	21070	18702	19002
XLT regular length, 4WD	22145	19648	19948
XLT extended, 4WD	23010	20409	20709
Eddie Bauer regular length, 2WD	23470	20814	21114
Eddie Bauer extended, 2WD	24270	21518	21818
Eddie Bauer regular length, 4WD	25380	22494	22794
Eddie Bauer extended, 4WD	26290	23296	23596
Destination charge	540	540	540

Standard Equipment:

XL: 3.0-liter V-6 with 5-speed manual transmission 2WD (4WD models have 4.0-liter V-6 with 4-speed automatic transmission, permanent 4WD), anti-lock rear brakes, driver-side air bag, power steering, cloth and vinyl front bucket seats, 3-passenger fold-down bench seat, tinted glass, dual outside mirrors, right visor mirror, rear wiper/washer, intermittent wipers, remote fuel door release, AM/FM radio, 215/70R14 tires. **XL Plus** adds: dual captain's chairs, 2-passenger middle and 3-passenger rear bench seats, cloth upholstery, storage bin under right front seat. **XLT** adds: 4-speed automatic transmission, dual captain's chairs with power lumbar support, front air conditioning, cruise control, tilt steering wheel, underseat storage bin, door and seatback map pockets, dual-note horn, 2-tone paint, liftgate convenience net, Light Group, leather-wrapped steering wheel. **Eddie Bauer** adds: 4.0-liter V-6 engine (ex. regular-length 2WD), front and rear air conditioning with auxiliary heater, Electronics Group, Power Convenience Group, luggage rack, mini console, AM/FM cassette, rear defogger, rear seat/bed, upgraded upholstery, 2-tone paint, floormats, forged alloy wheels.

Optional Equipment:

	Retail Price	Dealer Invoice	Fair Price
4.0-liter V-6, Ext. 2WD	300	255	262
4-speed automatic transmission, XL 2WD.	750	637	656
Limited-slip axle	252	215	220
Base Preferred Equipment Pkg. 400A, XL	37	31	32
Air conditioning, right underseat storage bin.			

Prices are accurate at time of publication; subject to manufacturer's change.

	Retail Price	Dealer Invoice	Fair Price
XL Preferred Equipment Pkg. 401A, XL Plus	$734	$623	$642
Deluxe paint stripe, air conditioning, privacy glass, cruise control, tilt steering wheel.			
XLT Preferred Equipment Pkg. 403A, XLT.	315	267	275
Privacy glass, rear defogger, power windows and locks, power mirrors, cassette player.			
Eddie Bauer Pkg. 405A	338	287	295
Privacy glass, floor console with storage and cup holders.			
Dual captain's chairs, XL	644	547	563
7-passenger seating: with front captain's chairs, XL	1043	886	912
with Pkg. 401A or 403A	552	470	483
with four captain's chairs, XLT	598	508	523
Four captain's chairs and seat/bed, XLT	622	528	544
Eddie Bauer	NC	NC	NC
with leather upholstery	848	720	742
Child safety seats	224	191	196
Front air conditioning, XL	857	729	749
High-capacity front air conditioning with rear heater	576	489	504
Floor console with storage and cup holders	174	147	152
Floor console delete (credit)	(61)	(52)	(52)
Rear defogger	168	142	147
Electronics Group, with Pkg. 403A	813	691	711
Electronic instruments, AM/FM stereo cassette with equalizer and clock, trip computer, autolamp and electrochromatic mirror.			
Exterior Appearance Group, XL with Pkg. 400A	576	522	504
XL Plus with Pkg. 401A	174	147	152
XLT with Pkg. 403A	94	79	82
XLT without privacy glass and Power Convenience Group	513	436	448
Styled wheel covers, privacy glass, 2-tone paint, swing-lock outside mirrors.			
Optional axle ratio	38	32	33
Light Group	159	135	139
Underhood, glove box and instrument panel lights, illuminated entry system.			
Luggage rack (std. Eddie Bauer)	143	121	125
Swing-lock mirrors (NA XLT and Eddie Bauer)	52	45	46
with Exterior Appearance Group and Power Convenience Group	NC	NC	NC

	Retail Price	Dealer Invoice	Fair Price
Bodyside molding	$63	$53	$55
Power Convenience Group	538	457	470
with Exterior Appearance Pkg.	485	413	424
Power windows and locks, power mirrors.			
Cruise control and tilt steering wheel	371	315	324
Sport Appearance Pkg.	733	623	641
High-gloss silver metallic treatment, color-keyed headlight frames and grille, striping, full wheel covers.			
Trailer Towing Pkg.	282	239	246
Class I wiring harness, heavy duty turn signal flasher, limited-slip axle with axle ratio upgrade.			
XL Plus Convenience Group, with Pkg. 401A	827	703	723
Privacy glass, cruise control, tilt steering wheel, deluxe paint stripe.			
XLT Convenience Group, with Pkg. 403A	901	766	788
with Exterior Appearance Group	849	721	742
Power Convenience Group, AM/FM cassette, rear defogger.			
Deluxe paint stripe	43	36	37
Delete for credit, XL Plus	(29)	(25)	(25)
Underseat storage bin	37	31	32
with captain's chairs	NC	NC	NC
Privacy glass	413	351	361
AM/FM cassette	195	165	170
Includes headphones.			
Forged alloy wheels	363	309	317
Engine block heater	33	28	29
215/70R14SL whitewall all-season tires	84	72	73

FORD ASPIRE

Specifications

Specifications	3-door hatchback	5-door hatchback
Wheelbase, in.	90.7	93.9
Overall length, in.	152.8	155.9
Overall width, in.	65.7	65.7
Overall height, in.	55.6	55.6
Curb weight, lbs.	2004	2053
Cargo vol., cu. ft.	37.7	41.0
Fuel capacity, gals.	10.0	10.0
Seating capacity	4	4

Prices are accurate at time of publication; subject to manufacturer's change.

Ford Aspire 5-door

	3-door hatchback	5-door hatchback
Front head room, in.	37.8	38.2
Max. front leg room, in.	41.6	41.6
Rear head room, in.	35.5	36.4
Min. rear leg room, in.	33.6	34.2

Powertrain layout: transverse front engine/front-wheel drive.

Engines	ohc I-4
Size, liters/cu. in.	1.3/81
Horsepower @ rpm	64 @ 5000
Torque (lbs./ft.) @ rpm	74 @ 3000
Availability	S
EPA city/highway mpg	
5-speed OD manual	36/43
3-speed automatic	29/34

Built in South Korea.

PRICES

Ford Aspire	Retail Price	Dealer Invoice	Fair Price
3-door hatchback	$8240	$7578	—
SE 3-door hatchback	8895	8175	—
5-door hatchback	8855	8138	—

Fair price and options not available at time of publication.

Standard Equipment:

1.3-liter 4-cylinder engine, 5-speed manual transmission, driver- and passenger-side air bags, reclining front seats, full folding rear bench seat, trip odometer, Radio Prep Pkg., body-color bumpers and grille, dual outside mirrors, floor console with cup holders, 165/70R13 all-season tires. **SE** adds: fog lamps, rear liftgate spoiler, split folding rear seat, upgraded upholstery and door trim panels, door map pockets.

FORD CROWN VICTORIA/ MERCURY GRAND MARQUIS

Ford Crown Victoria LX

Specifications	4-door notchback
Wheelbase, in.	114.4
Overall length, in.	212.4
Overall width, in.	77.8
Overall height, in.	56.8
Curb weight, lbs.	3776
Cargo vol., cu. ft.	20.6
Fuel capacity, gals.	20.0
Seating capacity	6
Front head room, in.	39.4
Max. front leg room, in.	42.5
Rear head room, in.	38.0
Min. rear leg room, in.	39.7

Powertrain layout: longitudinal front engine/rear-wheel drive.

FORD

Engines

	ohc V-8
Size, liters/cu. in.	4.6/281
Horsepower @ rpm	190 @ 4200[1]
Torque (lbs./ft.) @ rpm	260 @ 3200[2]
Availability	S
EPA city/highway mpg	
4-speed OD automatic	18/25

1. 210 with dual exhaust. 2. 270 with dual exhaust.

Built in Canada.

PRICES

Ford Crown Victoria	Retail Price	Dealer Invoice	Fair Price
4-door notchback	$19350	$17789	$18389
Special Value 4-door notchback with Preferred Equipment Pkg. 111A	19230	17736	—
LX 4-door notchback	20765	19142	19642
LX Special Value 4-door notchback with Preferred Equipment Pkg. 113A	21045	19450	—
LX Special Value 4-door notchback with Preferred Equipment Pkg. 114A	23635	21743	—
Destination charge	575	575	575

Fair price on Special Value models not available at time of publication. Special Value models include destination charge.

Standard Equipment:

4.6-liter V-8, 4-speed automatic transmission, 4-wheel disc brakes, variable-assist power steering, driver- and passenger-side air bags, air conditioning, cloth reclining split bench seat, map pockets, digital clock, power windows and mirrors, coolant temperature gauge, trip odometer, tilt steering wheel, tinted glass, automatic parking brake release, intermittent wipers, AM/FM radio, 215/70R15 all-season tires. **Special Value** adds Preferred Equipment Pkg. 111A. **LX** adds: upgraded interior trim, remote fuel door release, power driver's seat, carpeted spare tire cover. **LX Special Value** adds Preferred Equipment Pkg. 113A or 114A.

Optional Equipment:

Anti-lock brakes with Traction Assist	665	592	599

	Retail Price	Dealer Invoice	Fair Price
Preferred Equipment Pkg. 111A, base	$445	$406	$408
Group 1 plus front and rear floormats.			
Preferred Equipment Pkg. 113A, LX	845	767	770
Pkg. 111A plus Group 2 and 3, Light/Decor Group, power driver's seat.			
Pkg. 114A, LX	3435	3060	3091
Pkg. 113A plus Group 4, illuminated entry system, leather-wrapped steering wheel.			
Group 1, base	770	685	693
LX	670	596	603
Includes rear defogger, power door locks, remote fuel door and decklid releases, cruise control, cargo net, spare tire cover.			
Group 2, LX	245	218	220
AM/FM cassette player and power antenna.			
Group 3, LX	485	432	436
Alloy wheels and cornering lamps.			
Group 4, LX	2720	2421	2448
with Group 2	2555	2274	2299
Anti-lock brakes with Traction Assist, High level audio system, automatic air conditioning, trip computer, outside temperature indicator, heavy duty battery, electronic digital instruments, automatic day/night rearview mirror, rear air suspension, remote keyless entry system, power front seats. Requires Light/Decor Group.			
Cellular telephone, LX	745	663	670
Includes storage armrest.			
Leather upholstery, LX	625	557	562
with power passenger seat	530	472	477
Leather-wrapped steering wheel, LX	90	80	81
Illuminated entry system	80	71	72
Keyless entry, LX	215	191	193
Rear air suspension, LX	270	240	243
Power driver's seat, base	290	258	261
Power front passenger seat, LX	480	427	432
Includes power lumbar support and recliners for both front seats.			
Heavy Duty Trailer Towing Pkg.	690	614	621
with Pkg. 114A	395	352	355
Includes rear air spring suspension, heavy-duty battery, flasher system and U-joint, extra cooling, dual exhaust, wiring harness, power steering and transmission oil coolers, full-size spare tire, Traction-Lok axle (except with anti-lock brakes). Not available with Handling and Performance Package.			
Light/Decor Group	225	201	202
Includes illuminated visor mirrors, map and dome lights, engine compartment lights, bodyside paint stripes, secondary visors.			
Handling and Performance Pkg., LX	1765	1571	1588

	Retail Price	Dealer Invoice	Fair Price
with Group 3	$1345	$1197	$1210
with Group 4	830	739	747
with Pkg. 114A	410	365	369
Includes performance springs, shocks and stabilizer bars, alloy wheels, anti-lock brakes with Traction Assist, dual exhaust, 3.27 axle ratio, power steering cooler, rear air suspension, 225/60R15 tires.			
AM/FM cassette	165	147	148
High level audio system	480	427	432
with Group 2 or Pkg. 113A, 114A	315	280	283
AM/FM cassette, upgraded amplifier and speakers.			
JBL audio system, LX	500	445	448
Trunk mounted CD changer	785	699	706
215/70R15 whitewall tires	80	71	72
Full-size spare tire	80	71	72
with Handling and Performance Pkg.	198	168	178
Floormats, front	25	23	25
Floormats, rear	20	18	20
Engine block heater	25	23	25

Mercury Grand Marquis

	Retail Price	Dealer Invoice	Fair Price
GS 4-door notchback	$20330	$18690	$19190
GS Special Value 4-door notchback	19990	18435	—
LS 4-door notchback	21570	19916	20416
LS Special Value 4-door notchback	22060	20423	—
Destination charge	575	575	575

Special Value fair price not available at time of publication. Special Value prices include destination charge.

Standard Equipment:

GS: 4.6-liter V-8, 4-speed automatic transmission, 4-wheel disc brakes, power steering, driver- and passenger-side air bags, air conditioning, dual reclining seats, 6-way power driver's seat, dual front and rear folding armrests, power windows and mirrors, tinted glass, AM/FM cassette, right visor mirror, intermittent wipers, cargo net, digital clock, tilt steering wheel, trip odometer, Luxury Sound Insulation Pkg., remote fuel door release, automatic parking brake release, 215/70R15 all season whitewall tires. **GS Special Value** adds Preferred Equipment Pkg. 157A. **LS** adds: upgraded upholstery and door trim, luxury reclining twin comfort lounge seats, locking wire spoked wheel covers. **LS Special Value** adds Preferred Equipment Pkg. 172A.

Optional Equipment:	Retail Price	Dealer Invoice	Fair Price
Anti-lock brakes w/Traction-Assist	$665	$592	$599
Preferred Pkg. 157A, GS	225	204	208
Cruise control, rear defogger, Power Lock Group, floormats.			
Preferred Pkg. 172A, LS	1055	966	971
Pkg. 157A plus illuminated entry, bodyside paint stripe, leather-wrapped steering wheel, illuminated entry, Luxury Light Group (includes underhood light, dual dome/map lights, rear reading lights, dual secondary sun visors, lighted visor mirrors), alloy wheels, power antenna, cornering lights, rear license plate frame.			
Group 1	205	182	185
Rear defogger, floormats.			
Group 2	510	454	459
Power Lock Group (includes power locks, remote fuel door and decklid releases), cruise control.			
Group 3, LS	995	886	896
Illuminated entry, Luxury Light Group, bodyside paint stripe, leather-wrapped steering wheel, alloy wheels, power antenna, cornering lights, rear license plate frame.			
Luxury Light Group	190	169	171
Includes underhood light, dual dome/map lights, rear reading lights, dual secondary sun visors, lighted visor mirrors.			
Electronic Group, LS	515	458	463
Automatic climate control with outside temperature readout, digital instrumentation, tripminder computer. Requires rear window defogger.			
Illuminated entry system	80	71	72
Keyless entry system	215	191	193
Requires Group 2.			
Handling Pkg., LS	1485	1322	1336
with Pkg. 172A	1065	948	958
Includes rear air suspension, tuned suspension, larger stabilizer bars, anti-lock brakes with Traction-Assist, dual exhaust, 3.27 axle ratio, 225/70R15 whitewall tires, alloy wheels.			
Rear air suspension, LS	270	240	243
Trailer Tow III Pkg., LS	785	699	706
Includes rear air suspension, heavy duty battery, dual exhaust, trailer towing wiring harness, power steering and transmission oil coolers, heavy duty flashers, full-size spare tire, heavy duty U-joint, 3.27 Traction-Lok axle. Requires alloy wheels.			
Power front passenger's seat, LS	385	343	346
Includes power lumbar support and recliners for both front seats.			
Leather seat trim, LS	530	472	477
Premium electronic AM/FM cassette, LS	315	280	283
Locking radial-spoked wheel covers, GS	295	263	265

Prices are accurate at time of publication; subject to manufacturer's change.

	Retail Price	Dealer Invoice	Fair Price
Full-size conventional spare tire, LS .... *Includes alloy wheel.*	$185	$165	$166
Alloy wheels, LS	420	374	378
Front cornering lamps	65	58	59
Leather-wrapped steering wheel .... *Requires Group 2.*	90	80	81
Bodyside paint stripe	60	54	55

FORD ESCORT/ MERCURY TRACER

Ford Escort LX 4-door

Specifications	3-door hatchback	5-door hatchback	4-door notchback	5-door wagon
Wheelbase, in.	98.4	98.4	98.4	98.4
Overall length, in.	170.0	170.0	170.9	171.3
Overall width, in.	66.7	66.7	66.7	66.7
Overall height, in.	52.5	52.5	52.7	53.6
Curb weight, lbs.	2325	2419	2371	2419
Cargo vol., cu. ft.	35.2	36.0	12.1	66.9
Fuel capacity, gals.	11.9	11.9	11.9	11.9
Seating capacity	5	5	5	5
Front head room, in.	38.4	38.4	38.4	38.4
Max. front leg room, in.	41.7	41.7	41.7	41.7
Rear head room, in.	37.6	37.6	37.4	38.5
Min. rear leg room, in.	34.6	34.6	34.6	34.6

Powertrain layout: transverse front engine/front-wheel drive.

Engines

Engines	ohc I-4	dohc I-4
Size, liters/cu. in.	1.9/114	1.8/109
Horsepower @ rpm	88 @ 4400	127 @ 6500
Torque (lbs./ft.) @ rpm	108 @ 3800	114 @ 4500
Availability	S	S[1]
EPA city/highway mpg		
5-speed OD manual	30/37	26/31
4-speed OD automatic	25/33	23/30

1. Escort GT, Tracer LTS.

Built in Wayne, Mich., and Mexico.

PRICES

Ford Escort	Retail Price	Dealer Invoice	Fair Price
Std. 3-door hatchback	$9135	$8413	$8613
LX 3-door hatchback	9990	9191	9391
LX 4-door notchback	10650	9792	9992
LX 5-door hatchback	10425	9587	9787
LX 5-door wagon	10980	10091	10291
GT 3-door hatchback	12400	11384	11584
Destination charge	375	375	375

Standard Equipment:

Std.: 1.9-liter 4-cylinder engine, 5-speed manual transmission, driver-side air bag, motorized front passenger belt, cloth and vinyl reclining bucket seats, one-piece folding rear seatback, center console with cup holders, tinted glass, trip odometer, variable intermittent wipers, flip-out quarter window (3-door), cargo cover, door pockets, right visor mirror, 175/70R13 all-season tires. **LX** adds: upgraded upholstery and door trim panels, 60/40 split rear seatback, AM/FM radio, digital clock, bodyside molding, full wheel covers. **Wagon** adds: 175/65R14 all-season tires: **4-door** adds: tachometer, variable-intermittent wipers. **GT** adds: 1.8-liter DOHC engine, power steering, 4-wheel disc brakes, sport suspension, tachometer, cloth sport seats, leather-wrapped steering wheel, AM/FM cassette, Light Group, lighted visor mirrors, removable cup holder tray, remote fuel door and decklid releases, power mirrors, lighted visor mirrors, fog lamps, rear spoiler, rocker panel cladding, 185/60HR15 all-season tires, alloy wheels.

Prices are accurate at time of publication; subject to manufacturer's change.

Optional Equipment:	Retail Price	Dealer Invoice	Fair Price
4-speed automatic transmission	$790	$703	$771
LX requires power steering.			
Anti-lock brakes, GT	565	503	509
Air conditioning, LX and GT	725	646	653
LX requires power steering.			
Power steering, LX	250	223	225
Comfort Group, Std.	800	712	720
Air conditioning, power steering.			
Preferred Pkg. 320A, LX	235	211	212
Power steering, Light/Convenience Group, rear defogger.			
Preferred Pkg. 330A, GT	530	472	477
Rear defogger, air conditioning, tilt steering column, cruise control.			
One Price Pkg. 321A (5-speed) and 322A (automatic): LX 3-door, 5-speed	1130	1008	—
LX 3-door, automatic	1920	1711	—
LX 4-door, 5-speed	470	420	—
LX 4-door, automatic	1260	1123	—
LX 5-door, 5-speed	695	621	—
LX 5-door, automatic	1485	1324	—
LX wagon, 5-speed	140	126	—
LX wagon, automatic	930	829	
Air conditioning, power steering, cassette player, Light/Convenience Group, rear defogger. Pkg 322A includes 4-speed automatic transmission. Wagon adds Wagon Group.			
Sunrise Red Decor Group, GT	350	312	315
Sunrise red exterior, color-keyed wheels, gray cloth upholstery, front floormats with "GT" embroidered in red.			
Sport Appearance Group, LX 3-door	NC	NC	NC
Alloy wheels, tachometer, liftgate spoiler, rear cladding.			
Rear defogger	160	143	144
Light/Convenience Group, LX	300	268	270
Light Group, power mirrors, remote fuel door and hatch releases, removable cup holder tray.			
Light Group, LX	110	98	99
Removable cup holder tray, dual map, cargo area, underhood and ignition key lights, headlights-on warning chime, illuminated visor mirrors.			
Luxury Convenience Group, LX (except 4-door)	410	365	369
LX 4-door and GT	355	316	320
Tilt steering column, cruise control, tachometer.			
Power mirrors, LX	95	85	86
Power Equipment Group, 4-door, 5-door hatchback and wagon with Luxury Convenience Group	520	463	468

	Retail Price	Dealer Invoice	Fair Price
Wagon without Luxury Convenience Group	$575	$512	$518
3-door LX with Luxury Convenience Group and GT	460	410	414
3-door LX without Luxury Convenience Group	515	459	464
Power windows and locks, tachometer.			
Power moonroof, LX and GT (NA wagon)	525	468	473
LX requires Light/Convenience Group, power steering.			
Remote fuel door/liftgate releases, LX	95	85	86
AM/FM radio, Std.	300	267	270
AM/FM cassette, Std.	465	414	419
LX	165	147	149
CD player, Std.	740	658	666
LX	445	396	401
GT	280	249	252
Premium sound system	130	116	117
Requires AM/FM cassette.			
Radio delete (credit), LX	(300)	(267)	(267)
GT (credit)	(465)	(414)	(414)
Wagon Group	240	213	216
Luggage rack, rear wiper/washer. Requires Light/Convenience Group.			
Clearcoat paint	85	76	77
Engine block heater	20	18	19

Mercury Tracer

	Retail Price	Dealer Invoice	Fair Price
4-door notchback	$10350	$9519	$9719
5-door wagon	10620	9765	9965
LTS 4-door notchback	12660	11621	11921
Destination charge	375	375	375

Standard Equipment:

1.9-liter 4-cylinder engine, 5-speed manual transmission, driver-side air bag, cloth reclining front bucket seats, 60/40 split rear seatback, AM/FM radio, tachometer, trip odometer, digital clock, console, coolant temperature gauge, low fuel warning light, door map pockets, variable intermittent wipers, tinted glass, 175/70R13 tires. **Wagon** adds: power steering, remote fuel door release, power mirrors, rear defogger, cargo cover, rear wiper/washer, 175/65R14 tires, full wheel covers. **LTS** adds: 1.8-liter DOHC engine, 4-wheel disc brakes, sport suspension, tilt steering column, AM/FM cassette, remote decklid release, Light Group (includes dual map lights, lighted visor mirrors, trunk and engine compartment lights, rear door courtesy light), driver's seat tilt adjustment, cruise control, leather-wrapped steering wheel, 185/60HR14 tires, alloy wheels.

Optional Equipment:	Retail Price	Dealer Invoice	Fair Price
Preferred Pkg. 550A, base 4-door	NC	NC	NC
Wagon	NC	NC	NC
Power steering, power mirrors, AM/FM radio, rear defogger, driver's seat tilt adjustment, Light Group, remote fuel door release, remote decklid release (NA wagon).			
Preferred Equipment Pkg. 560A, LTS	NC	NC	NC
Power steering, power mirrors, AM/FM cassette, rear defogger, driver's seat tilt adjustment, Light Group, remote fuel door release, remote decklid release (NA wagon).			
4-speed automatic transmission	$790	$703	$711
Air conditioning	725	646	653
Anti-lock brakes, LTS	566	503	509
Power Group	520	463	468
Power door locks and windows.			
Convenience Group	355	316	320
Tilt steering wheel, cruise control.			
Power moonroof, LTS	525	468	473
Cassette player, base	165	147	149
Premium sound system	130	116	117
Requires cassette player.			
CD player and premium sound system, base	445	396	401
LTS	280	249	252
Luggage rack, wagon	110	98	99

FORD EXPLORER/ MAZDA NAVAJO

Specifications	3-door wagon	5-door wagon
Wheelbase, in.	102.1	111.9
Overall length, in.	174.4	184.3
Overall width, in.	70.2	70.2
Overall height, in.	67.5	67.3
Curb weight, lbs.	3844	4053

Ford Explorer XLT

	3-door wagon	5-door wagon
Cargo vol., cu. ft.	69.4	81.6
Fuel capacity, gals.	19.0	19.0
Seating capacity	4	6
Front head room, in.	39.9	39.9
Max. front leg room, in.	42.4	42.4
Rear head room, in.	39.1	39.3
Rear leg room, in.	36.6	37.7

Powertrain layout: longitudinal front engine/rear- or on-demand 4WD.

Engine	ohv V-6
Size, liters/cu. in.	4.0/245
Horsepower @ rpm	160 @ 4400
Torque (lbs./ft.) @ rpm	220 @ 2800
Availability	S
EPA city/highway mpg	
5-speed OD manual	17/21
4-speed OD automatic	15/20

Built in Louisville, Ky.

PRICES

Ford Explorer	Retail Price	Dealer Invoice	Fair Price
XL 3-door wagon, 2WD	$17470	$15564	$16064

Prices are accurate at time of publication; subject to manufacturer's change.

	Retail Price	Dealer Invoice	Fair Price
XL 3-door wagon, 4WD	$19220	$17104	$17604
Sport 3-door wagon, 2WD	18445	16421	16921
Sport 3-door wagon, 4WD	20155	17927	18427
Eddie Bauer 3-door wagon, 2WD	21405	19026	19526
Eddie Bauer 3-door wagon, 4WD	23105	20522	21022
XL 5-door wagon, 2WD	18360	16347	17047
XL 5-door wagon, 4WD	20130	17905	18605
XLT 5-door wagon, 2WD	20835	18525	19225
XLT 5-door wagon, 4WD	22635	20109	20809
Eddie Bauer 5-door wagon, 2WD	23400	20782	21482
Eddie Bauer 5-door wagon, 4WD	25205	22370	23070
Limited 5-door wagon, 2WD	26760	23739	24639
Limited 5-door wagon, 4WD	28560	25323	26223
Destination charge	485	485	485

Standard Equipment:

XL: 4.0-liter V-6, 5-speed manual transmission, anti-lock brakes, power steering, knitted vinyl front bucket seats, split folding rear seat, tinted glass, Light Group, intermittent wipers, dual outside mirrors, carpet, load floor tiedown hooks, rear seat heat duct, tachometer, coolant temperature gauge, tachometer, trip odometer, AM/FM radio, digital clock, 225/70R15 all-season tires, full-size spare tire. **Sport** adds: rear quarter and rear window privacy glass, rear wiper/washer, rear defogger, map light, load floor tiedown net, cargo area cover, leather-wrapped steering wheel, lighted visor mirrors, alloy wheels. **XLT** adds: cloth captain's chairs, floor console, power mirrors, upgraded door panels with pockets, power windows and locks, cruise control, tilt steering wheel, privacy glass rear door, rear quarter and liftgate, map pockets, floormats. **Eddie Bauer** adds to Sport: power driver's seat with lumbar support, power passenger seat (5-door), duffle and garment bags, luggage rack, privacy glass on rear quarter and liftgate windows (5-door includes rear door windows), 235/75R15 OWL tires. **Limited** adds: air conditioning, power luxury leather bucket seats with 3-position driver's-side memory, matching split/folding rear seat, floor console, color-keyed overhead console with compass, reading lamps and storage compartment, Electronic Group (remote keyless entry with theft-deterrent system, and electrochromic mirror with autolamp), color-keyed front bumper, front fascia with fog lamps, grille, bodyside moldings, striping, color-keyed leather-wrapped steering wheel, and spoke interior trim, heated mirrors, spoke alloy wheels. 4WD models have Touch Drive part-time 4WD.

Optional Equipment:	Retail Price	Dealer Invoice	Fair Price
4-speed automatic transmission	$890	$757	$845
Limited-slip rear axle	255	217	242
Optional axle ratio (upgrade)	45	38	42
Optional axle ratio (upgrade) with trailer tow	360	306	342
Air conditioning	805	684	765
with manual transmission	NC	NC	NC
Preferred Pkg. 931A, Sport 3-door	NC	NC	NC
Air conditioning, Power Equipment Group, cloth captain's chairs with console, 235/75R15 outlined white letter tires.			
Preferred Pkg. 932A, Eddie Bauer 3-door	125	106	119
Air conditioning, JBL audio system with cassette, leather seats.			
Preferred Pkg. 941A, XLT with automatic	470	400	447
XLT with 5-speed	25	21	24
Air conditioning, striping, premium cassette player.			
Preferred Pkg. 942A, Eddie Bauer 5-door	275	235	262
Air conditioning, premium cassette player, leather seats.			
Preferred Pkg. 943A, Limited	395	336	375
JBL Audio System with cassette, running boards (5-door), step bars (3-door).			
Electronics Group, XLT and Eddie Bauer 5-doors	485	413	460
Remote keyless entry with theft-deterrent system, electrochromatic mirror with autolamp feature.			
Cloth captain's chairs, XL and Sport	280	238	266
Cloth 60/40 split bench seat, XL 5-door	255	216	242
XLT (credit)	(20)	(17)	(17)
Power cloth sport bucket seats, Sport	1020	867	969
upgrade from captain's chairs	750	637	712
XLT	955	812	907
Power leather sport bucket seats, Sport	1600	1360	1520
upgrade from captain's chairs	1326	1127	1259
XLT	1530	1301	1453
Eddie Bauer	NC	NC	NC
Super engine cooling	55	47	52
Privacy glass	220	187	209
Floor-mounted transfer case w/manual locking hubs, 4WD (credit)	(105)	(89)	(89)
Bodyside molding	120	102	114
Luggage rack	140	119	133
with manual transmission and Pkg. 941A	NC	NC	NC

Prices are accurate at time of publication; subject to manufacturer's change.

FORD

	Retail Price	Dealer Invoice	Fair Price
Power Equipment Group, XL 3-door	$900	$765	$855
XL 5-door	1235	1050	1173
Power windows, locks and mirrors, rear defogger, rear wiper/washer, upgraded door trim panels.			
Power Equipment Group delete, Sport with Pkg. 931A (credit)	(190)	(162)	(162)
Power Equipment Group deleted without loss of Pkg. discount.			
Tilt-up sunroof	280	238	266
Cruise control and tilt steering wheel	385	328	365
Sport with manual transmission and Pkg. 931A	NC	NC	NC
Deep dish alloy wheels, XL and Sport	250	212	237
XLT and Eddie Bauer	NC	NC	NC
Trailer Towing Pkg.	105	89	99
Rear defogger and wiper/washer, XL	280	238	266
Premium AM/FM cassette	210	178	199
Sport with manual transmission and Pkg. 931A	NC	NC	NC
Ford JBL Audio System	700	595	665
Upgrade from premium cassette	490	416	465
Ford JBL Audio System with CD player	1000	850	950
Upgrade from premium cassette	790	672	750
Limited	300	255	285
Consolette, XL 5-door and XLT	30	26	28
Running boards, 5-door	395	336	375
Delete for credit, Limited	(395)	(336)	(336)
Step bars, 3-doors	245	208	232
Engine block heater	35	30	33
Deluxe tape stripe, 5-doors	55	47	52
Special Appearance Pkg.	285	243	270
Fog lamps, black bodyside molding, tape stripes.			
Deluxe 2-tone paint	120	102	114
Fog lamps, XL and Sport	185	158	175
235/75R15 outline white letter all-terrain tires	230	196	218
Floormats	45	38	42

Mazda Navajo

	Retail Price	Dealer Invoice	Fair Price
DX 3-door 2WD wagon	$17775	$15658	$15958
LX 3-door 2WD wagon	18995	16733	17033
DX 3-door 4WD wagon	19565	17234	17534
LX 3-door 4WD wagon	20785	18309	18609

	Retail Price	Dealer Invoice	Fair Price
Destination charge	$490	$490	$490

Prices are for vehicles distributed by Mazda Motor of America, Inc. Prices may be higher in areas served by independent distributors.

Standard Equipment:

DX: 4.0-liter V-6 engine, 5-speed manual transmission, anti-lock brakes, power steering, cloth reclining front bucket seats, split folding rear seat, intermittent wipers, tinted glass, AM/FM radio, skid plates, 225/70R15 tires. **LX** adds: power windows and locks, cassette player, rear window privacy glass, leather-wrapped steering wheel, power mirrors, lighted visor mirrors, upgraded door trim, retractable cargo cover, cargo net, alloy wheels. **4WD models** add part-time 4WD with electronic transfer case.

Optional Equipment:

	Retail Price	Dealer Invoice	Fair Price
4-speed automatic transmission (NA DX)	890	757	803
DX Special Equipment Pkg., 5-speed	295	251	266
Air conditioning, cassette player, console with armrest and cup holders, bodyside moldings,			
LX Premium Pkg., 5-speed	495	421	447
with automatic	1095	931	988
Air conditioning, premium cassette player, removable glass moonroof, cruise control, tilt steering wheel, sport front seats with power lumbar and adjustable side bolsters, rear defogger and wiper/washer, console with armrest and cup holders, roof rack, floormats, 235/75R15 all-terrain tires.			
LX Leather Pkg.	3995	3396	3605
Includes LX Premium Pkg. plus leather upholstery, automatic transmission, Towing Pkg., power driver's seat.			
Towing Pkg., LX	350	298	316
Performance axle, heavy duty cooling system, heavy duty flasher, trailer wiring harness, limited-slip differential. Requires automatic transmission.			
CD player, LX	300	255	271

FORD MUSTANG

Specifications

	2-door notchback	2-door conv.
Wheelbase, in.	101.3	101.3

Ford Mustang convertible

	2-door notchback	2-door conv.
Overall length, in.	181.5	181.5
Overall width, in.	71.8	71.8
Overall height, in.	52.9	52.8
Curb weight, lbs.	3055	3276
Cargo vol., cu. ft.	10.8	8.5
Fuel capacity, gals.	15.4	15.4
Seating capacity	4	4
Front head room, in.	38.1	37.9
Max. front leg room, in.	42.6	42.6
Rear head room, in.	35.9	35.8
Rear leg room, in.	30.3	30.3

Powertrain layout: longitudinal front engine/rear-wheel drive.

Engines	ohv V-6	ohv V-8	ohv V-8
Size, liters/cu. in.	3.8/232	5.0/302	5.0/302
Horsepower @ rpm	145 @ 4000	215 @ 2500	240 @ 4800
Torque (lbs./ft.) @ rpm	215 @ 4200	285 @ 3400	285 @ 4000
Availability	S	S[1]	S[2]
EPA city/highway mpg			
5-speed OD manual	20/30	17/25	NA
4-speed OD automatic	19/29	17/25	NA

1. Mustang GT. 2. Cobra.

Built in Dearborn, Mich.

PRICES

Ford Mustang	Retail Price	Dealer Invoice	Fair Price
2-door notchback	$13365	$12050	—
GT 2-door notchback	17280	15534	—
2-door convertible	20160	18098	—
GT 2-door convertible	21970	19708	—
Cobra 2-door notchback	20765	—	—
Cobra 2-door convertible	23535	—	—
Destination charge	475	475	475

Cobra dealer invoice and fair prices not available at time of publication.

Standard Equipment:

3.8-liter V-6 engine, 5-speed manual transmission, driver- and passenger-side air bags, 4-wheel disc brakes, variable-effort power steering, reclining cloth bucket seats with 4-way power driver-side adjustment, split folding rear seat, armrest storage console with cup holder and CD/cassette storage, visor mirrors, tachometer, trip odometer, coolant temperature and oil pressure gauges, tilt steering wheel, intermittent wipers, tinted glass, rear defogger, 205/65R15 all-season tires, wheel covers. **Convertible** adds: power convertible top, power mirrors, door locks and decklid release, power windows, lighted visor mirrors. **GT** adds to convertible: 5.0-liter V-8 engine, 4-way head restraint and power lumbar support for front seats, GT Suspension Pkg., Traction-Lok Axle, fog lamps, rear decklid spoiler, leather-wrapped steering wheel, shift and brake handles, 225/55ZR16 all-season tires, alloy wheels. **Cobra** adds: high-output 5.0-liter V-8 engine, anti-lock brakes, firmer suspension, 4-way power driver's seat, front air dam with fog lamps, unique headlamps and rear spoiler, Cobra interior trim and exterior badging, 255/45ZR17 all-season tires, 17-inch alloy wheels.

Optional Equipment:

	Retail Price	Dealer Invoice	Fair Price
4-speed automatic transmission	790	703	—
Anti-lock brakes	565	503	—
Preferred Pkg. 241A, base models	565	503	—
Air conditioning, AM/FM cassette.			
Preferred Pkg. 243A, base 2-door	1825	1626	—
base convertible	1415	1260	—

Air conditioning, power windows and door locks (std. convertible), illuminated remote keyless entry system, remote decklid release (std. convertible), cruise control, leather-wrapped shift knob and parking brake handle, cassette player with premium sound, lighted visor mirrors (std. convertible), cargo net, alloy wheels.

	Retail Price	Dealer Invoice	Fair Price
Preferred Pkg. 249A, GT models	$1405	$1251	—
Anti-lock brakes, air conditioning, cruise control, AM/FM cassette with premium sound.			
Group 1, base models	505	449	—
Power windows and door locks, remote decklid release.			
Group 2, base 2-door	870	775	—
base convertible	775	690	—
GT models	510	454	—
Cruise control, AM/FM cassette with premium sound, lighted visor mirrors (std. GT and convertibles), alloy wheels (std. GT).			
Group 3	310	276	—
Illuminated remote keyless entry system, cargo net.			
Air conditioning	780	694	—
Convertible hardtop	1545	1375	—
Leather upholstery, base models with Pkg. 243A, GT models	500	445	—
Rear defogger	160	143	—
AM/FM cassette	165	147	—
Mach 460 AM/FM cassette	1215	1081	—
with Group 2	920	819	—
Includes 460 watts peak power, AM stereo, 60 watt equalizer, CD changer compatability, soft touch tape controls, 10 speakers. Requires Group 1.			
CD player	475	423	—
Requires cassette player.			
Optional axle ratio, GT	NC	NC	NC
Alloy wheels, base	265	236	—
17-inch alloy wheels and 245/45ZR17 tires, GT	380	338	—
Bodyside moldings	50	45	—
Front floormats	30	27	—
Engine block heater	20	18	—

FORD TAURUS/ MERCURY SABLE

Specifications

Specifications	4-door notchback	5-door wagon
Wheelbase, in.	106.0	106.0
Overall length, in.	192.0	193.1

Ford Taurus LX 4-door

	4-door notchback	5-door wagon
Overall width, in.	70.7	70.7
Overall height, in.	54.1	55.5
Curb weight, lbs.	3104	3272
Cargo vol., cu. ft.	18.0	83.1
Fuel capacity, gals.	16.0	16.0
Seating capacity	6	8
Front head room, in.	38.3	38.6
Max. front leg room, in.	41.7	41.7
Rear head room, in.	37.6	38.1
Min. rear leg room, in.	37.7	36.9

Powertrain layout: transverse front engine/front-wheel drive.

Engines

	ohv V-6	ohv V-6	dohc V-6	dohc V-6
Size, liters/cu. in.	3.0/182	3.8/232	3.0/182	3.2/195
Horsepower @ rpm	140 @ 4800	140 @ 3800	220 @ 6200	220 @ 6000
Torque (lbs./ft.) @ rpm	165 @ 3250	215 @ 2200	200 @ 4800	215 @ 4800
Availability	S[1]	O[2]	S[3]	S[4]
EPA city/highway mpg				
5-speed OD manual			18/26	
4-speed OD automatic	20/29	19/28		18/26

1. Taurus GL, LX sedan; Sable. 2. Taurus GL, LX sedan; Sable. Standard Taurus LX wagon. 3. Taurus SHO with manual transmission. 4. Taurus SHO with automatic transmission.

Built in Atlanta, Ga., and Chicago, Ill.

Prices are accurate at time of publication; subject to manufacturer's change.

Ford Taurus	Retail Price	Dealer Invoice	Fair Price
GL 4-door notchback	$16240	$14608	$15108
LX 4-door notchback	18885	16963	17463
SHO 4-door notchback	24815	22240	22740
GL 5-door wagon	17320	15570	16070
LX 5-door wagon	20500	18400	18900
Destination charge	535	535	535

Standard Equipment:

GL: 3.0-liter V-6, 4-speed automatic transmission, power steering, driver- and passenger-side air bags, cloth reclining split bench seat with dual center armrests, tilt steering wheel, power mirrors, tinted glass, intermittent wipers, illuminated entry, door pockets, AM/FM radio, digital clock, trip odometer, wheel covers, luggage rack (wagon), 205/65R15 tires. **LX** adds: 3.8-liter V-6 on wagon, variable-assist power steering, air conditioning, reclining front bucket seats with lumbar support, console with with armrest and storage, 6-way power driver's seat, power windows and door locks, remote fuel door and decklid/liftgate releases, tachometer, diagnostic alert lights, automatic parking brake release, automatic on/off headlamps, cornering lamps, bodyside cladding, Convenience Kit (vinyl pouch with fluorescent lantern, tire pressure gauge, gloves, poncho, shop towel, distress flag, headlamp bulb), Light Group, illuminated entry, cargo tiedown net, alloy wheels. **SHO** deletes automatic parking brake release, and adds: 3.0-liter DOHC V-6 with dual exhaust, 5-speed manual transmission, anti-lock 4-wheel disc brakes, automatic air conditioner, cruise control, rear defogger, fog lamps, cloth and leather front bucket seats, rear spoiler, handling suspension, extended range fuel tank, cornering lights, high-level audio system, power antenna, leather-wrapped steering wheel, floormats, 215/60ZR16 tires.

Optional Equipment:

3.8-liter V-6 engine	555	472	500
Standard LX wagon. Requires Group 1. Not available GL with Pkg. 203A or SHO.			
Anti-lock 4-wheel disc brakes (std. SHO)	565	503	509
4-speed automatic transmission, SHO	790	703	711
Includes 3.2-liter DOHC V-6 engine and 215/60HR16 tires.			

	Retail Price	Dealer Invoice	Fair Price
Automatic air conditioning, LX	$175	$156	$158
Automatic air conditioning includes outside temperature readout.			
Preferred Pkg. 203A GL	650	579	585
Air conditioning, rear defogger.			
Preferred Pkg. 204A, GL	2070	1842	1863
Air conditioning, rear defogger, power windows and locks, power driver's seat, remote fuel door/decklid/liftgate releases, Light Group, cassette player, cruise control, floormats, deluxe wheel covers, cargo net, GL Equipment Group (variable-assist power steering, dual visor mirrors, driver's secondary visor, deluxe seat trim, striping).			
Preferred Pkg. 208A, LX 4-door	515	458	464
LX wagon	705	628	635
Rear defogger, cruise control, cassette player, power antenna, keyless entry, leather-wrapped steering wheel, floormats. Wagons add: cargo area cover, rear wiper/washer.			
Group 1, GL	960	855	864
LX	160	143	144
Air conditioning, rear defogger.			
Group 2, GL with Pkg. 204A	1115	992	1004
LX	380	338	342
Cruise control, cassette player, power windows and door locks, Light Group, remote fuel door/decklid/liftgate releases.			
Group 3	370	329	333
Power driver's seat, deluxe wheel covers.			
Group 4	405	360	365
Remote keyless entry system, leather-wrapped steering wheel, power antenna.			
Group 5, wagon	195	174	176
Rear wiper/washer, cargo area cover.			
Luxury Convenience Group, SHO	1555	1383	1400
Power front seats, power moonroof, Ford JBL audio system, remote keyless entry system.			
LX Convenience Group	1030	916	927
Power front seats, power moonroof.			
Bucket seats and console, GL with Pkg. 204A	NC	NC	NC
Leather bucket seats and console, GL with Pkg. 204A	595	530	536
LX	495	441	446
Leather bucket seats, SHO	495	441	446
Leather split bench seat, LX	495	441	446
6-way power driver's seat, GL	290	258	261
Power front passenger seat, LX	290	258	261
Rear facing third seat, wagons	150	134	135

Prices are accurate at time of publication; subject to manufacturer's change.

	Retail Price	Dealer Invoice	Fair Price
AM/FM cassette	$165	$147	$149
High-level audio system, LX	480	427	432
LX with Group 2	315	280	284
CD player (NA GL)	470	418	423
Ford JBL audio system, (NA GL and wagons)	500	445	450
Cellular telephone with storage armrest. *Requires split bench seat.*	500	445	450
Cruise control	215	191	194
Remote keyless entry, GL	310	276	279
with Group 2	215	191	194
Power windows	340	302	306
Power locks, GL *Requires power windows.*	257	219	231
Load floor extension "picnic table," wagon	85	76	77
Alloy wheels, GL with Pkg. 204A	230	205	207
Full-size spare tire (NA SHO)	70	62	63
Heavy duty battery (NA SHO)	30	27	28
Front and rear floormats	45	40	41

Mercury Sable

	Retail Price	Dealer Invoice	Fair Price
GS 4-door notchback	$17840	$16037	$16537
LS 4-door notchback	20100	18049	18549
GS 5-door wagon	19000	17070	17570
LS 5-door wagon	21210	19037	19537
Destination charge	525	525	525

Standard Equipment:

GS: 3.0-liter V-6, 4-speed automatic transmission, power steering, driver- and passenger-side air bags, air conditioning, cloth reclining 50/50 front seat with armrests, rear center armrest, tinted glass, intermittent wipers, rear defogger, tachometer, coolant temperature gauge, trip odometer, low fuel light, power mirrors, tilt steering wheel, AM/FM radio, Sound Insulation Pkg., dual visor mirrors, front door and seatback map pockets, 205/65R15 tires; **wagon** has 60/40 folding rear seat, tiedown hooks, luggage rack, rear wiper, lockable under floor storage. **LS** adds: anti-lock 4-wheel disc brakes, reclining bucket seats with power lumbar support (4-door), power driver's seat (4-door), cassette player, power windows, automatic parking brake release, remote fuel door and decklid releases, Light Group, bodyside cladding, 50/50 reclining front seats with power driver's seat (wagon), console, cargo net, lighted visor mirrors, alloy wheels.

Optional Equipment:	Retail Price	Dealer Invoice	Fair Price
3.8-liter V-6	$530	$472	$477
Includes heavy duty battery.			
3.0-liter V-6, LS with Pkgs. 461/462A and Group 4 (credit)	(530)	(472)	(472)
Anti-lock 4-wheel disc brakes, GS	565	503	509
Automatic climate control, LS	175	156	158
Preferred Pkg. 450A, GS	800	711	720
Power Lock Group (includes power locks, remote fuel door and decklid/liftgate releases), power windows, cruise control, Light Group (includes underhood light, courtesy lights, lighted visor mirrors), floormats, striping.			
Preferred Pkg. 451A, GS	1100	978	990
Pkg. 450A plus power driver's seat, cassette player, alloy wheels.			
Preferred Pkg. 461A, LS	975	868	878
3.8-liter V-6, leather-wrapped steering wheel, cruise control, Premium AM/FM cassette, power antenna, keyless entry system, Power Lock Group, Light Group, striping, floormats.			
Preferred Pkg. 462A, LS	1310	1166	1179
Pkg. 461A plus electronic instruments, autolamp system, air conditioning with automatic climate control.			
Group 1, GS	160	143	144
LS	105	94	95
Light Group, floormats, striping.			
Group 2, GS	895	795	806
LS	460	409	414
Power windows, Power Lock Group, cruise control.			
Group 3, GS (std. LS)	710	632	639
Power driver's seat, AM/FM cassette player, alloy wheels.			
Group 4, LS	1330	1184	1197
3.8-liter V-6 engine, keyless entry system, premium AM/FM cassette, leather-wrapped steering wheel, power antenna.			
Group 5, LS	535	476	482
Automatic climate control, autolamp system, electronic instrument cluster.			
Cargo area cover, wagons	65	58	59
Extended-range fuel tank	45	40	41
Not available with Group 5.			
Remote keyless entry	295	263	266
Includes illuminated entry; requires Group 2.			
Cassette player, GS	165	147	149
CD player	470	418	423
Requires Group 4.			
Rear-facing third seat, Wagons	150	134	135
Not available with conventional spare tire.			

	Retail Price	Dealer Invoice	Fair Price
Power moonroof, LS	$740	$658	$666
Power driver's seat, GS	290	258	261
Dual power seats, GS with Pkg. 450A	580	516	522
GS with Pkg. 451A and LS with 461A or 462A	290	258	261
Cloth individual seats, GS	NC	NC	NC
Leather Twin Comfort Lounge seats, LS	495	441	446
Leather individual seats, LS	495	441	446
Cellular telephone	500	445	450
Leather-wrapped steering wheel, LS *Requires Group 2.*	90	80	81
Heavy duty suspension	25	23	23
Full-size spare tire	70	62	63
Alloy wheels, GS	255	227	230
Heavy duty battery	30	27	27
Engine block heater	20	18	18

FORD THUNDERBIRD/ MERCURY COUGAR

Ford Thunderbird Super Coupe

Specifications

	2-door notchback
Wheelbase, in.	113.0
Overall length, in.	200.3

	2-door notchback
Overall width, in.	72.7
Overall height, in.	52.5
Curb weight, lbs.	3570
Cargo vol., cu. ft.	15.1
Fuel capacity, gals.	18.0
Seating capacity	5
Front head room, in.	38.1
Max. front leg room, in.	42.5
Rear head room, in.	37.5
Min. rear leg room, in.	35.8

Powertrain layout: longitudinal front engine/rear-wheel drive.

Engines	ohv V-6	ohc V-8	Supercharged ohv V-6
Size, liters/cu. in.	3.8/232	4.6/281	3.8/232
Horsepower @ rpm	140 @ 3800	205 @ 4500	230 @ 4400
Torque (lbs./ft.) @ rpm	215 @ 2400	265 @ 3200	330 @ 2500
Availability	S[1]	O[1]	S[2]
EPA city/highway mpg			
5-speed OD manual			18/26
4-speed OD automatic	19/26	18/25	18/24

1. Thunderbird LX, Cougar XR7. 2. Thunderbird Super Coupe.

Built in Lorain, Ohio.

PRICES

Ford Thunderbird	Retail Price	Dealer Invoice	Fair Price
LX 2-door notchback	$16930	$15213	$15713
Super Coupe 2-door notchback	22340	20027	20527
Destination charge	495	495	495

Standard Equipment:

LX: 3.8-liter V-6, 4-speed automatic transmission, driver- and passenger-side air bags, variable assist power steering, air conditioning, cruise control, cloth reclining front bucket seats with power driver's seat, center console with dual cup holders, rear seat center armrest, dual power mirrors, visor mirrors, tinted glass, coolant temperature gauge, tachometer, tilt steering wheel, trip odometer, fog lights, AM/FM cassette, power windows and door locks, leather-wrapped steering wheel and shift knob, illuminated entry system, remote fuel door and decklid release, body-color side moldings, intermittent wipers, 205/70R15 tires. **Super Coupe** deletes cruise control, power locks, power driver's seat and adds: 3.8-liter supercharged V-6 with dual exhaust, 5-speed manual transmission, anti-lock 4-wheel disc brakes, adjustable sport suspension, semi-automatic temperature control, Traction-Lok axle, articulated cloth/leather/vinyl sport seats with power lumbar and side bolsters, seatback pockets, tachometer, boost gauge, lower bodyside cladding, 225/60ZR16 tires, locking alloy wheels.

Optional Equipment:	Retail Price	Dealer Invoice	Fair Price
4.6-liter V-8, LX	$515	$459	$464
4-speed automatic transmission, SC	790	703	711
Includes Traction-Assist.			
Anti-lock 4-wheel disc brakes, LX	565	503	509
Includes Traction-Assist.			
Preferred Pkg. 155A, LX	NC	NC	NC
Semi-automatic temperature control, rear defogger, lighted visor mirrors, alloy wheels.			
Preferred Pkg. 157A, SC	NC	NC	NC
Power driver's seat, automatic climate control, rear defogger, cruise control, power door locks, remote fuel door and decklid releases.			
Group 1, SC	800	712	720
Power door locks, remote fuel door and decklid releases, cruise control, power driver's seat.			
Group 2, LX	315	280	284
SC	160	143	144
Semi-automatic temperature control (std. SC), rear defogger.			
Group 3, LX	305	271	275
SC	95	85	86
Lighted visor mirrors, 215/70R15 tires, alloy wheels.			
Luxury Group, LX	580	516	522
SC	555	494	500
Autolamp system, automatic day/night mirror, illuminated entry (SC), Light Group, power front passenger seat, integrated warning lamp.			
Leather seat trim, LX	490	436	441
SC	615	547	554
Traction-Assist, LX	210	187	189
Premium cassette player	370	329	333
Includes power antenna.			
Ford JBL audio system	500	445	450
Trunk mounted CD player	785	699	707
Remote keyless entry, LX and SC with Luxury Group	215	191	194
SC	295	263	266

	Retail Price	Dealer Invoice	Fair Price
Cold Weather Group, LX	$300	$267	$270
LX with Pkg. 155A	140	124	126
LX with 4.6-liter engine	275	245	248
LX with Pkg. 155A and 4.6-liter engine	115	102	104
LX with Traction-Assist and 4.6-liter engine, SC with automatic transmission	180	160	162
SC with automatic and Pkg. 157A, LX with Traction-Assist, Pkg. 155A and 4.6-liter engine	20	18	19
SC with manual transmission and LX with Traction-Assist	205	182	185
SC with manual transmission and Pkg. 157A, LX with Traction-Assist with Pkg. 155A	45	40	41

Includes engine block heater, heavy duty battery (std. SC w/automatic), heavy duty alternator, rear defogger.

	Retail Price	Dealer Invoice	Fair Price
Power moonroof	740	658	666
Voice activated cellular phone	530	472	477
Tri-coat paint	225	201	203
225/60ZR16 all-season performance tires, SC	70	62	63

Mercury Cougar

	Retail Price	Dealer Invoice	Fair Price
XR7 2-door notchback	$16360	$14706	$15206
Destination charge	495	495	495

Standard Equipment:

3.8-liter V-6, 4-speed automatic transmission, power steering, driver- and passenger-side air bags, air conditioning, reclining front bucket seats with power lumbar support, cloth and leather upholstery, floor storage console with cup holders, tilt steering wheel, intermittent wipers, tinted glass, power windows, AM/FM cassette, oil pressure and coolant temperature gauges, voltmeter, tachometer, center console with storage, power windows and mirrors, rear armrest, door map pockets, color-keyed bodyside moldings, bumpers and door trim panels, rear heater ducts, visor mirrors, cargo area net, 205/70R15 tires.

Optional Equipment:

	Retail Price	Dealer Invoice	Fair Price
4.6-liter V-8 engine	615	548	553

Prices are accurate at time of publication; subject to manufacturer's change.

	Retail Price	Dealer Invoice	Fair Price
Anti-lock 4-wheel disc brakes	$585	$503	$527
Preferred Pkg. 260A	990	881	891
Cruise control, rear defogger, power driver's seat, AM/FM cassette, Power Lock Group (includes power locks, remote fuel door and decklid releases), Light Group (includes underhood light, courtesy lights, lighted visor mirrors), illuminated entry, leather-wrapped steering wheel, 215/70R15 tires, alloy wheels, front floormats.			
Group 1	410	365	369
Rear defogger, illuminated entry, Light Group, front floormats.			
Group 2	515	458	464
Cruise control, leather-wrapped steering wheel, alloy wheels, 215/70R15 tires.			
Group 3	585	521	527
Power Lock Group, power driver's seat.			
Automatic air conditioning	155	138	140
Requires automatic headlamp on/off delay.			
Automatic headlamp on/off delay	70	62	63
Keyless entry system	215	191	194
Power moonroof	740	658	666
Includes dual reading lights, pop-up air deflector, sunshade, rear tilt-up. Requires Groups 1, 2, and 3.			
Premium electronic AM/FM cassette	370	329	333
Includes power antenna.			
Ford JBL audio system	500	445	450
Requires Premium electronic AM/FM cassette, trunk-mounted CD changer, Groups 1, 2, and 3.			
10-disc trunk-mounted CD changer	785	699	707
Requires Premium electronic AM/FM cassette, Ford JBL audio system, Groups 1, 2, and 3.			
Cellular phone	530	472	477
Requires Premium electronic AM/FM cassette.			
Dual power seats	290	258	261
Requires Pkg. 260A.			
Individual leather seats	490	436	441
Cold Weather Group	140	124	126
with 4.6-liter engine	115	102	104
with Traction-Assist	45	40	41
with 4.6-liter engine and Traction-Assist	20	18	18
Includes rear defogger, Traction-Lok axle, engine block heater, heavy duty battery.			
Traction-Assist	210	187	189
Requires anti-lock brakes.			
Tri-coat paint	225	201	203

1995 FORD WINDSTAR

1995 Ford Windstar LX

Specifications	4-door van
Wheelbase, in.	120.7
Overall length, in.	201.0
Overall width, in.	75.0
Overall height, in.	68.0
Curb weight, lbs.	3800
Cargo vol., cu. ft.	144.3
Fuel capacity, gals.	20.0
Seating capacity	7
Front head room, in.	39.3
Max. front leg room, in.	40.7
Rear head room, in.	38.9
Min. rear leg room, in.	39.2

Powertrain layout: transverse front engine/front-wheel drive.

Engines	ohv V-6
Size, liters/cu. in.	3.8/232
Horsepower @ rpm	155 @ 4000
Torque (lbs./ft.) @ rpm	220@ 3000
Availability	S

Prices are accurate at time of publication; subject to manufacturer's change.

EPA city/highway mpg	ohv V-6
4-speed OD automatic	17/24

Built in Canada.

PRICES

1995 Ford Windstar	Retail Price	Dealer Invoice	Fair Price
GL 4-door van	$19240	$17091	—
LX 4-door van	23000	20400	—
Destination charge	540	540	540

Fair price not available at time of publication.

Standard Equipment:

GL: 3.8-liter V-6 engine, 4-speed automatic transmission, driver- and passenger-side air bags, height-adjustable front shoulder belts, anti-lock brakes, power steering, 7-passenger seating (high- back front buckets, 2-place middle and 3-place rear bench seats), solar tinted windshield and front door glass, dual outside mirrors, AM/FM radio with digitial clock, intermittent wipers, rear wiper/ washer, cup holders, front-door map pockets, tachometer, color-keyed bodyside moldings, 205/705R15 tires, full wheel covers. **LX** adds: front air conditioning, power mirrors, power front windows with 30-second delay feature, power rear quarter vent windows, power locks, cassette player, Light Group, illuminated entry, illuminated visor vanity mirrors, low-back bucket seats with power lumbar adjustment, 6-way power driver's seat, map pockets on front seatbacks, 7-inch rear seat travel, storage drawer under front passenger seat, cargo net, 25-gallon fuel tank, 215/70R15 tires, alloy wheels.

Optional Equipment:

Preferred Pkg. 470A, GL	215	182	—
Includes air conditioning and 7-inch rear seat travel.			
Preferred Pkg. 471A, GL	1055	896	—
Pkg. 470A plus Light Group, Power Convenience Group, rear window defroster. Power Convenience Group includes power front windows with 30-second delay feature, power rear quarter vent windows, and power locks and mirrors.			
Preferred Pkg. 472A, GL	1495	1270	—
Pkg. 471A plus cassette player, cruise control, and tilt steering wheel.			
Preferred Pkg. 476A, LX	540	458	—
Rear window defroster, cruise control, tilt steering wheel, front and rear floor mats, luggage rack, 2-tone paint.			

	Retail Price	Dealer Invoice	Fair Price
Preferred Pkg. 477A, LX	$1620	$1377	—
Pkg. 476A plus electronic instrument cluster, privacy glass, remote entry, premium AM/FM cassette player.			
Front and rear air conditioning (NA GL w/Pkg. 470A)	465	395	—
Includes rear heater. Requires privacy glass. GL also requires cruise control, tilt steering wheel, and Light Group.			
Rear defroster, GL w/Pkg. 470A	170	144	—
Cruise control and tilt steering wheel, GL w/Pkg. 471A	370	314	—
Electronic instrument cluster, LX w/Pkg. 476A	490	417	—
Includes autolamp feature and electrochromatic mirror. Requires rear defroster.			
Floor console, LX, GL w/Pkg. 472A	140	119	—
Includes cup holders and covered storage bin. Requires rear air conditioning.			
Privacy glass (NA GL w/Pkg. 470A)	415	352	—
Keyless entry package, LX	340	289	—
Keyless entry system, anti-theft system, and heated mirrors. Requires remote entry and rear defroster.			
Light Group, GL w/Pkg. 470A (std. LX)	50	43	—
Front map/dome light and glove box, instrument panel and engine compartment lights.			
Luggage rack, GL w/Pkg. 472A	145	123	—
Remote entry, GL w/Pkgs. 471A, 472A, LX w/Pkg. 476A	145	123	—
Remote entry system and illuminated entry.			
Cassette player, GL w/Pkgs. 470A, 471A (std. LX)	170	144	—
Premium AM/FM CD player,			
LX w/Pkg. 477A	170	144	—
LX w/Pkg. 476A, GL w/Pkg. 472A	500	425	—
GL w/Pkg. 471A	670	569	—
GL requires cruise control and tilt steering wheel.			
JBL audio system, LX w/Pkg. 477A	510	433	—
Requires premium cassette or CD player.			
Quad bucket seats, LX	600	510	—
Integral child seats	225	192	—
Requires adjustable third seat track. NA with quad buckets.			
Floor mats, GL	70	59	—
Bodyside molding, GL w/Pkg. 470A (credit)	(80)	(68)	(68)

Prices are accurate at time of publication; subject to manufacturer's change.

GEO METRO

Geo Metro 3-door

Specifications

Specifications	3-door hatchback	5-door hatchback
Wheelbase, in.	89.2	93.1
Overall length, in.	147.4	151.4
Overall width, in.	62.7	62.7
Overall height, in.	52.4	53.5
Curb weight, lbs.	1650	1694
Cargo vol., cu. ft.	10.3	10.5
Fuel capacity, gals.	10.3	10.5
Seating capacity	4	4
Front head room, in.	37.8	38.8
Max. front leg room, in.	42.5	42.5
Rear head room, in.	36.5	38.0
Min. rear leg room, in.	29.8	32.6

Powertrain layout: transverse front engine/front-wheel drive.

Engines

Engines	ohc I-3
Size, liters/cu. in.	1.0/61
Horsepower @ rpm	55 @ 5700[1]
Torque (lbs./ft.) @ rpm	58 @ 3300
Availability	S

EPA city/highway mpg

5-speed OD manual	46/49[2]

	ohc I-3
3-speed automatic	36/39

1. XFi, 49 @ 4700. 2. XFi, 53/58.

Built in Canada.

PRICES

Geo Metro	Retail Price	Dealer Invoice	Fair Price
XFi 3-door hatchback	$7295	$6799	$6999
Base 3-door hatchback	7295	6799	6999
Base 5-door hatchback	7795	7265	7465
Destination charge	295	295	295

Standard Equipment:

XFi: 1.0-liter 3-cylinder engine, 5-speed manual transmission, door-mounted automatic front seatbelts, automatic power locks, cloth and vinyl reclining front bucket seats, one-piece folding rear seatback, temperature gauge, console with cup holders and storage tray, left door pocket, 145/80R12 tires. **Base** adds: left remote and right manual mirrors, intermittent wipers, bodyside moldings, wheel covers.

Optional Equipment:

3-speed automatic transmission, base	495	441	448
Air conditioning, base	720	641	652
UL1 AM/FM radio	301	268	272
Includes seek and scan, digital clock, and four speakers.			
UL0 AM/FM cassette player	496	441	449
Includes seek and scan, theft deterrent, tone select, digital clock, and four speakers.			
XFi Preferred Equipment Group 2	301	268	272
UL1 AM/FM radio.			
With UL0 AM/FM cassette player, add	195	174	176
Rear defogger	150	134	136
Base Preferred Group 2	1021	909	924
Air conditioning, UL1 AM/FM radio.			
With UL0 AM/FM cassette player, add	195	174	176
Rear wiper/washer, base	125	111	113
Requires rear defogger.			
Tachometer	50	45	46
Left remote and right manual mirrors, XFi	20	18	18
Bodyside moldings, XFi	50	45	46
Cargo security cover	50	45	46

Prices are accurate at time of publication; subject to manufacturer's change.

GEO PRIZM

Geo Prizm LSi

Specifications

Specifications	4-door notchback
Wheelbase, in.	97.1
Overall length, in.	172.6
Overall width, in.	66.3
Overall height, in.	52.8
Curb weight, lbs.	2347
Cargo vol., cu. ft.	12.7
Fuel capacity, gals.	13.2
Seating capacity	5
Front head room, in.	38.8
Max. front leg room, in.	42.4
Rear head room, in.	37.1
Min. rear leg room, in.	33.0

Powertrain layout: transverse front engine/front-wheel drive.

Engines

Engines	dohc I-4	dohc I-4
Size, liters/cu. in.	1.6/97	1.8/110
Horsepower @ rpm	108 @ 5800	115 @ 5600
Torque (lbs./ft.) @ rpm	105 @ 4800	115 @ 4800
Availability	S	O[1]
EPA city/highway mpg		
5-speed OD manual	27/34	28/34
3-speed automatic	26/29	

	dohc I-4	dohc I-4
4-speed OD automatic		26/32

1. LSi.

Built in Fremont, Calif.

PRICES

Geo Prizm	Retail Price	Dealer Invoice	Fair Price
4-door notchback	$11070	$10539	$10839
4-door notchback (California only)	10840	10320	10620
LSi 4-door notchback	11840	10916	11416
LSi 4-door notchback (California only)	11610	10704	11204
Destination charge	365	365	365

Standard Equipment:

1.6-liter DOHC 4-cylinder engine, 5-speed manual transmission, driver- and passenger-side air bags, left remote and right manual mirrors, reclining front bucket seats, cloth/vinyl upholstery, center console with storage tray and cup holders, remote fuel door release, tinted glass, rear-seat heating ducts, bodyside molding, 175/65R14 tires. **LSi** adds: tilt steering column, upgraded full-cloth upholstery, center console with armrest, dual front storage pockets, split-folding rear seat, visor mirrors, wheel covers.

Optional Equipment:

1.8-liter 4-cylinder engine, LSi	352	303	308
Includes rear stabilizer bar and 185/65R14 tires.			
3-speed automatic transmission	495	426	433
Requires 1.6-liter engine.			
4-speed automatic transmission, LSi	800	688	700
Requires 1.8-liter engine.			
Anti-lock brakes	595	512	521
Air conditioning	795	684	696
Cruise control, LSi w/Preferred Equipment Group 2	175	151	153
Rear defogger	170	146	149
Power locks	220	189	193
Power sunroof, LSi	660	568	578
Includes map light.			
Intermittent wipers	40	34	35
Tachometer	60	52	53
AM/FM cassette player	525	452	459
Includes seek and scan, theft deterrent, tone select, digital clock, and four speakers.			

	Retail Price	Dealer Invoice	Fair Price
AM/FM radio	$330	$284	$289
Includes seek and scan, digital clock, and four speakers.			
AM/FM radio with CD and cassette player, LSi	568	488	497
Includes seek and scan, theft deterrent, tone select, digital clock, and six speakers.			
Base Preferred Equipment Group 2	590	507	516
Power steering and AM/FM radio with digital clock.			
With AM/FM cassette player, add	195	168	171
LSi Preferred Equipment Group 2	1545	1329	1352
Air conditioning, AM/FM radio with digital clock, dual power mirrors, power steering, remote decklid release, intermittent wipers.			
With AM/FM cassette, add	195	168	171
With AM/FM radio, CD, and cassette player, add	568	488	497
LSi Preferred Equipment Group 3	2240	1926	1960
LSi Preferred Equipment Group 2 plus power windows and door locks, cruise control.			
With AM/FM cassette, add	195	168	171
With AM/FM radio, CD, and cassette player, add	568	488	497
Alloy wheels, LSi	335	288	293
Front and rear floormats	40	34	35

GEO TRACKER/ SUZUKI SIDEKICK

Specifications

Specifications	2-door wgn./conv.	5-door wagon
Wheelbase, in.	86.6	97.6
Overall length, in.	142.5	158.7
Overall width, in.	64.2	64.6
Overall height, in.	64.3	65.7
Curb weight, lbs.	2253	2571
Cargo vol., cu. ft.	32.9	45.0
Fuel capacity, gals.	11.1	14.5
Seating capacity	4	4
Front head room, in.	39.5	40.6
Max. front leg room, in.	42.1	42.1
Rear head room, in.	39.0	40.0

Geo Tracker convertible

	2-door wgn./conv.	5-door wagon
Min. rear leg room, in.	31.7	32.7

Powertrain layout: longitudinal front engine/rear-wheel drive or on-demand 4WD.

Engines

	ohc I-4	ohc I-4
Size, liters/cu. in.	1.6/97	1.6/97
Horsepower @ rpm	80 @ 5400	95 @ 5600
Torque (lbs./ft.) @ rpm	94 @ 3000	98 @ 4000
Availability	S[1]	S[2]
EPA city/highway mpg		
5-speed OD manual	25/27	24/26
3-speed automatic	23/24	23/24

1. 2-door models. 2. Sidekick 5-door and California 2-door models.

Built in Canada.

PRICES

Geo Tracker	Retail Price	Dealer Invoice	Fair Price
2-door convertible, 2WD	$11015	$10486	$10686
2-door wagon, 4WD	12445	11848	12048
LSi 2-door wagon, 4WD	13915	13247	13447
2-door convertible, 4WD	12285	11695	11895

Prices are accurate at time of publication; subject to manufacturer's change.

	Retail Price	Dealer Invoice	Fair Price
LSi 2-door convertible, 4WD	$13650	$12995	$13195
Destination charge	300	300	300

Standard Equipment:

1.6-liter 4-cylinder engine, 5-speed manual transmission, anti-lock rear brakes, rear defogger (wagon only), cloth/vinyl reclining front bucket seats, folding rear bench seat (4WD), center console with storage tray and cup holders, tachometer (4WD), trip odometer, dual mirrors, intermittent wipers, full-size lockable spare tire, spare tire cover, front and rear tow hooks, 195/75R15 tires, (205/75R15 tires 4WD). **LSi** adds: automatic locking front hubs, power steering, AM/FM radio, floormats, tinted glass, upgraded cloth/vinyl upholstery and door trim, adjustable rear bucket seats, rear wiper/washer (wagon only), bodyside moldings, styled steel wheels.

Optional Equipment:

	Retail Price	Dealer Invoice	Fair Price
3-speed automatic transmission	595	530	538
Air conditioning	745	663	674
Tilt steering wheel	115	102	104
UL1 AM/FM radio	306	272	277
Includes seek and scan, digital clock, and four speakers.			
UL0 AM/FM cassette player	501	446	453
LSi	195	174	176
Includes seek and scan, theft deterrent, tone select, digital clock, and four speakers.			
UP0 AM/FM radio with CD and cassette player, LSi	897	798	812
LSi	591	526	535
Includes seek and scan, theft deterrent, tone select, digital clock, and four speakers.			
Convertible 2WD Preferred Group 2	581	517	526
UL1 AM/FM radio, power steering.			
With UL0 AM/FM cassette, add	195	174	176
With UP0 AM/FM radio, CD, and cassette player, add	591	526	535
Base and convertible 4WD Preferred Equipment Group 2	581	517	526
UL1 AM/FM radio, power steering.			
With UL0 AM/FM cassette, add	195	174	176
With UP0 AM/FM radio, CD, and cassette player, add	591	526	535

	Retail Price	Dealer Invoice	Fair Price
Rear seat, 2WD	$445	$396	$403
Transfer case shield, 4WD	75	67	68
Alloy wheels	335	298	303
Bodyside moldings, base wagon	59	53	53
Convertibles	85	76	77

Suzuki Sidekick

	Retail Price	Dealer Invoice	Fair Price
JS 2WD 2-door soft top, 5-speed	$11449	$10762	$10962
JS 2WD 2-door soft top, 5-speed (New York and California)	11749	11044	11244
JS 2WD 2-door soft top, automatic	12049	11326	11526
JS 2WD 2-door soft top, automatic (New York and California)	12349	11608	11808
JX 4WD 2-door soft top, 5-speed	12849	11821	12021
JX 4WD 2-door soft top, 5-speed (New York and California)	13149	12097	12297
JX 4WD 2-door soft top, automatic	13449	12373	12573
JX 4WD 2-door soft top, automatic (New York and California)	13749	12649	12849
JS 2WD 5-door, 5-speed	12999	—	—
JS 2WD 5-door, automatic	14109	—	—
JX 4WD 5-door, 5-speed	14309	—	—
JX 4WD 5-door, automatic	15259	—	—
JLX 4WD 5-door, 5-speed	15719	—	—
JLX 4WD 5-door, automatic	16669	—	—
Destination charge, 2-door	330	330	330
5-door	350	350	350

5-door dealer invoice and fair price not available at time of publication.

Standard Equipment:

JS 2-door: 1.6-liter 4-cylinder engine, 5-speed manual transmission or 3-speed automatic transmission, rear-wheel drive, anti-lock rear brakes, cloth reclining front bucket seats and folding rear seat, center console, front door map pockets, fuel tank skid plate, folding canvas top, tinted glass, dual outside mirrors, intermittent wipers, trip odometer, carpeting, 195/75R15 tires. **JX 2-door** adds: part-time 4WD, automatic locking front hubs, 2-speed transfer case, power steering, power mirrors, tachometer, 205/75R15 tires. **JS 5-door** adds: 1.6-liter DOHC engine, 5-speed manual or 4-speed automatic transmission, rear-wheel drive, power steering, power mirrors, rear defogger, child-safety rear door locks, carpeting, center console, locking fuel door, tinted glass, front map pockets, AM/FM cassette, reclining front bucket seats, cloth upholstery, split folding rear seat, fuel tank skid plate, tachometer, intermittent wipers, 195/75R15 tires. **JX 5-door** adds: 5-speed manual or 4-speed automatic transmission, part-time 4WD, automatic locking front hubs, 2-speed transfer case, 205/75R15 mud and snow tires. **JLX 5-door** adds: tilt steering column, power windows and locks, cruise control, map lights, rear wiper/washer, remote fuel door release, deluxe upholstery, locking spare tire case, 205/75R15 outline white letter mud and snow tires, chrome wheels.

Options are available as dealer-installed accessories.

HONDA ACCORD

Honda Accord EX 4-door

Specifications	2-door notchback	4-door notchback	5-door wagon
Wheelbase, in.	106.9	106.9	106.9
Overall length, in.	184.0	184.0	187.8
Overall width, in.	70.1	70.1	70.1
Overall height, in.	54.7	55.1	55.9
Curb weight, lbs.	2756	2800	NA
Cargo vol., cu. ft.	13.0	13.0	25.7
Fuel capacity, gals.	17.0	17.0	17.0
Seating capacity	5	5	5
Front head room, in.	39.4	39.4	39.8
Max. front leg room, in.	42.9	42.7	42.7
Rear head room, in.	36.4	37.6	39.0
Min. rear leg room, in.	31.3	34.3	34.1

Powertrain layout: transverse front engine/front-wheel drive.

Engines

	ohc I-4	ohc I-4
Size, liters/cu. in.	2.2/132	2.2/132
Horsepower @ rpm	130 @ 5300	145 @ 5500
Torque (lbs./ft.) @ rpm	139 @ 4200	147 @ 4500
Availability	S[1]	S[2]
EPA city/highway mpg		
5-speed OD manual	25/31	25/31
4-speed OD automatic	23/29	23/30

1 DX, LX. 2. EX.

Built in Marysville, Ohio.

PRICES

Honda Accord	Retail Price	Dealer Invoice	Fair Price
DX 2-door notchback, 5-speed	$14130	$12011	—
DX 2-door notchback, automatic	14880	12648	—
DX 2-door notchback, 5-speed w/ABS	15080	12818	—
DX 2-door notchback, automatic w/ABS	15830	13456	—
LX 2-door notchback, 5-speed	17030	14476	—
LX 2-door notchback, automatic	17780	15113	—
LX 2-door notchback, 5-speed w/ABS	17980	15283	—
LX 2-door notchback, automatic w/ABS	18730	15921	—
EX 2-door notchback, 5-speed	19550	16618	—
EX 2-door notchback, automatic	20300	17255	—
EX 2-door notchback, 5-speed w/leather	20600	17510	—
EX 2-door notchback, automatic w/leather	21350	18148	—
DX 4-door notchback, 5-speed	14330	12181	—
DX 4-door notchback, automatic	15080	12818	—
DX 4-door notchback w/ABS, 5-speed	15280	12988	—
DX 4-door notchback w/ABS, automatic	16030	13626	—
LX 4-door notchback, 5-speed	17230	14646	—
LX 4-door notchback, automatic	17980	15283	—
LX 4-door notchback w/ABS, 5-speed	18180	15453	—
LX 4-door notchback w/ABS, automatic	18930	16091	—
EX 4-door notchback, 5-speed	19750	16788	—
EX 4-door notchback, automatic	20500	17425	—
EX 4-door notchback w/leather, 5-speed	20800	17680	—
EX 4-door notchback w/leather, automatic	21550	18318	—

	Retail Price	Dealer Invoice	Fair Price
LX 5-door wagon, 5-speed	$18180	$15453	—
LX 5-door wagon, automatic	18930	16091	—
LX 5-door wagon w/ABS, 5-speed	19130	16260	—
LX 5-door wagon w/ABS, automatic	19880	16898	—
EX 5-door wagon, 5-speed	20750	17638	—
EX 5-door wagon, automatic	21500	18275	—
Destination charge	350	350	350

Fair price not available at time of publication.

Standard Equipment:

DX: 2.2-liter 4-cylinder engine, 5-speed manual or 4-speed automatic transmission, variable-assist power steering, driver- and passenger-side air bags, cloth reclining front bucket seats, folding rear seatback, front console with armrest, tachometer, coolant temperature gauge, trip odometer, tinted glass, tilt steering column, intermittent wipers, rear defogger, dual remote mirrors, remote fuel door and decklid releases, door pockets, maintenance interval indicator, 185/70R14 tires. **Models with ABS** add 4-wheel anti-lock disc brakes. **LX** adds: air conditioning, cruise control, power windows and locks, power mirrors, AM/FM cassette, power antenna, rear armrest, beverage holder; wagon has cargo cover, full-size spare tire. **EX** adds: 145-horsepower VTEC engine, anti-lock 4-wheel disc brakes, driver's seat lumbar support and power height adjusters, power moonroof, upgraded audio system, 195/60HR15 tires, alloy wheels; wagon adds remote keyless entry.

Options are available as dealer-installed accessories.

HONDA CIVIC

Specifications	2-door notchback	3-door hatchback	4-door notchback
Wheelbase, in.	103.2	101.3	103.2
Overall length, in.	172.8	160.2	173.0
Overall width, in.	66.9	66.9	66.9
Overall height, in.	50.9	50.7	51.7
Curb weight, lbs.	2231	2108	2213
Cargo vol., cu. ft.	11.8	13.3	12.4
Fuel capacity, gals.	11.9	11.9	11.9
Seating capacity	5	5	5
Front head room, in.	38.5	38.6	39.1
Max. front leg room, in.	42.5	42.5	42.5

Honda Civic EX 4-door

	2-door notchback	3-door hatchback	4-door notchback
Rear head room, in.	34.9	36.6	37.2
Min. rear leg room, in.	31.1	30.5	32.8

Powertrain layout: transverse front engine/front-wheel drive.

Engines	ohc I-4	ohc I-4	ohc I-4	ohc I-4
Size, liters/cu. in.	1.5/91	1.5/91	1.5/91	1.6/97
Horsepower @ rpm	70 @ 5000	92 @ 5500	102 @ 5900	125 @ 6600
Torque (lbs./ft.) @ rpm	91 @ 2000	97 @ 4500	98 @ 5000	106 @ 5200
Availability	S[1]	S[2]	S[3]	S[4]
EPA city/highway mpg				
5-speed OD manual	42/46	47/56	34/40	29/35
4-speed OD automatic			29/36	26/33

1. CX. 2. VX. 3. DX, LX. 4. EX, Si.

Built in East Liberty, Ohio; Canada; and Japan.

PRICES

Honda Civic	Retail Price	Dealer Invoice	Fair Price
CX 3-door hatchback, 5-speed	$9400	$8460	$9360
DX 3-door hatchback, 5-speed	10800	9288	10188
DX 3-door hatchback, automatic	11780	10131	11031
VX 3-door hatchback, 5-speed	11500	9890	10790
Si 3-door hatchback, 5-speed	13170	11326	12226
Si 3-door hatchback w/ABS, 5-speed	14020	12057	12957
DX 2-door notchback, 5-speed	11220	9649	10549

Prices are accurate at time of publication; subject to manufacturer's change.

HONDA

	Retail Price	Dealer Invoice	Fair Price
DX 2-door notchback, automatic	$12200	$10492	$11392
EX 2-door notchback, 5-speed	13600	11696	12596
EX 2-door notchback, automatic	14350	12341	13241
EX 2-door notchback w/ABS, 5-speed	14450	12427	13327
EX 2-door notchback w/ABS, automatic	15200	13072	13972
DX 4-door notchback, 5-speed	11750	10105	11005
DX 4-door notchback, automatic	12500	10750	11650
LX 4-door notchback, 5-speed	12950	11137	12037
LX 4-door notchback, automatic	13700	11782	12682
LX 4-door notchback w/ABS, 5-speed	13800	11868	12768
LX 4-door notchback w/ABS, automatic	14550	12513	13413
EX 4-door notchback, 5-speed	15740	13536	14436
EX 4-door notchback, automatic	16490	14181	15081
Destination charge	350	350	350

Standard Equipment:

CX: 1.5-liter (70 horsepower) 4-cylinder engine, 5-speed manual transmission, driver- and passenger-side air bags, reclining cloth front bucket seats, 50/50 split folding rear seatback, remote fuel door and hatch releases, tinted glass, rear defogger, dual remote mirrors, 165/70R13 tires. **DX** adds: 1.5-liter (102 horsepower) engine, 5-speed manual or 4-speed automatic transmission, power steering (sedans; hatchbacks and coupes with automatic transmission only), rear wiper/washer (hatchback), tilt steering column, cargo cover (hatchback), intermittent wipers, bodyside moldings, 175/70R13 tires. **VX** adds to CX: 1.5-liter (92 horsepower) engine, tachometer, alloy wheels. **Si** adds to DX: 1.6-liter engine, 4-wheel disc brakes, power steering, dual power mirrors, power moonroof, digital clock, tachometer, sport seats, cruise control, rear wiper/washer, wheel covers, 185/60HR14 tires. **LX 4-door** adds to DX 4-door: power mirrors, power windows and locks, cruise control, digital clock, tachometer, front armrest, wheel covers, 175/65R14 tires. **Models with ABS** add: anti-lock 4-wheel disc brakes. **EX 4-door** adds to LX 4-door: 1.6-liter engine, anti-lock 4-wheel disc brakes, air conditioning, power moonroof, upgraded interior trim. **EX 2-door** adds to DX 2-door: 1.6-liter engine, power windows and locks, power mirrors, power moonroof, cruise control, AM/FM cassette, wheel covers, 185/60HR14 tires.

Options are available as dealer-installed accessories.

HONDA CIVIC DEL SOL

Honda Civic del Sol VTEC

Specifications

Specifications	2-door notchback
Wheelbase, in.	93.3
Overall length, in.	157.3
Overall width, in.	66.7
Overall height, in.	49.4
Curb weight, lbs.	2301
Cargo vol., cu. ft.	10.5
Fuel capacity, gals.	11.9
Seating capacity	2
Front head room, in.	37.5
Front leg room, max., in.	40.3
Rear head room, in.	—
Rear leg room, min. , in.	—

Powertrain layout: transverse front engine/front-wheel drive.

Engines

Engines	ohc I-4	ohc I-4	dohc I-4
Size, liters/cu. in.	1.5/91	1.6/97	1.6/97
Horsepower @ rpm	102 @ 5900	125 @ 6600	160 @ 7600
Torque (lbs/ft) @ rpm	98 @ 5000	106 @ 5200	111 @ 7000
Availability	S[1]	S[2]	S[3]

Prices are accurate at time of publication; subject to manufacturer's change.

EPA city/highway mpg	ohc I-4	ohc I-4	dohc I-4
5-speed OD manual	35/41	29/35	26/30
4-speed OD automatic	29/36	26/33	

1. S. 2. Si. 3. VTEC.

Built in Japan.

PRICES

Honda Civic del Sol	Retail Price	Dealer Invoice	Fair Price
S 2-door notchback, 5-speed	$14100	$12126	$13626
S 2-door notchback, automatic	15080	12969	14469
Si 2-door notchback, 5-speed	16100	13846	15346
Si 2-door notchback, automatic	16850	14491	15991
VTEC 2-door notchback, 5-speed	17500	15050	16550
Destination charge	350	350	350

Standard Equipment:

S: 1.5-liter 4-cylinder engine, driver- and passenger-side air bags, power steering (with automatic), reclining front bucket seats, center armrest with storage, power windows, rear defogger, intermittent wipers, tilt steering column, tachometer, remote fuel door release, 175/70R13 tires, wheel covers. **Si** adds: 1.6-liter 4-cylinder engine, power steering, 4-wheel disc brakes, cruise control, AM/FM cassette, power mirrors, 185/60HR14 tires, alloy wheels. **VTEC** adds: 1.6-liter DOHC VTEC engine, 195/60VR14 tires.

Options are available as dealer-installed accessories.

HONDA PRELUDE

Specifications	2-door notchback
Wheelbase, in.	100.4
Overall length, in.	174.8
Overall width, in.	69.5
Overall height, in.	50.8
Curb weight, lbs.	2765
Cargo vol., cu. ft.	7.9
Fuel capacity, gals.	15.9
Seating capacity	4
Front head room, in.	38.0
Max. front leg room, in.	44.2
Rear head room, in.	35.1

Honda Prelude Si

	2-door notchback
Min. rear leg room, in.	28.1

Powertrain layout: transverse front engine/front-wheel drive.

Engines	ohc I-4	dohc I-4	dohc I-4
Size, liters/cu. in.	2.2/132	2.3/138	2.2/132
Horsepower @ rpm	135 @ 5200	160 @ 5800	190 @ 6800
Torque (lbs./ft.) @ rpm	142 @ 4000	156 @ 4500	158 @ 5500
Availability	S[1]	S[2]	S[3]
EPA city/highway mpg			
5-speed OD manual	23/29	22/26	22/26
4-speed OD automatic	23/28	22/27	

1. S. 2. Si, Si 4WS. 3 VTEC.

Built in Japan.

PRICES

Honda Prelude	Retail Price	Dealer Invoice	Fair Price
S 2-door notchback, 5-speed	$18100	$15385	$16085
S 2-door notchback, automatic	18850	16023	16723
Si 2-door notchback, 5-speed	21400	18190	18890
Si 2-door notchback, automatic	22150	18828	19528
Si 4WS 2-door notchback, 5-speed	24160	20536	21236
Si 4WS 2-door notchback, automatic	24910	21174	21874
VTEC 2-door notchback, 5-speed	24500	20825	21525
Destination charge	350	350	350

Prices are accurate at time of publication; subject to manufacturer's change.

Dealer invoice and fair price not available at time of publication.

Standard Equipment:

S: 2.2-liter 4-cylinder engine, 5-speed manual or 4-speed automatic transmission, 4-wheel disc brakes, variable-assist power steering, driver- and passenger-side air bags, cloth reclining front bucket seats, folding rear seat, power moonroof, AM/FM cassette with power antenna, remote fuel door and decklid releases, rear defogger, intermittent wipers, power windows, power mirrors, cruise control, tilt steering column, tachometer, visor mirrors, 185/70HR14 tires, wheel covers. **Si** adds: 2.3-liter DOHC 4-cylinder engine, anti-lock brakes, air conditioning, power locks, driver-seat height and lumbar support adjusters, 205/55VR15 tires, alloy wheels. **Si 4WS** adds: 4-wheel steering, leather seats, rear spoiler. **VTEC** adds to Si: 2.2-liter DOHC VTEC engine, leather seats, rear spoiler.

Options are available as dealer-installed accessories.

HYUNDAI ELANTRA

Hyundai Elantra

Specifications	4-door notchback
Wheelbase, in.	98.4
Overall length, in.	172.8
Overall width, in.	66.1
Overall height, in.	52.0
Curb weight, lbs.	2500

	4-door notchback
Cargo vol., cu. ft.	11.8
Fuel capacity, gals.	13.7
Seating capacity	5
Front head room, in.	38.4
Max. front leg room, in.	42.6
Rear head room, in.	37.6
Min. rear leg room, in.	33.4

Powertrain layout: transverse front engine/front-wheel drive.

Engines	dohc I-4	dohc I-4
Size, liters/cu. in.	1.6/97	1.8/110
Horsepower @ rpm	113 @ 6000	124 @ 6000
Torque (lbs./ft.) @ rpm	102 @ 5000	116 @ 4500
Availability	S[1]	S
EPA city/highway mpg		
5-speed OD manual	22/29	21/28
4-speed OD automatic		23/28

1. Base model with manual transmission.

Built in South Korea.

PRICES

Hyundai Elantra	Retail Price	Dealer Invoice	Fair Price
4-door notchback, 5-speed	$9799	$8846	$9046
4-door notchback, automatic	11074	9993	10193
GLS 4-door notchback, 5-speed	11199	9881	10081
GLS 4-door notchback, automatic	11924	10532	10732
Destination charge	405	405	405

Standard Equipment:

1.6-liter DOHC 4-cylinder engine, 5-speed manual transmission, power steering, driver-side air bag, cloth reclining front bucket seats, center console, digital clock, remote fuel door and decklid releases, rear defogger, variable-intermittent wipers, coolant temperature gauge, trip odometer, tinted glass, dual remote outside mirrors, 175/65R14 tires. **Automatic** adds: 4-speed automatic transmission, 1.8-liter DOHC engine. **GLS** adds: 1.8-liter DOHC engine,

6-way adjustable driver's seat, split folding rear seat, upgraded upholstery, power mirrors, front map pockets, tachometer, power windows and locks, tilt steering column, AM/FM cassette, 185/60R14 tires.

Optional Equipment:	Retail Price	Dealer Invoice	Fair Price
Option Pkg. 2, base *AM/FM cassette.*	$350	$268	$305
Option Pkg. 3, base *Pkg. 2 plus air conditioning.*	1245	998	1108
Option Pkg. 4, base *Pkg. 3 plus cruise control.*	1465	1178	1305
Option Pkg. 10, GLS *Air conditioning, uplevel AM/FM cassette, cruise control.*	1303	1053	1163
Option Pkg. 11, GLS *Pkg. 10 plus alloy wheels.*	1643	1330	1468
Option Pkg. 12, GLS *Pkg. 10 plus sunroof.*	1813	1469	1621
Option Pkg. 13, GLS *Pkg. 10 plus anti-lock brakes.*	2075	1764	1896
Option Pkg. 14, GLS *Pkg. 13 plus high level AM/FM cassette, alloy wheels, and sunroof.*	3120	2605	2827
Option Pkg. 15, GLS *Deletes anti-lock brakes from Pkg. 14.*	2345	1894	2093
CD player	395	290	338
Front console armrest	108	70	88
Door edge guards	36	23	29
Mud guards, front and rear	78	47	62
Sunroof wind deflector	52	30	40
Floormats	58	38	47

HYUNDAI EXCEL

Specifications	3-door hatchback	4-door notchback
Wheelbase, in.	93.8	93.8
Overall length, in.	161.4	168.3
Overall width, in.	63.3	63.3
Overall height, in.	54.5	54.5
Curb weight, lbs.	2147	2224
Cargo vol., cu. ft.	37.9	11.4
Fuel capacity, gals.	11.9	11.9
Seating capacity	5	5

Hyundai Excel GL

	3-door hatchback	4-door notchback
Front head room, in.	37.8	37.8
Max. front leg room, in.	41.7	41.7
Rear head room, in.	37.6	37.6
Min. rear leg room, in.	33.1	33.1

Powertrain layout: transverse front engine/front-wheel drive.

Engines

	ohc I-4
Size, liters/cu. in.	1.5/90
Horsepower @ rpm	81 @ 5500
Torque (lbs./ft.) @ rpm	91 @ 3000
Availability	S

EPA city/highway mpg

5-speed OD manual	28/36
4-speed OD automatic	27/35

Built in South Korea.

PRICES

Hyundai Excel	Retail Price	Dealer Invoice	Fair Price
3-door hatchback, 5-speed manual	$7290	$6804	$7004
3-door hatchback, 4-speed automatic	7915	7365	7565
GS 3-door hatchback, 5-speed manual	8299	7492	7692

Prices are accurate at time of publication; subject to manufacturer's change.

	Retail Price	Dealer Invoice	Fair Price
GS 3-door hatchback, 4-speed automatic	$8924	$8053	$8253
GL 4-door notchback, 5-speed manual	8299	7661	7861
GL 4-door notchback, 4-speed automatic	8924	8222	8422
Destination charge	405	405	405

Standard Equipment:

1.5-liter 4-cylinder engine, 5-speed manual or 4-speed automatic transmission, door-mounted front shoulder belts, cloth and vinyl reclining front bucket seats, 60/40 folding rear seatback, dual remote outside mirrors, coolant temperature gauge, trip odometer, center bodyside molding, rear defogger, locking fuel door, intermittent wipers, cargo cover, 155/80R13 tires. **GL 4-door** adds: AM/FM cassette player, tinted glass, door map pockets, remote fuel door and decklid releases, lockable glove box, 175/70R13 tires. **GS 3-door** adds: tachometer, 5-way adjustable driver's seat, full cloth upholstery, digital clock, upgraded door trim, door map pockets, rear heater ducts, rear spoiler, passenger-side visor mirror, console with cassette storage, rear wiper/washer.

Optional Equipment:

	Retail Price	Dealer Invoice	Fair Price
Option Pkg. 2, base *AM/FM cassette.*	340	260	293
Option Pkg. 3, base *Pkg. 2 plus power steering and tinted glass.*	660	541	586
Option Pkg. 4, base *Pkg. 3 plus air conditioning.*	1545	1263	1370
Option Pkg. 5, GL and Option Pkg. 10, GS *Power steering.*	260	232	240
Option Pkg. 6, GL and Option Pkg. 11, GS *Pkg. 5, GS and Pkg. 10, GL plus air conditioning.*	1155	994	1048
Option Pkg. 12, GS *Pkg. 11 plus sunroof.*	1646	1394	1483
Sunroof air deflector	62	30	40
Console armrest	105	64	82
Mud guards, rear	40	26	32
Floormats	62	38	47

HYUNDAI SCOUPE

Hyundai Scoupe Turbo

Specifications

Specifications	2-door notchback
Wheelbase, in.	93.8
Overall length, in.	165.9
Overall width, in.	63.9
Overall height, in.	50.0
Curb weight, lbs.	2176
Cargo vol., cu. ft.	9.3
Fuel capacity, gals.	11.9
Seating capacity	4
Front head room, in.	38.1
Max. front leg room, in.	42.8
Rear head room, in.	34.3
Min. rear leg room, in.	29.4

Powertrain layout: transverse front engine/front-wheel drive.

Engines

Engines	ohc I-4	Turbo ohc I-4
Size, liters/cu. in.	1.5/91	1.5/91
Horsepower @ rpm	92 @ 5500	115 @ 5500
Torque (lbs./ft.) @ rpm	97 @ 4500	123 @ 4000
Availability	S	S[1]

Prices are accurate at time of publication; subject to manufacturer's change.

HYUNDAI

EPA city/highway mpg	ohc I-4	Turbo ohc I-4
5-speed OD manual	26/33	26/31
4-speed OD automatic	26/33	

1. Scoupe Turbo.

Built in South Korea.

PRICES

Hyundai Scoupe	Retail Price	Dealer Invoice	Fair Price
2-door notchback, 5-speed	$9799	$8846	$9046
2-door notchback, automatic	10474	9459	9659
LS 2-door notchback, 5-speed	11099	9793	9993
LS 2-door notchback, automatic	11774	10406	10606
Turbo 2-door notchback, 5-speed	11899	10498	10698
Destination charge	405	405	405

Standard Equipment:

1.5-liter 4-cylinder engine, 5-speed manual or 4-speed automatic transmission, door-mounted front shoulder belts, cloth reclining front bucket seats, 60/40 folding rear seatback, tachometer, coolant temperature gauge, trip odometer, remote outside mirrors, rear window defroster, tinted glass, intermittent wipers, remote fuel door and decklid releases, digital clock, door map pockets, rear spoiler, passenger-side visor mirror, 175/70R13 tires. **LS** adds: power steering, power windows and mirrors, 6-way adjustable driver's seat, 4-way adjustable passenger's seat, full cloth upholstery, AM/FM cassette, cup holders, 185/60HR14 tires. **Turbo** adds to LS: turbocharged 1.5-liter engine, LED turbo boost gauge, sport suspension, leather-wrapped steering wheel and shift knob, fog lamps, alloy wheels.

Optional Equipment:

Option Pkg. 2, base *AM/FM cassette, power steering.*	610	496	540
Option Pkg. 3, base *Pkg. 2 plus air conditioning.*	1505	1235	1337
Option Pkg. 10, LS *Air conditioning.*	895	739	797
Option Pkg. 11, LS *Pkg. 10 plus sunroof.*	1190	983	1060
Option Pkg. 12, LS *Pkg. 11 plus high-level AM/FM cassette, air conditioning.*	1715	1405	1522

	Retail Price	Dealer Invoice	Fair Price
Option Pkg. 15, Turbo	$1385	$1132	$1228
High-level AM/FM cassette, air conditioning, sunroof.			
CD player	395	290	334
Console armrest	105	64	82
Sunshade	58	38	47
Floormats	58	38	47

1995 HYUNDAI SONATA

1995 Hyundai Sonata GLS

Specifications	4-door notchback
Wheelbase, in.	106.3
Overall length, in.	185.0
Overall width, in.	69.7
Overall height, in.	55.3
Curb weight, lbs.	3025
Cargo vol., cu. ft.	13.2
Fuel capacity, gals.	16.9
Seating capacity	5
Front head room, in.	38.5
Max. front leg room, in.	43.3
Rear head room, in.	NA
Min. rear leg room, in.	NA

Powertrain layout: transverse front engine/front-wheel drive.

HYUNDAI

Engines

Engines	dohc I-4	ohc V-6
Size, liters/cu. in.	2.0/122	3.0/181
Horsepower @ rpm	137 @ 5800	142 @ 5000
Torque (lbs./ft.) @ rpm	129 @ 4000	168 @ 2400
Availability	S[1]	S[2]
EPA city/highway mpg		
5-speed OD manual	21/29	
4-speed OD automatic	21/28	18/24

1. Base, GL. 2. GLS; optional, GL.

Built in South Korea.

PRICES

1995 Hyundai Sonata	Retail Price	Dealer Invoice	Fair Price
4-door notchback, 5-speed	$13299	$11937	—
4-door notchback, automatic	14079	12701	—
GL 4-door notchback, automatic	14799	13133	—
GL 4-door notchback, V-6 automatic	15699	13826	—
GLS 4-door notchback, V-6 automatic	17199	14912	—
Destination charge	405	405	405

Fair price not available at time of publication.

Standard Equipment:

2.0-liter DOHC 4-cylinder or 3.0-liter V-6 engine, 5-speed manual or 4-speed automatic transmission, air conditioning, power steering, driver- and passenger-side air bags, cloth reclining front bucket seats with 4-way adjustable driver's seat, center console, tachometer, coolant temperature gauge, trip odometer, AM/FM cassette, tilt steering column, digital clock, remote fuel door and decklid releases, rear defogger, door pockets, remote outside mirrors, bodyside molding, tinted glass, intermittent wipers, visor mirrors, 195/70R14 tires. **GL** adds: power windows and door locks, power mirrors. **GLS** adds to GL: 3.0-liter V-6 engine, 6-way adjustable driver's seat, 60/40 split folding rear seat with center armrest, dual map lights, power antenna, upgraded cloth upholstery and door trim, upgraded AM/FM cassette player, lighted passenger-side visor mirror, front seatback pockets, 205/60HR15 tires, alloy wheels.

Optional Equipment:

Front console armrest	135	84	—

	Retail Price	Dealer Invoice	Fair Price
Option Pkg. 5, GL and GL V-6	$230	$188	—
Cruise control.			
Option Pkg. 6, GL and GL V-6	830	678	—
Cruise control, sunroof.			
Option Pkg. 7, GL V-6	1710	1504	—
Anti-lock brakes, cruise control, sunroof.			
Option Pkg. 10, GLS	600	490	—
Sunroof.			
Option Pkg. 11, GLS	1400	1214	—
Leather Pkg. (leather upholstery, leather-wrapped steering wheel), CD player.			
Option Pkg. 12, GLS	1630	1438	—
Anti-lock brakes, CD player.			
Option Pkg. 13, GLS	2880	2530	—
Anti-lock brakes, Leather Pkg., CD player, sunroof.			

INFINITI G20

Infiniti G20

Specifications	4-door notchback
Wheelbase, in.	100.4
Overall length, in.	174.8
Overall width, in.	66.7
Overall height, in.	54.7
Curb weight, lbs.	2877
Cargo vol., cu. ft.	14.2

	4-door notchback
Fuel capacity, gals.	15.9
Seating capacity	5
Front head room, in.	38.8
Max. front leg room, in.	42.0
Rear head room, in.	37.3
Min. rear leg room, in.	32.2

Powertrain layout: transverse front engine/front-wheel drive.

Engines

	dohc I-4
Size, liters/cu. in.	2.0/122
Horsepower @ rpm	140 @ 6400
Torque (lbs./ft.) @ rpm	132 @ 4800
Availability	S
EPA city/highway mpg	
5-speed OD manual	24/32
4-speed OD automatic	22/29

Built in Japan.

PRICES

Infiniti G20	Retail Price	Dealer Invoice	Fair Price
4-door notchback, 5-speed	$21975	—	—
4-door notchback, automatic	22975	—	—
G20t with Touring Package, 5-speed	24875	—	—
G20t with Touring Package, automatic	25875	—	—
Destination charge	450	450	450

Dealer invoice and fair prices not available at time of publication.

Standard Equipment:

2.0-liter DOHC 4-cylinder engine, 5-speed manual or 4-speed automatic transmission, anti-lock 4-wheel disc brakes, power steering, driver- and passenger-side air bags, automatic climate control, cloth reclining front bucket seats, tachometer, coolant temperature gauge, trip odometer, power windows and locks, power mirrors, AM/FM radio with CD player, power antenna, leather-wrapped steering wheel, remote fuel door and decklid releases, tinted glass, anti-theft device, 195/65HR14 all-season tires, alloy wheels. **G20t** adds: Touring Package (limited-slip differential, performance tires, rear spoiler, fog lamps, Leather Appointment Group, fold-down rear seat).

Optional Equipment:	Retail Price	Dealer Invoice	Fair Price
Power glass sunroof, base	$1000	$820	—
Leather Appointment Group, base	2200	1804	—

Includes leather seats, 4-way power front seats, padded leather center console armrest, remote keyless entry system, power glass sunroof.

INFINITI J30

Infiniti J30t

Specifications	4-door notchback
Wheelbase, in.	108.7
Overall length, in.	191.3
Overall width, in.	69.7
Overall height, in.	54.7
Curb weight, lbs.	3527
Cargo vol., cu. ft.	10.1
Fuel capacity, gals.	19.0
Seating capacity	5
Front head room, in.	37.7
Max. front leg room, in.	41.3
Rear head room, in.	36.7
Min. rear leg room, in.	30.5

Powertrain layout: longitudinal front engine/rear-wheel drive.

Engines	dohc V-6
Size, liters/cu. in.	3.0/181

	dohc V-6
Horsepower @ rpm	210 @ 6400
Torque (lbs./ft.) @ rpm	193 @ 4800
Availability	S

EPA city/highway mpg

4-speed OD automatic	18/23

Built in Japan.

PRICES

Infiniti J30	Retail Price	Dealer Invoice	Fair Price
4-door notchback	$36950	$29930	$32930
J30t with Touring Package	39250	31793	34793
Destination charge	450	450	450

Standard Equipment:

3.0-liter DOHC V-6 engine, 4-speed automatic transmission, anti-lock 4-wheel disc brakes, variable-assist power steering, limited-slip differential, driver- and passenger-side air bags, 8-way heated power front bucket seats, leather upholstery, walnut inlays, automatic climate control, cruise control, tilt steering column, AM/FM cassette and CD player with six speakers, power sunroof, tinted glass, power windows and locks, 8-way power front seats, heated power mirrors, remote fuel door and decklid releases, remote keyless entry and anti-theft alarm systems, intermittent wipers, tachometer, trip odometer, leather-wrapped steering wheel, rear folding armrest, floormats, 215/60HR15 all-season tires, cast alloy wheels. **J30t** adds: Touring Package (Super HICAS 4-wheel steering, rear spoiler, firmer suspension, larger stabilizer bars, 215/60HR15 performance tires, forged alloy wheels).

INFINITI Q45

Specifications	4-door notchback
Wheelbase, in.	113.2
Overall length, in.	199.8
Overall width, in.	71.9
Overall height, in.	56.5

Infiniti Q45

	4-door notchback
Curb weight, lbs.	4039
Cargo vol., cu. ft.	14.8
Fuel capacity, gals.	22.5
Seating capacity	5
Front head room, in.	38.2
Max. front leg room, in.	43.9
Rear head room, in.	36.3
Min. rear leg room, in.	32.0

Powertrain layout: longitudinal front engine/rear-wheel drive.

Engines

	dohc V-8
Size, liters/cu. in.	4.5/274
Horsepower @ rpm	278 @ 6000
Torque (lbs./ft.) @ rpm	292 @ 4000
Availability	S

EPA city/highway mpg

4-speed OD automatic	17/22

Built in Japan.

PRICES

Infiniti Q45	Retail Price	Dealer Invoice	Fair Price
4-door notchback	$50450	$41055	$44555
Q45t with Touring Pkg.	53550	43566	47066

Prices are accurate at time of publication; subject to manufacturer's change.

	Retail Price	Dealer Invoice	Fair Price
Q45a with Full-Active Suspension	$57050	$46610	$50110
Destination charge	450	450	450

Prices include Gas Guzzler tax.

Standard Equipment:

4.5-liter DOHC V-8, 4-speed automatic transmission, 4-wheel anti-lock disc brakes, power steering, limited-slip differential, driver- and passenger-side air bags, cruise control, automatic climate control, leather reclining front bucket seats (wool is available at no charge), wood interior trim, Nissan/Bose AM/FM cassette, power antenna, power sunroof, tinted glass, power windows and locks, remote keyless entry system, power driver's seat with 2-position memory (memory includes tilt/telescopic steering column), power passenger seat, heated power mirrors, fog lights, remote fuel door and decklid releases, intermittent wipers, front and rear folding armrests, theft deterrent system, 215/65VR15 tires, alloy wheels. **Q45t** adds to base: Touring Pkg. (includes Super HICAS 4-wheel steering, rear spoiler, forged alloy wheels, revised front stabilizer bar diameter, rear stabilizer bar, performance tires, heated front seats). **Q45a** adds to base: Full-Active Suspension, all-season tires, heated front seats, traction control, trunk-mounted CD changer, revised front stabilizer bar diameter, rear stabilizer bar, alloy wheels.

Optional Equipment:

	Retail Price	Dealer Invoice	Fair Price
Traction control, base	1600	1296	1520
with Touring Pkg.	1500	1215	1425
Includes all-season tires, heated front seats.			

ISUZU RODEO/ HONDA PASSPORT

Specifications

	5-door wagon
Wheelbase, in.	108.7
Overall length, in.	176.5
Overall width, in.	66.5
Overall height, in.	66.5
Curb weight, lbs.	3545

Isuzu Rodeo S

	5-door wagon
Cargo vol., cu. ft.	74.9
Fuel capacity, gals.	21.9
Seating capacity	6
Front head room, in.	38.0
Max. front leg room, in.	42.5
Rear head room, in.	38.0
Min. rear leg room, in.	36.0

Powertrain layout: longitudinal front engine/rear-wheel drive or on-demand 4WD.

Engines	ohc I-4	ohc V-6
Size, liters/cu. in.	2.6/156	3.2/193
Horsepower @ rpm	120 @ 4600	175 @ 5200
Torque (lbs./ft.) @ rpm	150 @ 2600	188 @ 4000
Availability	S[1]	S
EPA city/highway mpg		
5-speed OD automatic	16/20	16/19
4-speed OD automatic		15/18

1. Rodeo 2WD S, Passport DX.

Built in Lafayette, Ind.

PRICES

Isuzu Rodeo	Retail Price	Dealer Invoice	Fair Price
S 4-cylinder 2WD 5-door wagon, 5-speed	$14969	$13472	$13972

Prices are accurate at time of publication; subject to manufacturer's change.

	Retail Price	Dealer Invoice	Fair Price
S V-6 2WD 5-door wagon, 5-speed	$17499	$15311	$15811
S V-6 2WD 5-door wagon, automatic	18399	16099	16599
LS V-6 2WD 5-door wagon, automatic	22729	19887	20387
S V-6 4WD 5-door wagon, 5-speed	19249	16746	17246
S V-6 4WD 5-door wagon, automatic	20349	17703	18203
LS V-6 4WD 5-door wagon, 5-speed	23799	20705	21205
LS V-6 4WD 5-door wagon, automatic	24899	21662	22162
Destination charge	375	375	375

Standard Equipment:

S: 2.6-liter 4-cylinder engine, 5-speed manual transmission, anti-lock rear brakes, power steering, cloth front bench seat with folding armrest, folding rear seat, rear defogger, tinted glass, day/night mirror, cargo rope hooks, carpet, 225/75R15 all-terrain tires, styled steel wheels with bright center caps. **S V-6** adds: 3.2-liter V-6, 5-speed manual or 4-speed automatic transmission, 4-wheel disc brakes, reclining front bucket seats, center console, tachometer, oil pressure and coolant temperature gauges, voltmeter, intermittent rear wiper/washer, carpeted floormats, outside spare tire, wheel trim rings. **LS** adds: air conditioning, tilt steering column, split folding rear seat, power windows and doors, cruise control, cassette player, velour upholstery, map and courtesy lights, intermittent wipers, right visor mirror, leather-wrapped steering wheel, bright exterior trim, roof rack, privacy rear quarter and rear side glass, cargo net, alloy wheels. **4WD** adds: part-time 4WD automatic locking hubs, tow hooks, skid plates, 245/70R16 tires, alloy wheels.

Optional Equipment:

	Retail Price	Dealer Invoice	Fair Price
Air conditioning, S	850	722	786
Preferred Equipment Pkg., S V-6	1990	1690	1840
Air conditioning, power windows and locks, cruise control, intermittent rear wiper/washer, roof rack, 4-speaker cassette player, cargo net.			
Alloy Wheel Pkg., S 4WD	990	847	919
16-inch alloy wheels, 245/70R16 tires, limited-slip differential.			
Limited-slip differential, LS 4WD	260	210	235
Sunroof, LS	300	255	278
Rear wiper/washer, S 4-cylinder	185	158	172
Outside spare tire carrier, S 4-cylinder	275	234	255
Brush/grille guard	305	216	261
AM/FM cassette, S	585	410	498
CD player, LS	550	385	468
Aero roof rack, S	195	137	166
Carpeted floormats (std. V-6)	55	39	47

Honda Passport

	Retail Price	Dealer Invoice	Fair Price
DX 2WD 5-door wagon, 5-speed	$15660	$13577	—
LX 2WD 5-door wagon, 5-speed	18870	16360	—
LX 2WD 5-door wagon, automatic	19770	17141	—
LX 4WD 5-door wagon, 5-speed	21350	18510	—
LX 4WD 5-door wagon with 16-inch Wheel Pkg., 5-speed	21950	19031	—
LX 4WD 5-door wagon, automatic	22450	19464	—
LX 4WD 5-door wagon with 16-inch Wheel Pkg., automatic	23050	19984	—
EX 4WD 5-door wagon, 5-speed	23900	20721	—
EX 4WD 5-door wagon, automatic	25000	21675	—
EX 4WD 5-door wagon with 16-inch Wheel Pkg., 5-speed	24500	21242	—
EX 4WD 5-door wagon with 16-inch Wheel Pkg., automatic	25600	22195	—
Destination charge	375	375	375

Fair price not available at time of publication.

Standard Equipment:

DX: 2.6-liter 4-cylinder engine, 5-speed manual transmission, anti-lock rear brakes, variable-assist power steering, front bench seat with folding center armrest, folding rear seatback, tinted glass, rear defogger, cargo area light, fuel tank skid plate, full-size spare tire, outside mounted spare tire carrier, 225/75R15 mud and snow tires, styled steel wheels. **LX 2WD** adds: 3.2-liter V-6 engine, 5-speed manual or 4-speed automatic transmission, 4-wheel disc brakes, cruise control, power windows and door locks, reclining front bucket seats, center storage console, tilt steering column, remote tailgate release, tachometer, upgraded door trim panels, door courtesy lights, AM/FM cassette player. **LX 4WD** adds to LX 2WD: part-time 4-wheel drive, automatic locking front hubs, air conditioning, 2-speed transfer case, transfer case skid plate, alloy wheels. **EX** adds to LX 4WD: removable tilt-up moonroof, heated power mirrors, 60/40 split folding rear bench seat, rear chrome bumpers, rear privacy glass, rear wiper/washer, leather-wrapped steering wheel, intermittent wipers, cargo net, passenger-side visor mirror, map lights. 16-inch Wheel Pkg. adds: limited-slip differential, flared wheel opening moldings, splash guards, 245/70R16 tires, 16-inch alloy wheels.

Options are available as dealer-installed accessories.

ISUZU TROOPER

Isuzu Trooper LS

Specifications

Specifications	2-door wagon	4-door wagon
Wheelbase, in.	91.7	108.7
Overall length, in.	166.5	183.5
Overall width, in.	68.7	68.7
Overall height, in.	72.8	72.8
Curb weight, lbs.	4060	4210
Cargo vol., cu. ft.	68.3	90.0
Fuel capacity, gals.	22.5	22.5
Seating capacity	5	5
Front head room, in.	39.8	39.8
Max. front leg room, in.	40.8	40.8
Rear head room, in.	39.8	39.8
Min. rear leg room, in.	32.2	39.1

Powertrain layout: longitudinal front engine/rear-wheel drive with on-demand 4WD.

Engines

Engines	ohc V-6	dohc V-6
Size, liters/cu. in.	3.2/193	3.2/193
Horsepower @ rpm	175 @ 5200	190 @ 5600
Torque (lbs./ft.) @ rpm	188 @ 4000	195 @ 3800
Availability	S[1]	S[2]

EPA city/highway mpg	ohc V-6	dohc V-6
5-speed OD manual	16/18	15/17
4-speed OD automatic	15/18	15/18

1. S. 2. LS, RS.

Built in Japan.

PRICES

Isuzu Trooper	Retail Price	Dealer Invoice	Fair Price
S 4-door 4WD wagon, 5-speed	$21250	$18381	$18881
S 4-door 4WD wagon, automatic	22400	19376	19876
LS 4-door 4WD wagon, 5-speed	26850	22822	23322
LS 4-door 4WD wagon, automatic	28000	23800	24300
RS 2-door 4WD wagon, 5-speed	24000	21120	21620
RS 2-door 4WD wagon, automatic	25150	22132	22632
Destination charge	400	400	400

Standard Equipment:

S: 3.2-liter V-6 engine, 5-speed manual transmission, power steering, 4-wheel disc brakes, anti-lock rear brakes, part-time 4WD system with automatic locking front hubs, cloth reclining front bucket seats, folding rear seat, full door trim, AM/FM cassette, center console, dual outside mirrors, rear defogger, tilt steering column, intermittent wipers, rear wiper/washer, skid plates, tachometer, voltmeter, oil pressure gauge, visor mirrors, tinted glass, rear step pad, rear air deflector, 245/70R16 tires, wheel trim rings. **LS** adds: 3.2-liter DOHC engine, 4-wheel anti-lock brakes, limited-slip differential, air conditioning, power windows and locks, cruise control, multi-adjustable driver's seat, split folding rear seat, bright exterior trim, color-keyed bumpers, variable intermittent wipers, headlamp wiper/washer, leather-wrapped steering wheel, heated power mirrors, privacy glass, premium cassette system with six speakers, power antenna, anti-theft alarm, visor mirrors, fog lamps, cargo floor rails, retractable cargo cover, cargo net, alloy wheels. **RS** deletes 4-wheel anti-lock brakes, bright exterior trim and adds: anti-lock rear brakes, sport cloth interior, one-piece folding and reclining rear seat, flip-out quarter windows, color-keyed grille, 2-tone paint, gas shocks.

Optional Equipment:

4-wheel anti-lock brakes, S and RS	1100	880	990
Limited slip-differential, S	260	210	235
Requires Preferred Equipment Pkg.			
Air conditioning, S	900	720	810

Prices are accurate at time of publication; subject to manufacturer's change.

	Retail Price	Dealer Invoice	Fair Price
Preferred Equipment Pkg., S	$1880	$1600	$1740
Air conditioning, power windows and locks, 6-speaker radio, split-folding rear seat, power mirrors, cruise control, retractable cargo cover, cargo net.			
Appearance Pkg., S	750	600	675
Alloy wheels with locks, bright radiator grille and mirrors, color-keyed bumpers. Requires Preferred Equipment Pkg.			
Power sunroof, LS	1100	880	990
Heated leather power seats, LS 2250	2250	1915	2083
Split folding rear seat, S	250	200	225
CD player, S with Preferred Equipment Pkg., RS and LS	550	385	468
2-tone paint, LS	280	225	253
Retractable cargo cover, S	120	84	102
Cargo net, S	30	21	26

JEEP CHEROKEE

Jeep Cherokee Sport 3-door

Specifications	3-door wagon	5-door wagon
Wheelbase, in.	101.4	101.4
Overall length, in.	168.8	168.8
Overall width, in.	67.7	67.7
Overall height, in.	63.9	63.9
Curb weight, lbs.	3042	3090

	3-door wagon	5-door wagon
Cargo vol., cu. ft.	71.8	71.8
Fuel capacity, gals.	20.0	20.0
Seating capacity	5	5
Front head room, in.	38.3	38.3
Max. front leg room, in.	41.0	41.0
Rear head room, in.	38.0	38.0
Min. rear leg room, in.	35.3	35.3

Powertrain layout: longitudinal front engine/rear-wheel drive or on-demand 4WD.

Engines	ohv I-4	ohv I-6
Size, liters/cu. in.	2.5/151	4.0/242
Horsepower @ rpm	130 @ 5250	190 @ 4750
Torque (lbs./ft.) @ rpm	149 @ 3000	225 @ 4000
Availability	S[1]	O[2]
EPA city/highway mpg		
5-speed OD manual	19/22	17/21
3-speed automatic	NA	
4-speed OD automatic		15/19

1. SE. 2. SE; standard, Sport and Country.

Built in Toledo, Ohio.

PRICES

Jeep Cherokee	Retail Price	Dealer Invoice	Fair Price
SE 3-door 2WD	$13427	$12674	$12874
SE 3-door 4WD	14912	14040	14240
SE 5-door 2WD	14437	13608	14058
SE 5-door 4WD	15922	14979	15429
Sport 3-door 2WD	15584	14169	14369
Sport 3-door 4WD	17069	15491	15691
Sport 5-door 2WD	16594	15073	15523
Sport 5-door 4WD	18079	16400	16850
Country 3-door 2WD	17221	15609	15859
Country 3-door 4WD	18706	16931	17181
Country 5-door 2WD	18231	16513	16963
Country 5-door 4WD	19716	17840	18290
Destination charge	495	495	495

Prices are accurate at time of publication; subject to manufacturer's change.

Standard Equipment:

SE: 2.5-liter 4-cylinder engine, 5-speed manual transmission, power steering, vinyl front bucket seats, front armrest, folding rear seat, mini console, AM/FM radio with two speakers, tinted glass, dual remote mirrors, 215/75R15 tires; 4WD system is Command-Trac part-time. **Sport** adds: 4.0-liter 6-cylinder engine, cloth reclining front bucket seats, tachometer, trip odometer, oil pressure and coolant temperature gauges, voltmeter, intermittent wipers, Sport Decor Group, spare tire cover, cargo tiedown hooks, 2-tone paint, 225/75R15 outlined white letter all-terrain tires. **Country** adds: front console with armrest and storage, rear seat heater ducts, AM/FM stereo with four speakers, Light Group, leather-wrapped steering wheel, roof rack, rear wiper/washer, dual remote breakaway mirrors, Country Decor Group, Extra-Quiet Insulation Pkg., front floormats, bodyside cladding, 225/70R15 tires, lattice-design alloy wheels.

Optional Equipment:

	Retail Price	Dealer Invoice	Fair Price
Pkg. 23B/25B/26B, SE	$492	$418	$431
Cloth reclining bucket seats, floor console with armrest, Visibility Group. Pkg. 25B requires 4.0-liter V-6. Pkg. 26B requies 4.0-liter V-6 and automatic transmission.			
Pkg. 26E, Sport	897	762	785
Adds 4-speed automatic transmission.			
Pkg. 25E/26E, Sport	1169	994	1023
Air conditioning, floor console with armrest, roof rack, leather-wrapped tilt steering wheel, rear wiper/washer, floormats. Pkg. 26E requires automatic transmission.			
Pkg. 25H/26H, Country	824	700	721
Air conditioning, cruise control, cassette player with four speakers, tilt steering wheel. Pkg. 26H requires automatic transmission.			
4.0-liter 6-cylinder engine, SE	612	520	536
4-speed automatic transmission	897	762	785
Selec-Trac full-time 4WD, Sport, Country	394	335	345
Requires automatic transmission.			
Trac-Lok rear differential	285	242	249
Requires conventional spare tire.			
Anti-lock brakes	599	509	524
Requires 4.0-liter engine.			
Heavy Duty Alternator/Battery Group	135	115	118
with rear defogger	63	54	55
Air conditioning	836	711	732
Includes Heavy Duty Alternator/Battery Group.			
Rear defogger	161	137	141
Requires air conditioning or Heavy Duty Alternator/Battery Group.			

	Retail Price	Dealer Invoice	Fair Price
Visibility Group, SE	$208	$177	$182
Intermittent wipers, rear wiper/washer.			
Fog lamps, Sport, Country	110	94	96
Requires air conditioning or Heavy Duty Alternator/Battery Group.			
Rear wiper/washer, Sport	147	125	129
Deep-tinted glass, Sport and Country			
3-doors	305	259	267
Sport and Country 5-doors	144	122	126
Front vent windows	91	77	80
Power Windows and Door Locks Group,			
Sport and Country 3-doors	437	371	382
Sport and Country 5-doors	582	495	509
Power windows and locks, remote keyless entry.			
Dual remote break-away mirrors, SE,			
Sport	22	19	20
Power mirrors, Country	100	85	88
Requires Power Windows and Door Locks Group.			
Tilt steering wheel	132	112	116
SE requires Visibility Group.			
Cruise control	230	196	201
SE requires Visibility Group.			
Leather-wrapped steering wheel, SE,			
Sport	48	41	42
Cassette player with four speakers, SE,			
Sport	291	247	255
Country	201	171	176
Premium speakers (six), Country	128	109	112
Requires Power Windows and Door Locks Group.			
Fabric seats, SE	137	116	120
SE w/Pkgs. 23B, 25B, 26B	NC	NC	NC
Power driver's seat, Country	296	252	259
Leather seats, Country 5-door	831	706	727
Floor console with armrest, SE, Sport	147	125	129
Overhead console, Sport, Country	203	173	178
Includes compass and thermometer, reading lights. Requires Power Windows and Door Locks Group.			
Cargo area cover	72	61	63
Roof rack, SE, Sport	139	118	122
Light Group, SE, Sport	195	166	171
Headlamp-off delay system, lighted visor mirrors, misc. lights.			
Bright Group, Country	202	172	177
Bright dual power remote mirrors, front and rear bumpers, grille and headlamp bezels, door handles and escutcheons, windshield and drip rail moldings. Requires Power Windows and Door Locks Group.			

	Retail Price	Dealer Invoice	Fair Price
Trailer Tow Group	$358	$304	$313
4WD models with Off-Road Suspension	242	206	212
Requires 4.0-liter engine, automatic transmission, Heavy Duty Alternator/ Battery Group, conventional spare tire.			
Off-Road Suspension (4WD only), SE	761	647	666
Sport	448	381	392
Country	360	306	315
Requires Heavy Duty Alternator/Battery Group, dual remote breakaway mirrors (SE and Sport).			
Skid Plates Group, 4WD models	144	122	126
225/75R15 outlined white letter tires (four), SE	313	266	274
spare 225/75R15 tire (required), SE	116	99	102
Conventional (215/75R15) spare tire, SE	71	60	62
Conventional (225/75R15 outlined white letter) spare tire, Sport	116	99	102
Conventional (225/70R15) spare tire, Country	140	119	123
10-hole alloy wheels, SE	435	370	381
Sport	332	282	291
Country	87	74	76
Requires conventional spare tire.			
Matching fifth alloy wheel, Sport	26	22	23
Country	87	74	76
Requires conventional spare tire.			

JEEP GRAND CHEROKEE

Specifications

	5-door wagon
Wheelbase, in.	105.9
Overall length, in.	179.0
Overall width, in.	70.9
Overall height, in.	64.8
Curb weight, lbs.	3674
Cargo vol., cu. ft.	81.0
Fuel capacity, gals.	23.0
Seating capacity	5
Front head room, in.	38.9

Jeep Grand Cherokee Limited

	5-door wagon
Max. front leg room, in.	40.8
Rear head room, in.	39.1
Min. rear leg room, in.	35.7

Powertrain layout: longitudinal front engine/rear-wheel drive or on-demand or permanent 4WD.

Engines	ohv I-6	ohv V-8
Size, liters/cu. in.	4.0/242	5.2/318
Horsepower @ rpm	190 @ 4750	220 @ 4800
Torque (lbs./ft.) @ rpm	225 @ 4000	285 @ 3600
Availability	S	O
EPA city/highway mpg		
5-speed OD manual	16/20	
4-speed OD automatic	15/20	14/18

Built in Detroit, Mich.

PRICES

Jeep Grand Cherokee	Retail Price	Dealer Invoice	Fair Price
SE 5-door 2WD	$21156	$19242	$19942
SE 5-door 4WD	22096	20109	20809
Limited 5-door 4WD	29643	26751	27651

Prices are accurate at time of publication; subject to manufacturer's change.

	Retail Price	Dealer Invoice	Fair Price
Destination charge	$495	$495	$495

Standard Equipment:

SE: 4.0-liter 6-cylinder engine, 5-speed manual transmission (4WD) or 4-speed automatic transmission (2WD), driver-side air bag, anti-lock brakes, power steering, cloth reclining front bucket seats, split folding rear seat, air conditioning, leather-wrapped tilt steering wheel, cruise control, tachometer, voltage and temperature gauges, console with armrest and cupholders, AM/FM cassette, tinted glass, rear defogger, intermittent rear wiper/washer, dual outside mirrors, remote fuel door release, trip odometer, map lights, roof rack, striping, 215/75R15 tires, wheel covers. 4WD system is Command-Trac part-time. **Limited** adds: 4-speed automatic transmission, 4-wheel disc brakes, automatic temperature control, leather power front seats, automatic day/night rearview mirror, automatic headlamp system, illuminated entry system, anti-theft alarm, overhead console with compass and temperature display, trip computer, heated power mirrors, fog lamps, deep tinted side and rear glass, 6-speaker AM/FM cassette with equalizer and amplifier, power antenna, 225/70R15 outlined white letter tires, alloy wheels, full-size spare tire. 4WD system is Quadra-Trac permanent 4WD.

Optional Equipment:

	Retail Price	Dealer Invoice	Fair Price
Laredo Pkg. 25E/26E, SE	1286	1093	1221
Power windows and locks, power mirrors, remote keyless entry system, lighted visor mirrors, Laredo Decor Group, Protection Group, cargo area tie-down hooks and skid strips, 225/75R15 outline white letter tires, alloy wheels. Pkg. 26E requires automatic transmission.			
Laredo Pkg. 26F, 2WD SE	3120	2652	2964
Laredo Pkg. 26F/28F, 4WD SE	3564	3029	3386
Package 26E plus Luxury Group, Security Group, overhead console, deep-tinted glass, cassette player with equalizer and six speakers. Pkg. 26F (4WD) requires automatic transmission. Pkg. 28F includes Quadra-Trac permanent 4WD and requires 5.2-liter V-8 engine, automatic transmission.			
5.2-liter V-8 engine, 4WD SE and Laredo	1176	1000	1117
Laredo Pkg. 28F and Limited	732	622	695
Includes Quadra-Trac permanent 4WD (SE and Laredo). Requires automatic transmission (std. Limited).			
4-speed automatic transmission, SE, Laredo	897	762	852
Selec-Trac full-time 4WD, SE, Laredo	394	335	374
Limited	NC	NC	NC

	Retail Price	Dealer Invoice	Fair Price
Requires automatic transmission. Not available with 5.2-liter V-8.			
Quadra-Trac permanent 4WD,			
SE, Laredo	$444	$377	$422
Requires automatic transmission.			
Trac-Lok rear differential	285	242	271
Requires automatic transmission.			
Power Group, SE	616	524	585
Power windows and locks, remote keyless entry.			
Luxury Group, Laredo 4WD	593	504	563
4WD with automatic transmission,			
2WD	688	585	654
Power front seats, automatic day/night rearview mirror, automatic headlamp system.			
Protection Group, SE	146	124	139
Cargo area cover and net, floormats.			
Security Group, SE, Laredo	226	192	215
Theft security system, illuminated entry system. Requires Power Group.			
Trailer Tow Prep Group	100	85	95
Requires automatic transmission.			
Trailer Tow Group III	358	304	340
Requires automatic transmission.			
Trailer Tow Group IV	242	206	230
Requires automatic transmission and 5.2-liter V-8.			
Fog lamps, 2WD SE and Laredo	110	94	105
Fog Lamp/Skid Plate Group (4WD),			
SE, Laredo	254	216	241
w/Up Country Suspension Group	110	94	105
Limited with 4.0-liter engine	144	122	137
Up Country Suspension Group,			
SE 4WD	720	612	684
Laredo 4WD	504	428	479
Limited	349	297	332
Skid Plate Group, tow hooks, high-pressure gas shocks, 245/70R15 outlined white letter all-terrain tires, conventional spare tire, matching fifth wheel.			
Overhead console, Laredo	232	197	220
Includes compass, thermometer, and trip computer.			
Leather seats, Laredo	576	490	547
Requires Luxury Group.			
Luxury leather seats, Limited	300	255	285
Power mirrors, SE	95	81	90
Heated power mirrors, SE	140	119	133
Laredo	45	38	43

	Retail Price	Dealer Invoice	Fair Price
Deep tinted glass, SE, Laredo	$226	$192	$215
AM/FM cassette with equalizer,			
SE, Laredo	617	524	586
Includes amplifier, power antenna.			
AM/FM with CD and equalizer,			
SE, Laredo	787	669	748
Laredo Pkg. 26F, 28F, Limited	170	145	162
Includes six speakers, amplifier, power antenna.			
Conventional spare tire, SE	130	111	124
Laredo, Limited	160	136	152
225/75R15 outlined white letter tires, SE	246	209	234
225/75R15 outlined white letter			
all-terrain tires, SE	313	266	297
Laredo	67	57	64
Limited	NC	NC	NC
Engine block heater	31	26	29

JEEP WRANGLER

Jeep Wrangler Sahara

Specifications	2-door conv.
Wheelbase, in.	93.4
Overall length, in.	151.9
Overall width, in.	66.0
Overall height, in.	71.9

	2-door conv.
Curb weight, lbs.	2943
Cargo vol., cu. ft.	53.4
Fuel capacity, gals.	15.0
Seating capacity	4
Front head room, in.	41.4
Max. front leg room, in.	39.4
Rear head room, in.	40.3
Min. rear leg room, in.	35.0

Powertrain layout: longitudinal front engine/rear-wheel drive with on-demand 4WD.

Engines

	ohv I-4	ohv I-6
Size, liters/cu. in.	2.5/150	4.0/242
Horsepower @ rpm	123 @ 5250	180 @ 4750
Torque (lbs./ft.) @ rpm	139 @ 3250	220 @ 4000
Availability	S[1]	S[2]
EPA city/highway mpg		
5-speed OD manual	19/20	16/18
3-speed automatic	17/18	15/17

1. S. 2. SE.

Built in Toledo, Ohio.

PRICES

Jeep Wrangler	Retail Price	Dealer Invoice	Fair Price
S soft top	$11480	$11071	$11371
SE soft top	14544	13194	13494
Destination charge	495	495	495

Standard Equipment:

S: 2.5-liter 4-cylinder engine, 5-speed manual transmission, vinyl front bucket seats, tachometer, coolant temperature and oil pressure gauges, voltmeter, trip odometer, tinted windshield, fuel tank skid plate, swingaway outside spare tire carrier, 205/75R15 tires. **SE** adds: 4.0-liter engine, reclining front seats, fold-and-tumble rear seat, right outside mirror, AM/FM radio, 215/75R15 all-terrain tires, 6-spoke steel wheels.

Prices are accurate at time of publication; subject to manufacturer's change.

Optional Equipment:

	Retail Price	Dealer Invoice	Fair Price
Pkg. 22A, S	$624	$530	$543
Adds automatic transmission. Requires tilt steering wheel.			
Pkg. 23B/22B, S	1030	876	896
Power steering, vinyl reclining front bucket seats, rear seat, right outside mirror, carpeting, rear bumperettes. Pkg. 22B requires automatic transmission and tilt steering wheel.			
Pkg. 24C, SE	624	530	543
Adds automatic transmission. Requires tilt steering wheel.			
Pkg. 25D/24D, SE	973	827	847
Power steering, tilt steering wheel, Convenience Group, carpeting, 20-gallon fuel tank, conventional spare tire. Pkg. 24 D requires automatic transmission.			
Sport Pkg. 25F/24F, SE	1640	1394	1427
Sport Pkg. (Convenience Group, power steering, tilt steering wheel, Sound Bar, sport striping, body-color fender flares and bodyside steps, carpeting, 215/75R15 outlined white letter all-terrain tires, full face steel wheels). Pkg. 24F requires automatic transmission.			
Sahara Pkg. 25H/24H, SE	2423	2060	2108
Sahara Decor Group (black exterior trim, tilt steering wheel, fog lights, vinyl spare tire cover, exterior graphics, color-keyed fender flares and bodyside steps, cloth upholstery, map pockets, leather-wrapped steering wheel, carpeting, front floormats, Convenience Group, power steering, 20-gallon fuel tank, off road gas shocks, full face steel wheels), AM/FM cassette, Sound Bar, conventional spare tire. Pkg. 24H requires automatic transmission.			
Renegade Pkg. 25K/24K, SE	4252	3614	3699
Renegade Decor Group (Sahara Pkg. plus: unique lower body panels and fascias, color-keyed bumpers with steps, bodyside steps, unique exterior graphics, five 29-9.5R15LT outlined white letter all-terrain tires, alloy wheels). Pkg. 24K requires automatic transmission.			
3-speed automatic transmission	624	530	543
Requires tilt steering wheel.			
Anti-lock brakes, SE	599	509	521
Trac-Lok rear differential, SE	278	236	242
Requires conventional spare tire and 215 or 225 tires.			
Air conditioning, SE	878	746	764
Requires 4.0-liter engine, power steering, carpeting. Includes Heavy Duty Alternator/Battery Group.			
Power steering	300	255	261
Vinyl reclining front seats, S	75	64	65
Requires rear seat and carpeting.			
Cloth reclining front bucket seats with reclining rear seat, SE	107	91	93
Rear seat, S	455	387	396

	Retail Price	Dealer Invoice	Fair Price
Requires carpeting and reclining front seats.			
Add-A-Trunk lockable storage	$125	$106	$109
Requires carpeting.			
Carpeting	137	116	119
Requires reclining front seats and rear seat.			
Hardtop	755	642	657
SE with Sahara or Renegade Pkg.	923	785	803
Includes dual outside mirrors, rear wiper/washer, tinted glass (deep-tinted on Sahara and Renegade), full doors with vent windows.			
Bright Exterior Group, SE	197	167	171
Includes bright bumpers, grille overlay, and headlamp bezels.			
Bodyside steps, SE	73	62	64
Convenience Group	233	198	203
SE with tilt steering column	170	145	148
Intermittent wipers, center console with cup holders, misc. lights, glove box lock.			
Heavy Duty Alternator/Battery Group	135	115	117
Rear defogger for hardtop	164	139	143
Off-Road Pkg., SE	129	110	112
Heavy duty shock absorbers, draw bar, tow hooks.			
Sound bar with 2 rear speakers, SE	204	173	177
AM/FM radio with 2 speakers, S	270	230	235
AM/FM cassette with 2 speakers, S	534	454	465
S with Sound Group, SE	264	224	230
Sound Group, S	494	420	430
AM/FM stereo, Sound Bar, sport bar padding.			
Right outside mirror, S	27	23	24
Tilt steering wheel	193	164	168
Leather-wrapped steering wheel, SE	48	41	42
Five 215/75R15 outlined white letter all-terrain tires (and wheels), S	272	231	237
SE	228	194	198
SE w/Pkgs. 25D, 24D, 25F, 24F, Sahara Pkg.	117	99	102
Requires 15 x 7 wheels.			
Five 225/75R15 outlined white letter all-terrain tires (and wheels), S	463	394	403
SE	419	356	365
SE w/Pkgs. 25D, 24D, Renegade Pkg.	308	262	268
SE w/Pkgs. 25F, 24F	191	162	166
Requires 15 x 7 wheels.			
Conventional spare tire	111	94	97
Five 15 x 7 styled steel wheels, S	NC	NC	NC
Requires 215 or 225 tires and conventional spare tire.			

Prices are accurate at time of publication; subject to manufacturer's change.

	Retail Price	Dealer Invoice	Fair Price
Four 15 x 7 full face steel wheels, SE	$102	$87	$89
Five 15 x 7 full face steel wheels, SE	128	109	111
Requires conventional spare tire.			
15 x 7 alloy wheels, S, SE	339	288	295
SE w/Pkg. 25F, 24F	211	179	184
Requires conventional spare and 215 or 225 tires.			
Five 15 x 7 five-spoke alloy wheels, SE w/Sahara Pkg.	237	201	206
Rear bumperettes, S	36	31	32
20-gallon fuel tank	62	53	54
Engine block heater (Alaska only)	31	26	27

LEXUS ES 300

Lexus ES 300

Specifications	4-door notchback
Wheelbase, in.	103.1
Overall length, in.	187.8
Overall width, in.	70.0
Overall height, in.	53.9
Curb weight, lbs.	3374
Cargo vol., cu. ft.	14.3
Fuel capacity, gals.	18.5
Seating capacity	5
Front head room, in.	37.8
Max. front leg room, in.	43.5
Rear head room, in.	36.6

	4-door notchback
Min. rear leg room, in.	33.1

Powertrain layout: transverse front engine/front-wheel drive.

Engines	dohc V-6
Size, liters/cu. in.	3.0/181
Horsepower @ rpm	188 @ 5200
Torque (lbs./ft.) @ rpm	203 @ 4400
Availability	S
EPA city/highway mpg	
4-speed OD automatic	18/24

Built in Japan.

PRICES

Lexus ES 300	Retail Price	Dealer Invoice	Fair Price
4-door notchback	$31200	$25584	$30200
Destination charge	470	470	470

Standard Equipment:

3.0-liter DOHC V-6, 4-speed automatic transmission, anti-lock 4-wheel disc brakes, variable-assist power steering, driver- and passenger-side air bags, tilt steering column, automatic climate control, cruise control, power windows and locks, AM/FM cassette, cloth multi-adjustable power front bucket seats, split folding rear seatback, rear defogger, variable intermittent wipers, lighted visor mirrors, outside temperature indicator, automatic on/off headlamps, remote fuel door and decklid releases, tool kit, first aid kit, cellular phone pre-wiring, remote keyless entry system, theft deterrent system, 205/65VR15 tires, alloy wheels.

Optional Equipment:

Leather Trim Pkg.	1300	1040	1235
Heated front seats	400	320	380
Power moonroof with sunshade	900	720	855
Remote 6-CD auto changer	1000	750	950
205/65VR15 all-season tires	NC	NC	NC

Prices are accurate at time of publication; subject to manufacturer's change.

LEXUS GS 300

Lexus GS 300

Specifications	4-door notchback
Wheelbase, in.	109.4
Overall length, in.	194.9
Overall width, in.	70.7
Overall height, in.	55.1
Curb weight, lbs.	3660
Cargo vol., cu. ft.	13.0
Fuel capacity, gals.	21.1
Seating capacity	5
Front head room, in.	36.9
Max. front leg room, in.	44.0
Rear head room, in.	35.6
Min. rear leg room, in.	33.8

Powertrain layout: longitudinal front engine/rear-wheel drive.

Engines	dohc I-6
Size, liters/cu. in.	3.0/183
Horsepower @ rpm	220 @ 5800
Torque (lbs./ft.) @ rpm	210 @ 4800

	dohc I-6
Availability	S
EPA city/highway mpg	
4-speed OD automatic	17/23

Built in Japan.

PRICES

Lexus GS 300	Retail Price	Dealer Invoice	Fair Price
4-door notchback	$41100	$33702	$39100
Destination charge	470	470	470

Standard Equipment:

3.0-liter DOHC 6-cylinder engine, 4-speed automatic transmission, anti-lock 4-wheel disc brakes, driver- and passenger-side air bags, variable-assist power steering, dual power/heated outside mirrors, electronic analog instruments, power tilt/telescopic steering column, cloth power driver and front passenger seats, power windows and door locks, walnut wood trim, automatic climate control, automatic on/off headlamps, remote entry system, illuminated entry system, rear defogger, variable intermittent wipers, theft-deterrent system, illuminated visor mirrors, remote electric trunk and fuel-filler door releases, Lexus Premium Audio System with AM/FM/cassette and seven speakers, power diversity antenna, cellular phone pre-wiring, outside temperature indicator, illuminated entry system, tool kit, first aid kit, 215/60VR16 tires, alloy wheels.

Optional Equipment:

	Retail Price	Dealer Invoice	Fair Price
Traction Control System	1800	1440	1710
Includes heated front seats. Requires Leather Trim Package and all-season tires.			
Leather Trim Package	1300	1040	1235
Lexus/Nakamichi Premium Audio System	1100	825	1045
Requires Leather Trim Package and remote 12-CD auto-changer.			
Remote 12-CD auto-changer	1000	750	950
Power tilt and slide moonroof with sunshade	900	720	855
All-season tires	NC	NC	NC
Wheel locks	50	30	48
Floormats	115	69	109
Carpeted trunk mat	68	41	65

Prices are accurate at time of publication; subject to manufacturer's change.

LEXUS LS 400

Lexus LS 400

Specifications	4-door notchback
Wheelbase, in.	110.8
Overall length, in.	196.7
Overall width, in.	71.7
Overall height, in.	55.3
Curb weight, lbs.	3859
Cargo vol., cu. ft.	14.4
Fuel capacity, gals.	22.5
Seating capacity	5
Front head room, in.	38.6
Max. front leg room, in.	43.8
Rear head room, in.	36.8
Min. rear leg room, in.	34.3

Powertrain layout: longitudinal front engine/rear-wheel drive.

Engines	dohc V-8
Size, liters/cu. in.	4.0/242
Horsepower @ rpm	250 @ 5600
Torque (lbs./ft.) @ rpm	260 @ 4400
Availability	S

EPA city/highway mpg

4-speed OD automatic	18/23

Built in Japan.

PRICES

Lexus LS 400	Retail Price	Dealer Invoice	Fair Price
4-door notchback	$51200	$40960	$48200
Destination charge	470	470	470

Standard Equipment:

4.0-liter DOHC V-8 engine, 4-speed automatic transmission, anti-lock 4-wheel disc brakes, driver- and passenger-side air bags, variable-assist power steering, seatbelt pretensioners, air conditioning with automatic climate control, cloth reclining front bucket seats with 7-way power adjustment, power windows and locks, cruise control, remote entry system, walnut wood trim, heated power mirrors, tachometer, trip odometer, coolant temperature gauge, outside temperature indicator, remote fuel door and decklid releases, lighted visor mirrors, theft-deterrent system, automatic on/off headlamps, power tilt/telescopic steering column, AM/FM cassette with seven speakers and power diversity antenna, intermittent wipers, cellular phone pre-wiring, tool kit, first aid kit, 225/60VR16 tires, alloy wheels.

Optional Equipment:

	Retail Price	Dealer Invoice	Fair Price
Power moonroof with sunshade	1000	800	950
Traction control with heated front seats	1900	1520	1805
Electronic air suspension	1700	1360	1615
Requires moonroof and memory system.			
Seat memory system	800	640	760
Lexus/Nakamichi Premium Audio System	1100	825	1045
Requires CD changer.			
Remote 6-CD auto-changer	1000	750	950
All-season tires	NC	NC	NC
Wheel locks	50	30	48
Floormats	115	69	109
Carpeted trunk mat	68	41	65

1995 LEXUS SC 300/400

Specifications	2-door notchback
Wheelbase, in.	105.9

1995 Lexus SC 400

	2-door notchback
Overall length, in.	191.1
Overall width, in.	70.5
Overall height, in.	52.4
Curb weight, lbs.	3506
Cargo vol., cu. ft.	9.3
Fuel capacity, gals.	20.6
Seating capacity	4
Front head room, in.	38.3
Max. front leg room, in.	44.1
Rear head room, in.	36.1
Min. rear leg room, in.	27.2

Powertrain layout: longitudinal front engine/rear-wheel drive.

Engines	dohc I-6	dohc V-8
Size, liters/cu. in.	3.0/183	4.0/242
Horsepower @ rpm	225 @ 6000	250 @ 5600
Torque (lbs./ft.) @ rpm	210 @ 4800	260 @ 4400
Availability	S[1]	S[2]
EPA city/highway mpg		
5-speed OD manual	18/23	
4-speed OD automatic	17/23	18/23

1. SC 300. 2. SC 400.

Built in Japan.

PRICES

1995 Lexus SC 300/400	Retail Price	Dealer Invoice	Fair Price
300 2-door notchback, 5-speed	$40000	—	—
300 2-door notchback, automatic	40900	—	—
400 2-door notchback	47500	—	—
Destination charge	470	470	470

Dealer invoice and fair prices not available at time of publication

Standard Equipment:

300: 3.0-liter DOHC 6-cylinder engine, 5-speed manual or 4-speed automatic transmission, anti-lock 4-wheel disc brakes, variable-assist power steering, driver- and passenger-side air bags, air conditioning with automatic climate control, tinted glass, power front seats, tilt/telescoping steering column, rear defogger, heated power mirrors, power windows and door locks, remote entry system, illuminated entry system, cruise control, tachometer, AM/FM cassette with seven speakers and automatic power diversity antenna, automatic on/off headlamps, lighted visor mirrors, remote fuel door and decklid releases, variable intermittent wipers, theft-deterrent system, cellular phone pre-wiring, tool kit, first aid kit, 215/60VR15 tires, 225/55VR16 tires, alloy wheels. **400** adds: 4.0-liter DOHC V-8 engine, 4-speed automatic transmission, power tilt/telescoping steering column, leather upholstery, driver-side seat memory system.

Optional Equipment:

	Retail Price	Dealer Invoice	Fair Price
Traction control system with heated front seats	1800	1440	1710
Requires automatic transmission.			
Remote 12-CD auto changer	1000	750	950
Lexus/Nakamichi Premium Audio System	1100	825	1045
Requires remote CD changer; 300 also requires Leather Trim Pkg. with seat memory system.			
Leather Trim Pkg. with seat memory system, 300	1800	1440	1710
Power moonroof with sunshade	900	720	855
Heated front seats, 300 with manual transmission..	400	320	380
Rear spoiler, 400	400	320	380

Prices are accurate at time of publication; subject to manufacturer's change.

LINCOLN CONTINENTAL

Lincoln Continental Signature Series

Specifications

Specifications	4-door notchback
Wheelbase, in.	109.0
Overall length, in.	205.1
Overall width, in.	72.3
Overall height, in.	55.4
Curb weight, lbs.	3576
Cargo vol., cu. ft.	19.1
Fuel capacity, gals.	18.4
Seating capacity	6
Front head room, in.	38.7
Max. front leg room, in.	41.7
Rear head room, in.	38.4
Min. rear leg room, in.	39.2

Powertrain layout: transverse front engine/front-wheel drive.

Engines

Engines	ohv V-6
Size, liters/cu. in.	3.8/232
Horsepower @ rpm	160 @ 4400
Torque (lbs./ft.) @ rpm	225 @ 3000
Availability	S

EPA city/highway mpg

4-speed OD automatic	18/26

Built in Wixom, Mich.

PRICES

Lincoln Continental

	Retail Price	Dealer Invoice	Fair Price
Executive 4-door notchback	$33750	$29296	$29796
Signature Series 4-door notchback	35600	30886	31386
Destination charge	625	625	625

Standard Equipment:

Executive: 3.8-liter V-6, 4-speed automatic transmission, anti-lock 4-wheel disc brakes, power steering, driver- and passenger-side air bags, automatic climate control, 50/50 leather front seat, power driver's seat with power recliner, tilt steering wheel, cruise control, automatic parking brake release, rear defogger, heated power mirrors, power windows and locks, remote fuel door and decklid releases, power decklid pulldown, AM/FM cassette, automatic power antenna, tinted glass, intermittent wipers, cornering lamps, electronic instruments, coolant temperature and oil pressure gauges, voltmeter, trip odometer, trip computer, service interval reminder, door pockets, rear courtesy lights, leather-wrapped steering wheel, right visor mirror, 205/70R15 tires, alloy wheels. **Signature Series** adds: 6-way power remote memory front seats with power recliners, remote keyless illuminated entry, Headlight Convenience Group, automatic dimmer, lighted visor mirrors, bodyside accent stripe, floormats.

Optional Equipment:

	Retail Price	Dealer Invoice	Fair Price
Anti-theft alarm system	290	250	255
Executive requires Preferred Equipment Pkg. 952A.			
Comfort/Convenience Group, Executive	700	602	616
Power passenger seat with power recliner, Headlight Convenience Group, lighted visor mirrors, power decklid pulldown, rear floormats.			
Preferred Equipment Pkg. 952A, Executive	NC	NC	NC
Comfort/Convenience Group, remote keyless illuminated entry.			
Preferred Equipment Pkg. 953A, Executive	1325	1140	1166
Power moonroof, 5-passenger seating with remote memory.			
Overhead Console Group	350	303	308
Includes compass and automatic day/night mirror, electrochromatic outside mirror; Executive requires Preferred Equipment Pkg.			
Remote keyless illuminated entry, Executive	300	257	264
5-passenger seating, Executive	890	767	783

	Retail Price	Dealer Invoice	Fair Price
Power moonroof	$1515	$1303	$1333
Not available with Overhead Console Group.			
CD player	600	516	528
Ford JBL audio system	565	486	497
Executive requires Preferred Equipment Pkg.			
Voice-activated cellular telephone	690	593	607
White opalescent clearcoat paint	235	201	207

LINCOLN MARK VIII

Lincoln Mark VIII

Specifications

	2-door notchback
Wheelbase, in.	113.0
Overall length, in.	206.9
Overall width, in.	74.6
Overall height, in.	53.6
Curb weight, lbs.	3768
Cargo vol., cu. ft.	14.4
Fuel capacity, gals.	18.0
Seating capacity	5
Front head room, in.	38.1
Max. front leg room, in.	42.6
Rear head room, in.	37.5
Min. rear leg room, in.	32.5

Powertrain layout: longitudinal front engine/rear-wheel drive.

Engines

	dohc V-8
Size, liters/cu. in.	4.6/281

	dohc V-8
Horsepower @ rpm	280 @ 5500
Torque (lbs./ft.) @ rpm	285 @ 4500
Availability	S

EPA city/highway mpg

4-speed OD automatic	18/25

Built in Wixom, Mich.

PRICES

Lincoln Mark VIII	Retail Price	Dealer Invoice	Fair Price
2-door notchback	$38050	$33034	$34234
Destination charge	625	625	625

Standard Equipment:

4.6-liter DOHC V-8 engine, 4-speed automatic transmission, 4-wheel anti-lock disc brakes, driver- and passenger-side air bags, automatic air conditioning, variable-assist power steering, tilt steering wheel, analog instrumentation with message center and programmable trip functions, service interval reminder, console with cup holder and storage bin, leather seat trim, Autoglide dual reclining 6-way power front seats with power lumbar supports and remote driver-side memory, leather wrapped steering wheel, automatic headlamps, door map pockets, solar-control tinted glass, anti-theft alarm system, cruise control, power windows and locks, heated power mirrors with remote 3-position memory, lighted visor mirrors, rear defogger, remote decklid and fuel door releases, illuminated and remote keyless entry systems, AM/FM cassette stereo with premium sound system, automatic power antenna, intermittent wipers, cargo net, floormats, 225/60VR16 tires, alloy wheels.

Optional Equipment:

	Retail Price	Dealer Invoice	Fair Price
Traction Assist	215	184	204
Power moonroof	1515	1302	1439
Voice-activated celluar telephone *Requires JBL Audio System.*	690	594	655
Electrochromatic auto dimming inside/outside mirrors	215	184	204
AM/FM stereo with CD player *Requires JBL Audio System.*	290	250	275

	Retail Price	Dealer Invoice	Fair Price
JBL Audio System	$565	$486	$536
Trunk-mounted CD changer	815	700	774
Requires JBL Audio System.			
Chrome wheels	845	726	802

LINCOLN TOWN CAR

Lincoln Town Car

Specifications	4-door notchback
Wheelbase, in.	117.4
Overall length, in.	218.9
Overall width, in.	76.9
Overall height, in.	56.9
Curb weight, lbs.	4039
Cargo vol., cu. ft.	22.3
Fuel capacity, gals.	20.0
Seating capacity	6
Front head room, in.	39.0
Max. front leg room, in.	42.6
Rear head room, in.	38.0
Min. rear leg room, in.	41.6

Powertrain layout: longitudinal front engine/rear-wheel drive.

Engines	ohc V-8
Size, liters/cu. in.	4.6/281
Horsepower @ rpm	210 @ 4600

	ohc V-8
Torque (lbs./ft.) @ rpm	270 @ 3400
Availability	S

EPA city/highway mpg

4-speed OD automatic	18/25

Built in Wixom, Mich.

PRICES

Lincoln Town Car	Retail Price	Dealer Invoice	Fair Price
Executive 4-door notchback	$34750	$30166	$30666
Signature Series 4-door notchback	36050	31284	31784
Cartier Designer Series 4-door notchback	38100	33046	33546
Destination charge	625	625	625

Standard Equipment:

Executive: 4.6-liter V-8, 4-speed automatic transmission, 4-wheel anti-lock disc brakes, power steering, driver- and passenger-side air bags, automatic climate control, 6-way power twin-comfort lounge seats with 2-way front head restraints, front and rear folding armrests, power windows and locks, tilt steering wheel, leather wrapped steering wheel, cruise control, automatic parking brake release, heated power mirrors, rear defogger, AM/FM cassette with premium sound, power antenna, solar-control tinted glass, remote fuel door and decklid release, power decklid pulldown, illuminated and remote keyless entry systems, cornering lamps, intermittent wipers, electronic instruments, digital clock, map pockets on front doors, dual lighted visor mirrors, front and rear floormats, dual exhaust, 215/70R15 whitewall tires. **Signature Series** adds: dual shade paint, dual footwell lights, front seat storage with cup holders, map pockets on front seatbacks, striping. **Cartier Designer Series** adds: cloth and leather upholstery, driver's seat position memory and power lumbar support, power front recliners, Ford JBL audio system, upgraded door trim panels.

Optional Equipment:

Traction Assist	215	184	193
Leather seat trim (std. Cartier)	555	479	499
Anti-theft alarm system	290	248	261
Automatic day/night mirror	110	94	99

	Retail Price	Dealer Invoice	Fair Price
Programmable memory seat (std. Cartier)	$535	$460	$481
Power moonroof	1515	1302	1363
Ford JBL audio system, (std. Cartier)	565	486	508
Trunk-mounted CD changer	815	700	733
Ride Control Pkg.	285	246	256
Auxiliary power steering fluid cooler, larger front and rear stabilizer bars, firmer front and rear springs, 225/70R15 whitewall tires. Not available with Heavy Duty Pkg., Livery Pkg., Trailer Tow III Pkg. or any other tire and wheel combination.			
Heavy Duty Pkg., Executive and Signature	805	692	724
3.55 Traction-Lok axle, heavy duty cooling, transmission oil and steering fluid coolers, heavy duty suspension, full-size spare tire, heavy duty alternator and battery, 225/75R15 whitewall tires, steel wheels. Not available with Traction Assist, power moonroof, Livery Pkg., Trailer Tow III Pkg., conventional axle, 225/70R15 or 215/70R15 tires.			
Trailer Tow III Pkg.	465	400	418
3.55 axle ratio, heavy duty cooling, transmission oil and steering fluid coolers, heavy duty suspension, larger front stabilizer bar, heavy duty shock absorbers, heavy duty turn signals and flashers, full-size spare tire, trailer wiring harness. Not available with Livery Pkg.			
Livery Pkg, Executive and Signature	325	280	292
Same as Heavy Duty Pkg. but with standard cooling system and 215/70R15 tires.			
Voice activated cellular telephone	690	594	621
White opalescent clearcoat paint	235	202	211
Engine block heater	60	52	54
Full-size spare tire	220	190	198

MAZDA MIATA

Specifications

	2-door convertible
Wheelbase, in.	89.2
Overall length, in.	155.4
Overall width, in.	65.9
Overall height, in.	48.2
Curb weight, lbs.	2293
Cargo vol., cu. ft.	3.6
Fuel capacity, gals.	12.7
Seating capacity	2

Mazda Miata

	2-door convertible
Front head room, in.	37.1
Max. front leg room, in.	42.7
Rear head room, in.	—
Min. rear leg room, in.	—

Powertrain layout: longitudinal front engine/rear-wheel drive.

Engines

	dohc I-4
Size, liters/cu. in.	1.8/112
Horsepower @ rpm	128 @ 6500
Torque (lbs./ft.) @ rpm	110 @ 5000
Availability	S
EPA city/highway mpg	
5-speed OD manual	22/27
4-speed OD automatic	23/28

Built in Japan.

PRICES

Mazda Miata	Retail Price	Dealer Invoice	Fair Price
2-door convertible	$16650	$14835	$16150
M-Edition 2-door convertible	21500	—	—
Destination charge	395	395	395

M-Edition dealer invoice and fair price not available at time of publication. Prices are for vehicles distributed by Mazda Motor of America, Inc. Prices may be higher in areas served by independent distributors.

Standard Equipment:

1.8-liter DOHC 4-cylinder engine, 5-speed manual transmission, 4-wheel disc brakes, driver- and passenger-side air bags, cloth reclining bucket seats, tachometer, coolant temperature gauge, trip odometer, intermittent wipers, AM/FM cassette, passenger visor mirror, dual outside mirrors, center console, dual courtesy lights, tinted glass, remote fuel door release, 185/60HR14 tires, alloy wheels. **M-Edition** adds: tan leather interior, tan vinyl top, wood interior accents, Montego Blue Mica paint, polished alloy wheels.

Optional Equipment:	Retail Price	Dealer Invoice	Fair Price
4-speed automatic transmission	$850	$739	$765
Requires Pkg. A, B, or C.			
Anti-lock brakes	900	765	810
Requires Pkg. A, B, or C.			
Air conditioning	830	680	765
Detachable hardtop	1500	1215	1350
Requires Pkg. A, B, or C.			
Sensory Sound System	700	560	630
Requires Pkg. B or C.			
Option Pkg. A, 5-speed	1710	1436	1539
Automatic	1320	1109	1188
Power steering, alloy wheels with locks, power mirrors, leather-wrapped steering wheel, headrest speakers, limited-slip differential (5-speed).			
Option Pkg. B, 5-speed	2410	2024	2169
Automatic	2020	1697	1818
Pkg. A plus power windows, cruise control, power antenna.			
Option Pkg. C, 5-speed	3110	2612	2799
Automatic	2720	2285	2448
Pkg. B plus tan interior with leather seating surfaces, tan vinyl top.			
Option Pkg. R	1500	1260	1350
Limited-slip differential, sport suspension, front and rear spoilers, locking alloy wheels. Not available with Option Pkgs. A, B, or C.			
Floormats	65	47	59

1995 MAZDA MILLENIA

Specifications	4-door notchback
Wheelbase, in.	108.3
Overall length, in.	189.8
Overall width, in.	69.7

1995 Mazda Millenia S

	4-door notchback
Overall height, in.	54.5
Curb weight, lbs.	3216
Cargo vol., cu. ft.	13.3
Fuel capacity, gals.	18.0
Seating capacity	5
Front head room, in.	NA
Max. front leg room, in.	NA
Rear head room, in.	NA
Min. rear leg room, in.	NA

Powertrain layout: transverse front engine/front-wheel drive.

Engines	dohc V-6	dohc V-6
Size, liters/cu. in.	2.5/152	2.3/138
Horsepower @ rpm	170 @ 5800	210 @ 4800
Torque (lbs./ft.) @ rpm	160 @ 4800	210 @ 3500
Availability	S	S[1]
EPA city/highway mpg		
4-speed OD automatic	20/27	20/28

1. S model.

Built in Japan.

PRICES

1995 Mazda Millenia	Retail Price	Dealer Invoice	Fair Price
4-door notchback	$25995	—	—

Prices are accurate at time of publication; subject to manufacturer's change.

	Retail Price	Dealer Invoice	Fair Price
4-door notchback w/Leather Pkg.	$28300	—	—
S 4-door notchback	31400	—	—
Destination charge	395	395	395

Dealer invoice and fair price not available at time of publication. Prices are for vehicles distributed by Mazda Motor America, Inc. Prices may be higher in areas served by independent distributors.

Standard Equipment:

2.5-liter DOHC V-6 engine, 4-speed automatic transmission, anti-lock 4-wheel disc brakes, driver- and passenger-side air bags, automatic climate control, power steering, 8-way power driver's seat, power tilt steering column, power windows and locks, heated power mirrors, anti-theft alarm, illuminated entry system, projector low-beam headlamps, integrated projector fog lamps, wood console trim, 205/65HR15 tires, alloy wheels. **Leather Pkg.** adds: leather upholstery, 4-way power front passenger seat, remote keyless entry, power glass moonroof. **S** adds: 2.3-liter DOHC Miller-cycle V-6 engine, traction control, Leather Package, 215/55VR16 tires.

Optional Equipment:

4-Seasons Package, base	600	—	—
S	300	—	—
Traction control, heated front seats, heavy-duty wipers.			
CD changer	900	—	—
Base model requires Leather Pkg.			
Bose audio system with CD changer	1200	—	—
Base model requires Leather Pkg.			
Protection Package	125	—	—
Carpeted floormats and wheel locks.			

MAZDA MPV

Specifications	4-door van	4WD 4-door van
Wheelbase, in.	110.4	110.4
Overall length, in.	175.8	175.8
Overall width, in.	71.9	72.3

Mazda MPV

	4-door van	4WD 4-door van
Overall height, in.	68.1	70.8
Curb weight, lbs.	3515	4010
Cargo vol., cu. ft.	37.5	37.5
Fuel capacity, gals.	15.9	19.8
Seating capacity	8	7
Front head room, in.	40.0	40.0
Max. front leg room, in.	40.6	40.6
Rear head room, in.	39.0	39.0
Min. rear leg room, in.	34.8	34.8

Powertrain layout: longitudinal front engine/rear-wheel drive or on-demand 4WD.

Engines	ohc I-4	ohc V-6
Size, liters/cu. in.	2.6/159	3.0/180
Horsepower @ rpm	121 @ 4600	155 @ 5000
Torque (lbs./ft.) @ rpm	149 @ 3500	169 @ 4000
Availability	S	S
EPA city/highway mpg		
4-speed OD automatic	18/24	16/22

Built in Japan.

PRICES

Mazda MPV	Retail Price	Dealer Invoice	Fair Price
4-door van, 5-passenger, 4-cyl.	$18195	$16212	$16712

Prices are accurate at time of publication; subject to manufacturer's change.

MAZDA

	Retail Price	Dealer Invoice	Fair Price
4-door van, 7-passenger, 4-cyl.	$19595	$17460	$17960
4-door van, 7-passenger, V-6	20395	18172	18672
4WD van, 7-passenger, V-6	23395	20845	21345
Destination charge	445	445	445

Prices are for vehicles distributed by Mazda Motor of America, Inc. Prices may be higher in areas served by independent distributors.

Standard Equipment:

5-passenger: 2.6-liter 4-cylinder engine, 4-speed automatic transmission, anti-lock rear brakes, driver-side air bag, power steering, cloth reclining front bucket seats, removable reclining 3-passenger bench seat, remote mirrors, tachometer, coolant temperature gauge, trip odometer, intermittent wipers, rear defogger and wiper/washer, tinted glass, door pockets, remote fuel door release, tilt steering column, AM/FM cassette w/four speakers, digital clock, wheel covers, 195/75R15 tires. **7-passenger:** 2.6-liter 4-cylinder or 3.0-liter V-6, removable reclining 2-passenger middle and flip-fold 3-passenger rear bench seats, AM/FM cassette with six speakers, power mirrors. 4WD has on-demand 4WD, 215/65R15 tires, alloy wheels.

Optional Equipment:

	Retail Price	Dealer Invoice	Fair Price
Touring Pkg. 1, V-6 2WD	570	490	537
8-passenger seating, 3-passenger middle seat with fold-down armrests, cup holders, and outboard armrests. Requires Option Pkg. B or D.			
Cold Pkg.	300	258	283
Heavy duty battery, larger windshield washer solvent reservoir, rear heater.			
Option Pkg. A, 2WD	1050	872	973
Power windows and locks, cruise control, bronze-tinted windshield, rear privacy glass.			
Option Pkg. B, 2WD V-6	1350	1121	1251
Pkg. A plus keyless entry system, body-color grille, rear license plate illumination bar.			
Option Pkg. C, 4WD	1350	1121	1251
Pkg. A plus keyless entry system, body-color grille, rear license plate illumination bar.			
Luxury Pkg. (Option Pkg. D), 2WD V-6	3995	3316	3702
4WD	3550	2947	3290
Pkg. B (2WD), Pkg. C (4WD), leather upholstery, leather-wrapped steering wheel, color-keyed bodyside moldings, 2-tone paint, lace alloy wheels; requires dual air conditioning, Towing Pkg. and moonroof.			
CD player, 2WD V-6, 4WD	700	560	638
Requires Pkg. D.			

	Retail Price	Dealer Invoice	Fair Price
Single air conditioning	$860	$705	$792
Dual air conditioning	1500	1230	1382
Requires V-6 engine and Pkg. A, B, C, or D.			
Power moonroof, 2WD V6, 4WD	1000	820	922
Requires Pkg. B, C, or D.			
2-tone paint	300	246	276
Towing Pkg., 2WD V-6	500	430	471
4WD	400	344	377
Transmission oil cooler, automatic load leveling, heavy duty cooling fan (2WD), conventional spare (2WD). 2WD requires Alloy wheel Pkg. or Pkg. D; 4WD requires Pkg. C or D.			
Alloy wheel Pkg., 2WD V-6	450	374	417
215/65R15 tires, alloy wheels. Requires Pkg. B.			
Floormats, 5-passenger	65	47	57
7-passenger	90	65	78
8-passenger	95	69	83

MAZDA MX-3

Mazda MX-3 GS

Specifications

	3-door hatchback
Wheelbase, in.	96.3
Overall length, in.	165.7
Overall width, in.	66.7
Overall height, in.	51.6
Curb weight, lbs.	2443
Cargo vol., cu. ft.	36.6
Fuel capacity, gals.	13.2

Prices are accurate at time of publication; subject to manufacturer's change.

	3-door hatchback
Seating capacity	4
Front head room, in.	38.2
Max. front leg room, in.	42.6
Rear head room, in.	33.9
Min. rear leg room, in.	31.1

Powertrain layout: transverse front engine/front-wheel drive.

Engines

	dohc I-4	dohc V-6
Size, liters/cu. in.	1.6/98	1.8/113
Horsepower @ rpm	105 @ 6200	130 @ 6500
Torque (lbs./ft.) @ rpm	100 @ 3600	115 @ 4500
Availability	S	S[1]
EPA city/highway mpg		
5-speed OD manual	29/37	23/29
4-speed OD automatic	25/34	20/27

1 GS.

Built in Japan.

PRICES

Mazda MX-3	Retail Price	Dealer Invoice	Fair Price
3-door hatchback	$13595	$12251	$12651
GS 3-door hatchback	16095	14341	14841
Destination charge	395	395	395

Prices are for vehicles distributed by Mazda Motor of America, Inc. Prices may be higher in areas served by independent distributors.

Standard Equipment:

1.6-liter DOHC 4-cylinder engine, 5-speed manual transmission, driver- and passenger-side air bags, cloth reclining front bucket seats, power steering, tachometer, AM/FM cassette stereo, coolant temperature gauge, variable-intermittent wipers, rear defogger, folding rear seat, power mirrors, tinted glass, tilt steering column, remote fuel door and hatch releases, rear cargo cover, wheel covers, 185/65R14 tires. **GS** adds: 1.8-liter DOHC V-6, 4-wheel disc brakes, rear wiper/washer, front and rear spoilers, 205/55R15 tires, alloy wheels.

Optional Equipment:

	Retail Price	Dealer Invoice	Fair Price
Anti-lock brakes, base	$950	$808	$879
Includes rear disc brakes. Requires 5-speed manual transmission.			
Anti-lock brakes, GS	800	680	740
Requires 5-speed manual transmission.			
4-speed automatic transmission	750	675	713
Air conditioning	850	680	765
Power Pkg., base	300	261	281
Power windows and locks.			
Power Pkg., GS	500	430	465
Power windows and locks, cruise control.			
Power sunroof, GS	560	448	504
Alloy wheels, base	425	340	383
Armrest	65	52	59
Floormats	70	51	61

MAZDA MX-6/ FORD PROBE

Mazda MX-6 LS

Specifications

	MX-6 2-door notchback	Probe 3-door hatchback
Wheelbase, in.	102.8	102.8
Overall length, in.	181.5	178.7
Overall width, in.	68.9	69.8
Overall height, in.	51.6	51.6
Curb weight, lbs.	2625	2690

MAZDA

	MX-6 2-door notchback	Probe 3-door hatchback
Cargo vol., cu. ft.	12.4	18.0
Fuel capacity, gals.	15.5	15.5
Seating capacity	4	4
Front head room, in.	38.1	37.8
Max. front leg room, in.	44.0	43.1
Rear head room, in.	34.7	34.8
Min. rear leg room, in.	27.7	28.5

Powertrain layout: transverse front engine/front-wheel drive.

Engines

	dohc I-4	dohc V-6
Size, liters/cu. in.	2.0/122	2.5/153
Horsepower @ rpm	118 @ 5500	164 @ 5600
Torque (lbs./ft.) @ rpm	127 @ 4500	160 @ 4800
Availability	S[1]	S[2]
EPA city/highway mpg		
5-speed OD manual	26/34	21/26
4-speed OD automatic	23/31	20/26

1 Base models. 2. MX-6 LS, Probe GT.

Built in Flat Rock, Mich.

PRICES

Mazda MX-6	Retail Price	Dealer Invoice	Fair Price
MX-6 2-door notchback	$17495	$15411	$15911
MX-6 LS 2-door notchback	21495	18717	19517
Destination charge	395	395	395

Prices are for vehicles distributed by Mazda Motor of America, Inc. Prices may be higher in areas served by independent distributors.

Standard Equipment:

2.0-liter DOHC 4-cylinder engine, 5-speed manual transmission, power steering, driver- and passenger-side air bags, cloth reclining front bucket seats, driver's-seat thigh support adjustment, 60/40 folding rear seat with armrest, console with storage, power windows and locks, cruise control, power mirrors, visor mirrors, AM/FM cassette with power antenna, tachometer, coolant temperature gauge, trip odometer, tilt steering column, intermittent wipers, dual remote mirrors, door pockets, tinted glass, remote fuel door and decklid releases, rear defogger, 195/65R14 tires, full wheel covers. **LS** adds: 2.5-liter DOHC V-6 engine, 4-wheel disc brakes, air conditioning, power sunroof, leather-wrapped steering wheel, anti-theft alarm, fog lamps, 205/55VR15 tires, alloy wheels.

Optional Equipment:	Retail Price	Dealer Invoice	Fair Price
4-speed automatic transmission	$800	$696	$760
Anti-lock 4-wheel disc brakes, base	950	808	902
Anti-lock brakes, LS	800	680	760
Air conditioning, base	850	680	807
Popular Equipment Group, base	1250	1000	1188
Power sunroof, anti-theft alarm, alloy wheels.			
Leather Pkg., LS	1000	800	950
Leather seats, power driver's seat, heated outside mirrors.			
Rear spoiler	375	300	356
Floormats	70	51	66

Ford Probe	Retail Price	Dealer Invoice	Fair Price
3-door hatchback	$13755	$12387	$12887
GT 3-door hatchback	16085	14461	15261
Destination charge	360	360	360

Standard Equipment:

Base: 2.0-liter DOHC 4-cylinder engine, 5-speed manual transmission, power steering, driver- and passenger-side air bags, cloth reclining front bucket seats with memory, split folding rear seat, tachometer, coolant temperature and oil pressure gauges, voltmeter, trip odometer, tinted rear and quarter windows, right visor mirror, center console, dual remote mirrors, AM/FM radio, 195/65R14 all-season tires, wheel covers. **GT** adds: 2.5-liter DOHC V-6 engine, 4-wheel disc brakes, full console with armrest and storage, door pockets, multi-adjustable power seats w/driver-side lumbar support and side bolsters, leather-wrapped steering wheel and shift knob, front seatback storage compartment, cargo net, fog lights, lower bodyside cladding, 225/50VR16 tires, alloy wheels.

Optional Equipment:	Retail Price	Dealer Invoice	Fair Price
Anti-lock brakes, Base	735	654	661
GT	565	503	508
Includes 4-wheel disc brakes and sport suspension (std. GT).			
Air conditioning	780	695	702
Requires Group 2.			

	Retail Price	Dealer Invoice	Fair Price
4-speed automatic transmission	$790	$703	$711
Preferred Pkg. 251A, Base	370	329	333
Power mirrors, rear defogger, Convenience Group, tilt steering column.			
Preferred Pkg. 253A, Base	2340	2082	2106
Preferred Pkg. 251A plus air conditioning, power windows and door locks, AM/FM cassette with premium sound, color-keyed bodyside moldings, remote keyless entry, cruise control, Light Group, Power Group.			
Preferred Pkg. 261A, GT	1385	1233	1246
Air conditioning, power mirrors, tilt steering column, cassette player with premium sound, Convenience Group, rear defogger.			
Preferred Pkg. 263A, GT	2790	2484	2511
Pkg. 261A plus anti-lock brakes, color-keyed bodyside moldings, remote keyless entry, cruise control, Light Group, Power Group, rear wiper/washer, heated power mirrors.			
Group 1	260	232	234
Rear defogger, power mirrors.			
Group 2	495	440	445
Tilt steering column, Convenience Group (tinted glass, intermittent wipers, remote fuel door and liftgate releases, battery saver, headlamp warning chime, convenience lights).			
Group 3	1105	984	994
Air conditioning, AM/FM cassette with premium sound.			
Group 4	1145	1019	1030
Light Group, Power Group, color-keyed bodyside moldings.			
Group 5	740	658	666
Anti-lock brakes, rear wiper/washer.			
Light Group	395	352	355
Illuminated entry, lighted visor mirrors, remote keyless entry, fade-to-off dome light with map lights.			
Power Group	700	623	630
Power windows and door locks, cruise control.			
Sport Edition, Base	760	677	684
Body-color bodyside cladding, front fascia, 205/55R15 tires, alloy wheels.			
Rear wiper/washer with heated power mirrors	175	156	157
Power driver's seat	290	258	261
Requires Power Group.			
Leather seats, GT	500	445	450
Manual driver seat height adjuster, Base	35	31	32
Power antenna	80	71	72
Requires cassette or CD player.			

	Retail Price	Dealer Invoice	Fair Price
Feature Car, GT	$215	$191	$193
Wild orchid exterior, unique black GT bucket seats and floormats. Requires Power Group and rear wiper/washer with heated power mirrors.			
Cassette player	325	290	292
CD player, Base with Pkg. 251A	800	712	720
Base with 253A, GT with 261A or 263A	475	423	427
Graphic equalizer	135	120	121
Anti-theft system	190	169	171
Console with storage armrest and cup holder, Base	60	54	55
Color-keyed bodyside moldings	50	45	46
Sliding power roof	615	547	553
Includes dome light with map lights.			
Alloy wheels and 205/55R15 tires	430	383	387
Floormats	30	27	28

MAZDA RX-7

Mazda RX-7

Specifications	3-door hatchback
Wheelbase, in.	95.5
Overall length, in.	168.5
Overall width, in.	68.9
Overall height, in.	48.4
Curb weight, lbs.	2826

	3-door hatchback
Cargo vol., cu. ft.	17.0
Fuel capacity, gals.	20.0
Seating capacity	2
Front head room, in.	37.6
Max. front leg room, in.	44.1
Rear head room, in.	—
Min. rear leg room, in.	—

Powertrain layout: longitudinal front engine/rear-wheel drive.

Engines

	Turbo 2-rotor Wankel
Size, liters/cu. in.	1.3/81
Horsepower @ rpm	255 @ 6500
Torque (lbs./ft.) @ rpm	217 @ 5000
Availability	S

EPA city/highway mpg

5-speed OD manual	17/25
4-speed OD automatic	18/24

Built in Japan.

PRICES

Mazda RX-7	Retail Price	Dealer Invoice	Fair Price
3-door hatchback	$34000	$30618	$32118
Destination charge	375	375	375

Prices are for vehicles distributed by Mazda Motor of America, Inc. Prices may be higher in areas served by independent distributors.

Standard Equipment:

1.3-liter turbocharged rotary engine, 5-speed manual transmission, limited-slip differential, 4-wheel anti-lock disc brakes, variable-assist power steering, driver- and passenger-side air bags, cloth highback sport bucket seats, air conditioning, power windows and locks, dual storage compartments, power mirrors, AM/FM cassette, power antenna, tachometer and gauges, trip odometer, cruise control, tinted glass, intermittent wipers, leather-wrapped steering wheel, anti-theft alarm, remote fuel door and decklid releases, 225/50VR16 tires, alloy wheels.

Optional Equipment:	Retail Price	Dealer Invoice	Fair Price
4-speed automatic transmission	$900	$783	$810
Not available with R-2 Pkg. or Popular Equipment Group.			
R-2 Pkg.	2000	1640	1800
Dual oil coolers, special suspension tuning, front brake air ducts, rear spoiler, front air dam, front shock tower support brace, upgraded cloth upholstery, Pirelli Z-rated tires; deletes cruise control. Not available with Touring Pkg. or Popular Equipment Group.			
Touring Pkg.	4200	3444	3780
Leather seats, power glass moonroof, cargo cover, rear wiper/ washer, Bose Acoustic Wave music system with CD player, fog lights, rear cargo cover, additional sound insulation. Not available with R-2 Pkg.			
Popular Equipment Group	1800	1476	1620
Leather seats, power steel sunroof, rear cargo cover. Not available with automatic transmission.			
Floormats	70	51	63

MAZDA 323/PROTEGE

Mazda Protege LX

Specifications	3-door hatchback	4-door notchback
Wheelbase, in.	96.5	98.4
Overall length, in.	163.6	171.5
Overall width, in.	65.7	65.9
Overall height, in.	54.3	54.1
Curb weight, lbs.	2238	2359
Cargo vol., cu. ft.	15.8	12.8
Fuel capacity, gals.	13.2	14.5

Prices are accurate at time of publication; subject to manufacturer's change.

MAZDA

	3-door hatchback	4-door notchback
Seating capacity	5	5
Front head room, in.	38.6	38.6
Max. front leg room, in.	42.2	42.2
Rear head room, in.	37.6	37.1
Min. rear leg room, in.	34.2	34.6

Powertrain layout: transverse front engine/front-wheel drive.

Engines	ohc I-4	ohc I-4	dohc I-4
Size, liters/cu. in.	1.6/97	1.8/112	1.8/112
Horsepower @ rpm	82 @ 5000	103 @ 5500	125 @ 6500
Torque (lbs./ft.) @ rpm	92 @ 2500	111 @ 4000	114 @ 4500
Availability	S[1]	S[2]	S[3]
EPA city/highway mpg			
5-speed OD manual	29/36	28/36	24/30
4-speed OD automatic	26/33	24/31	23/29

1 323. 2. Protege DX. 3. Protege LX.

Built in Japan.

PRICES

Mazda 323/Protege	Retail Price	Dealer Invoice	Fair Price
323 3-door hatchback	$8395	$7990	$8190
Protege DX 4-door notchback	11495	10475	10675
Protege LX 4-door notchback	13195	11891	12091
Destination charge	395	395	395

Standard Equipment:

323: 1.6-liter 4-cylinder engine, 5-speed manual transmission, motorized front shoulder belts, vinyl reclining front bucket seats, one-piece folding rear seat, left remote mirror, coolant temperature gauge, trip odometer, cargo cover, console with storage, rear defogger, 155/SR13 tires. **Protege DX**: 1.8-liter 4-cylinder engine, 5-speed manual transmission, power steering, cloth reclining front bucket seats, 60/40 folding rear seat, remote mirrors, coolant temperature gauge, trip odometer, console with storage, tinted glass, bodyside moldings, door pockets, remote fuel door and decklid releases, intermittent wipers, color-keyed bumpers, right visor mirror, digital clock, rear defogger, 175/70R13 tires. **Protege LX** adds to DX:

1.8-liter DOHC engine, 4-wheel disc brakes, power windows and locks, tilt steering column, cruise control, AM/FM cassette, power mirrors, rear center folding armrest, driver seat adjustable thigh support, trunk light, tachometer, left visor mirror, 185/60R14 tires.

Optional Equipment:	Retail Price	Dealer Invoice	Fair Price
4-speed automatic transmission	$750	$675	$695
Power steering, 323	250	—	—
Air conditioning	850	680	746
Plus Pkg., 323	650	—	—
Cloth upholstery, AM/FM cassette, 60/40 split folding rear seat, full wheel covers.			
DX Convenience Group, Protege DX	650	520	571
Tilt steering column, tachometer, AM/FM cassette with four speakers, trunk light, diagnostic warning lights.			
Power sunroof, Protege LX	560	408	472
Alloy wheels, Protege LX	425	340	373
Floormats	65	47	55

MAZDA 626

Mazda 626 LX

Specifications	4-door notchback
Wheelbase, in.	102.8
Overall length, in.	184.4
Overall width, in.	68.9
Overall height, in.	51.6
Curb weight, lbs.	2626
Cargo vol., cu. ft.	13.8

Prices are accurate at time of publication; subject to manufacturer's change.

MAZDA

	4-door notchback
Fuel capacity, gals.	15.9
Seating capacity	5
Front head room, in.	39.2
Max. front leg room, in.	43.5
Rear head room, in.	37.8
Min. rear leg room, in.	35.8

Powertrain layout: transverse front engine/front-wheel drive.

Engines	dohc I-4	dohc V-6
Size, liters/cu. in.	2.0/122	2.5/153
Horsepower @ rpm	118 @ 5500	164 @ 5600
Torque (lbs./ft.) @ rpm	127 @ 4500	160 @ 4800
Availability	S[1]	S[2]
EPA city/highway mpg		
5-speed OD manual	26/34	21/26
4-speed OD automatic	23/31	20/26

1 DX, LX. 2. LX V6, ES.

Built in Flat Rock, Mich.

PRICES

Mazda 626	Retail Price	Dealer Invoice	Fair Price
626 DX 4-door notchback	$14255	$13134	$13634
626 LX 4-door notchback	16540	14737	15237
626 LX V-6, 4-door notchback	18700	16472	17172
626 ES V-6, 4-door notchback	21545	18761	19461
Destination charge	395	395	395

Prices are for vehicles distributed by Mazda Motor of America, Inc. Prices may be higher in areas served by independent distributors.

Standard Equipment:

DX: 2.0-liter DOHC 4-cylinder engine, 5-speed manual transmission, power steering, driver- and passenger-side air bags, cloth reclining front bucket seats, driver's-seat thigh support adjustment, 60/40 folding rear seat with armrest, console with storage, tachometer, coolant temperature gauge, trip odometer, tilt steering column, intermittent wipers, dual remote mirrors, door pockets, tinted glass, remote fuel door and decklid release, rear defogger,

195/65R14 tires, full wheel covers. **LX** adds: air conditioning, power windows and locks, cruise control, power mirrors, AM/FM cassette with power antenna, map lights. **LX V-6** adds: 2.5-liter DOHC V-6 engine, 4-wheel disc brakes, 205/55VR15 tires, alloy wheels. **ES** adds: anti-lock brakes, anti-theft alarm, power moonroof, leather seats, heated power mirrors, fog lamps.

Optional Equipment:	Retail Price	Dealer Invoice	Fair Price
4-speed automatic transmission	$800	$696	$760
Anti-lock 4-wheel disc brakes, LX	950	808	903
Anti-lock brakes, LX V-6	800	680	760
Luxury Pkg., LX	1500	1200	1425
Power moonroof, heated power mirrrors, anti-theft alarm, alloy wheels.			
Premium Pkg., LX V-6	1875	1500	1781
Anti-lock brakes, power driver's seat, power moonroof, heated power mirrors, anti-theft alarm.			
Floormats	70	51	67

MAZDA 929

Mazda 929

Specifications	4-door notchback
Wheelbase, in.	112.2
Overall length, in.	193.7
Overall width, in.	70.7
Overall height, in.	54.9
Curb weight, lbs.	3596
Cargo vol., cu. ft.	12.4
Fuel capacity, gals.	18.5

Prices are accurate at time of publication; subject to manufacturer's change.

	4-door notchback
Seating capacity	5
Front head room, in.	37.4
Max. front leg room, in.	43.4
Rear head room, in.	37.4
Min. rear leg room, in.	37.0

Powertrain layout: longitudinal front engine/rear-wheel drive.

Engines

	dohc V-6
Size, liters/cu. in.	3.0/180
Horsepower @ rpm	193 @ 5750
Torque (lbs./ft.) @ rpm	200 @ 3500
Availability	S

EPA city/highway mpg

4-speed OD automatic	19/24

Built in Japan.

PRICES

Mazda 929	Retail Price	Dealer Invoice	Fair Price
4-door notchback	$31500	$26791	$27543
Destination charge	395	395	395

Prices are for vehicles distributed by Mazda Motor of America, Inc. Prices may be higher in areas served by independent distributors.

Standard Equipment:

3.0-liter DOHC V-6 engine, 4-speed automatic transmission, anti-lock 4-wheel disc brakes, variable-assist power steering, driver- and passenger-side air bags, automatic climate control, cloth reclining front bucket seats, power driver's seat, console with storage, tachometer, coolant temperature gauge, voltmeter, trip odometer, heated power mirrors, analog clock, variable intermittent wipers, cruise control, AM/FM cassette, power antenna, diversity antenna system, power sunroof, tinted glass, remote fuel door and decklid releases, map lights, lighted visor mirrors, rear defogger, 205/65R15 tires, alloy wheels.

Optional Equipment:

Floormats	100	77	86

	Retail Price	Dealer Invoice	Fair Price
Premium Pkg.	$4100	$3362	$3731
Leather Pkg., premium audio system with multi-disc CD changer, keyless entry system, reflective solar-control tinted glass, wood trim, cellular phone pre-wiring.			
Leather Pkg.	1850	1517	1684
Leather upholstery, rear storage armrest, power front passenger seat.			
Cold Pkg.	600	498	549
Heated front seats, all-season tires, limited-slip differential, heavy duty wiper motor, larger washer reservoir, heavy duty battery. NA California.			
Solar Ventilation System	650	533	592
Requires Premium Pkg.			

MERCEDES-BENZ C-CLASS

Mercedes-Benz C280

Specifications	4-door notchback
Wheelbase, in.	105.9
Overall length, in.	177.4
Overall width, in.	67.7
Overall height, in.	56.1
Curb weight, lbs.	3173
Cargo vol., cu. ft.	13.7
Fuel capacity, gals.	16.4
Seating capacity	5

Prices are accurate at time of publication; subject to manufacturer's change.

	4-door notchback
Front head room, in.	37.2
Max. front leg room, in.	41.5
Rear head room, in.	37.0
Min. rear leg room, in.	32.8

Powertrain layout: longitudinal front engine/rear-wheel drive.

Engines	dohc I-4	dohc I-6
Size, liters/cu. in.	2.2/132	2.8/173
Horsepower @ rpm	147 @ 5500	194 @ 5500
Torque (lbs./ft.) @ rpm	155 @ 4000	199 @ 3750
Availability	S[1]	S[2]
EPA city/highway mpg		
4-speed automatic	22/28	20/26

1. C220. 2. C280.

Built in Germany.

PRICES

Mercedes-Benz C-Class	Retail Price	Dealer Invoice	Fair Price
C220 4-door notchback	$29900	$25440	—
C280 4-door notchback	34900	29690	—
Destination charge	475	475	475

Fair price not available at time of publication.

Standard Equipment:

C220: 2.2-liter DOHC 4-cylinder engine, 4-speed automatic transmission, anti-lock 4-wheel disc brakes, driver- and passenger-side air bags, power steering, air conditioning, automatic climate control, cruise control, power windows, heated power mirrors, 10-way power driver's seat, 10-way manual adjustable passenger seat, center console with armrest and bi-level storage, folding rear armrest, cellular phone and CD pre-wiring, tinted glass, fog lamps, AM/FM cassette, automatic power antenna, power steel sunroof, lighted visor mirrors, cup holder, rear defogger, sunroof, first aid kit, 195/65HR15 tires, alloy wheels. **C280** adds: 2.8-liter DOHC 6-cylinder engine, Bose sound system, power passenger seat.

Optional Equipment:

C1 Option Pkg., C220	1560	1295	—

	Retail Price	Dealer Invoice	Fair Price
C280	$2750	$2283	—
ASD automatic locking differential (C220), ASR automatic slip control (C280), headlamp washer/wipers, heated front seats.			
C2 Option Pkg., C220 and C280	320	266	—
Split folding rear seat.			
C3 Option Pkg., C280	1710	1419	—
Leather upholstery, power glass sunroof, retractable rear head restraints.			
ASD automatic locking differential, C220	1110	921	—
ASR automatic slip control, C280	2615	2170	—
Leather upholstery, C280	1580	1311	—
Anti-theft alarm system	575	477	—
Headlamp washer/wipers	310	257	—
Bose sound system, C220	485	403	—
Rear head restraints	330	274	—
Power glass sunroof	220	183	—
Power passenger seat, C220	560	465	—
Heated front seats	550	457	—
Power front seat orthopedic backrests (each)	355	295	—
Split folding rear seat	270	224	—
Metallic paint	560	469	—

MERCEDES-BENZ E-CLASS

Specifications	2-door notchback	4-door notchback	5-door wagon	2-door conv.
Wheelbase, in.	106.9	110.2	110.2	106.9
Overall length, in.	183.9	187.2	188.2	183.9
Overall width, in.	68.5	68.5	68.5	68.5
Overall height, in.	54.9	56.3	59.8	54.8
Curb weight, lbs.	3525	3525	3750	4025
Cargo vol., cu. ft.	14.4	14.6	76.8	10.5
Fuel capacity, gals.	18.5	18.5	19.0	18.5
Seating capacity	4	5	5	4
Front head room, in.	36.0	36.9	37.4	37.6
Max. front leg room, in.	41.9	41.7	41.7	41.9

Mercedes-Benz E320

	2-door notchback	4-door notchback	5-door wagon	2-door conv.
Rear head room, in.	36.8	36.9	36.8	35.5
Min. rear leg room, in.	29.6	33.5	33.9	24.8

Powertrain layout: longitudinal front engine/rear-wheel drive.

Engines	Diesel dohc I-6	dohc I-6	dohc V-8	dohc V-8
Size, liters/cu. in.	3.0/181	3.2/195	4.2/256	5.0/303
Horsepower @ rpm	134 @ 5000	217 @ 5500	275 @ 5700	315 @ 5600
Torque (lbs./ft.) @ rpm	155 @ 2600	229 @ 3750	295 @ 3900	347 @ 3900
Availability	S[1]	S[2]	S[3]	S[4]
EPA city/highway mpg				
4-speed automatic	26/32	19/25	18/24	16/19

1. E300D 2. E300 3. E420 5. E500.

Built in Germany.

PRICES

Mercedes-Benz E-Class	Retail Price	Dealer Invoice	Fair Price
E300 Diesel 4-door notchback	$40000	$34030	—
E320 4-door notchback	42500	36160	—
E320 2-door notchback	61600	51130	—
E320 2-door convertible	77300	64160	—
E320 5-door wagon	46200	39310	—
E420 4-door notchback	51000	43390	—
E500 4-door notchback	80800	67060	—

	Retail Price	Dealer Invoice	Fair Price
Destination charge	$475	$475	$475
Gas Guzzler Tax, E500	1700	1700	1700

Fair price not available at time of publication.

Standard Equipment:

E300 Diesel/E320: 3.0-liter DOHC 6-cylinder diesel engine (E300 Diesel), 3.2-liter DOHC 6-cylinder engine (E320), 4-speed automatic transmisssion, driver- and passenger-side air bags, anti-lock 4-wheel disc brakes, power steering, cruise control, automatic climate control, cloth power front seats, rear head rests, seat pockets, anti-theft alarm system, power windows and door locks, AM/FM cassette, automatic power antenna, tinted glass, rear defogger, visor mirrors, leather-wrapped steering wheel, cellular phone and CD pre-wiring, power steel sunroof, first aid kit, fog lamps, outside temperature indicator, 195/65R15 tires, alloy wheels. **E320 4-door** adds to E300 Diesel: leather upholstery. **E320 2-door** adds to E320 4-door: high performance sound system, headlamp washers/wipers, rear console storage box, adjustable steering column with memory, memory driver's seat. **E320 convertible** adds to E320 2-door: wind deflector, power convertible top; deletes rear console storage box. **E320 wagon** adds to E320 4-door: cloth upholstery, luggage rack, rear facing third seat. **E420 4-door** adds to E320 4-door: 4.2-liter DOHC V-8 engine, headlamp washers/wipers, high performance sound system, adjustable steering column with memory, memory driver's seat. **E500 4-door** adds to E420 4-door: 5.0-liter DOHC V-8 engine, ASR automatic slip control, rear console storage box, heated front seats, rear reading lamps, rear axle level control, rear window sunshade, metallic paint.

Optional Equipment:

	Retail Price	Dealer Invoice	Fair Price
E1 Option Pkg. , E300 Diesel	1560	1295	—
E320 4-door and E320 wagon	2750	2283	—
E320 2-door, E320 Cabriolet and E420 4-door	2500	2075	—
ASD automatic locking differential (E320 Diesel), ASR automatic slip control (NA E320 Diesel), headlamp washers/wipers (std. E320 2-door and Cabriolet, E420), heated front seats.			
E2 Option Pkg., E300 Diesel and E320 4-door	1050	872	—
Memory driver's seat, adjustable steering column with memory, high performance sound system.			
E3 Option Pkg., E320 wagon	1000	830	—

	Retail Price	Dealer Invoice	Fair Price
Memory driver's seat, adjustable steering column with memory, partition net and luggage cover.			
Sportline Pkg., E320 4-door	$1850	$1536	—
E320 2-door	1060	880	—
4-place sport seats (4-door), sport suspension and steering.			
Leather upholstery, E300 Diesel and E320 wagon	1580	1311	—
ASD automatic locking differential, E320 Diesel	1110	921	—
ASR automatic slip control (Std. E500; NA E320 Diesel)	2615	2170	—
Rear axle level control (NA 300 Diesel)	675	560	—
Headlamp washers/wipers	310	257	—
High performance sound system	485	403	—
Power adjustable steering column	355	295	—
Heated front seats	550	457	—
Memory driver's seat	450	374	—
Power front seat orthopedic backrests (each)	355	295	—
Not available with Sportline Pkg.			
Rear window sunshade	400	332	—
Rear reading lamps	85	71	—
Metallic paint	645	535	—
E320 2-door, Cabriolet and E420 4-door	NC	NC	NC

MERCEDES-BENZ S-CLASS

Specifications	2-door notchback	4-door notchback	4-door notchback
Wheelbase, in.	115.9	119.7	123.6
Overall length, in.	199.4	201.3	205.2
Overall width, in.	74.6	74.3	74.3
Overall height, in.	57.1	58.7	58.9
Curb weight, lbs.	4785	4630	4760
Cargo vol., cu. ft.	14.2	15.6	15.6
Fuel capacity, gals.	26.3	26.4	26.4
Seating capacity	4	5	5
Front head room, in.	36.5	38.0	38.0

Mercedes-Benz S420

	2-door notchback	4-door notchback	4-door notchback
Max. front leg room, in.	41.7	41.3	41.3
Rear head room, in.	37.2	37.8	38.5
Min. rear leg room, in.	31.5	36.1	39.6

Powertrain layout: longitudinal front engine/rear-wheel drive.

Engines	dohc I-6	Turbodiesel ohc I-6	dohc V-8	dohc V-8	dohc V-12
Size, liters/cu. in	3.2/195	3.5/210	4.2/256	5.0/303	6.0/365
Horsepower @ rpm	228 @ 5600	148 @ 4000	275 @ 5700	315 @ 5600	389 @ 5200
Torque (lbs./ft.) @ rpm	232 @ 3750	229 @ 2200	295 @ 3900	345 @ 3900	421 @ 3800
Availability	S[1]	S[2]	S[3]	S[4]	S[5]
EPA city/highway mpg					
5-speed OD automatic	17/24				
4-speed automatic		21/28	15/20	14/19	12/16

1. S320. 2. S350 Turbodiesel. 3. S420. 4. S500. 5. S600.

Built in Germany.

PRICES

Mercedes-Benz S-Class	Retail Price	Dealer Invoice	Fair Price
S350 Turbodiesel 4-door notchback (NA California and New York)	$70600	$58600	—
S320 4-door notchback	70600	58600	—
S420 4-door notchback	79500	65990	—
S500 4-door notchback	95300	79100	—

Prices are accurate at time of publication; subject to manufacturer's change.

MERCEDES-BENZ

	Retail Price	Dealer Invoice	Fair Price
S500 2-door notchback	$99800	$82830	—
S600 4-door notchback	130300	108150	—
S600 2-door notchback	133300	110640	—
Destination charge	475	475	475
Gas Guzzler Tax, S420	1700	1700	1700
S500	2100	2100	2100
S600 2-door notchback	3000	3000	3000
S600 4-door notchback	3700	3700	3700

Fair price not available at time of publication.

Standard Equipment:

S350 Turbodiesel: 3.5-liter 6-cylinder turbodiesel engine, 4-speed automatic transmission, power steering, anti-lock 4-wheel disc brakes, driver- and passenger-side air bags, anti-theft alarm, power windows and locks, automatic climate control, AM/FM cassette, CD and cellular phone pre-wiring, automatic power antenna, power leather front seats with 3-position memory, power telescopic steering column with memory, leather-wrapped steering wheel and shift knob, rear defogger, cruise control, headlamp wipers/washers, speed-sensitive intermittent wipers, heated windshield washer jets, power sunroof, heated power memory mirrors, automatic day/night memory rearview mirror, outside temperature indicator, tachometer, coolant temperature and oil pressure gauges, trip odometer, first aid kit, lighted visor mirrors, 225/60HR16 tires, alloy wheels. **S320** adds: 3.2-liter DOHC 6-cylinder engine, 5-speed automatic transmission. **S420** adds: 4.2-liter DOHC V-8 engine, 4-speed automatic transmission, 235/60HR16 tires. **S500** adds: 5.0-liter DOHC V-8 engine, ASR Automatic Slip Control, rear axle level control, heated front and rear seats (sedan), power rear seat (sedan), active charcoal ventilation filter, rear storage console (coupe), rear reading lamps (sedan). **S600** adds to S500: 6.0-liter DOHC V-12 engine, ADS Adaptive Damping System, rear air conditioner, 10-disc CD changer, cellular telephone, rear window sunshade, orthopedic front backrests, 235/60ZR16 tires.

Optional Equipment:

	Retail Price	Dealer Invoice	Fair Price
Rear air conditioner (std. 600)	1840	1527	—
ADS (Adaptive Damping System), 350, 320, and 420	2750	2283	—
500	2040	1693	—
ASD (Automatic Locking Differential), 350	1110	921	—

	Retail Price	Dealer Invoice	Fair Price
ASR (Automatic Slip Control), 320 and 420	$2615	$2170	—
Rear window sunshade (std. 600)	400	332	—
Orthopedic front backrests, each (std. 600)	355	295	—
4-place seating (NA 500 and 600 2-doors)	5220	4333	—
600	3908	3303	—
Power rear seats 350, 320, and 420	1040	863	—
Heated front and rear seats, each	575	481	—
Heated rear seat	580	481	—
Active charcoal filter	500	415	—
Rear axle level control	860	714	—
Power glass sunroof	390	324	—

MERCURY TOPAZ/ FORD TEMPO

Mercury Topaz GS 4-door

Specifications

	2-door notchback	4-door notchback
Wheelbase, in.	99.9	99.9
Overall length, in.	176.7	177.0
Overall width, in.	68.3	68.3
Overall height, in.	52.8	52.9
Curb weight, lbs.	2531	2588
Cargo vol., cu. ft.	13.2	12.9
Fuel capacity, gals.	15.9	15.9
Seating capacity	5	5

Prices are accurate at time of publication; subject to manufacturer's change.

MERCURY

	2-door notchback	4-door notchback
Front head room, in.	37.5	37.5
Max. front leg room, in.	41.5	41.5
Rear head room, in.	36.8	37.0
Min. rear leg room, in.	36.0	36.0

Powertrain layout: transverse front engine/front-wheel drive.

Engines	ohv I-4	ohv V-6
Size, liters/cu. in.	2.3/141	3.0/182
Horsepower @ rpm	96 @ 4200	135 @ 4800
Torque (lbs./ft.) @ rpm	126 @ 2600	150 @ 4250
Availability	S	O
EPA city/highway mpg		
5-speed OD manual	24/33	21/28
3-speed automatic	22/27	20/23

Built in Kansas City, Mo., and Canada.

PRICES

Mercury Topaz	Retail Price	Dealer Invoice	Fair Price
GS 2-door notchback	$11420	$10498	$10698
GS 2-door notchback (Great Lakes, Central, and Southwest regions)	10470	—	—
GS 4-door notchback	11420	10498	10698
Destination charge	485	485	485

Dealer invoice and fair price for Great Lakes, Central, and Southwest regions GS 2-door not available at time of publication.

Standard Equipment:

2.3-liter 4-cylinder engine, 5-speed manual transmission, power steering, motorized front shoulder belts, cloth reclining front bucket seats, tinted glass, intermittent wipers, door map pockets, digital clock, dual visor mirrors, power mirrors, tachometer, coolant temperature gauge, trip odometer, AM/FM radio, center console, 185/70R14 all season tires, floormats.

Optional Equipment:

3.0-liter V-6 engine	655	583	590

Requires air conditioning.

	Retail Price	Dealer Invoice	Fair Price
3-speed automatic transmission	$535	$476	$482
Driver-side air bag	465	414	419
Requires 3-speed automatic transmission. NA with tilt steering wheel, cruise control, or 3.0-liter V-6 engine.			
Air conditioning	780	694	702
Rear defogger	160	143	144
Power windows, 4-door	315	280	284
Power driver's seat	290	258	261
Preferred Pkg. 352A, 2-door	830	739	747
4-door and 4-door Great Lakes, Central and Southwest regions	870	774	783
Automatic transmission, Comfort/Convenience Group, rear defogger, air conditioning, Power Lock Group.			
Preferred Pkg. 353A, 4-door and 4-door Great Lakes, Central, and Southwest regions	1245	1108	1121
Pkg. 352A plus power windows, tilt steering wheel, cruise control, cassette player.			
Preferred Pkg. 354A, 2-door	830	739	747
2-door Great Lakes, Central and Southwest regions	NC	NC	NC
Comfort/Convenience Group, rear defogger, AM/FM cassette, air conditioning, luggage rack, alloy wheels.			
Comfort/Convenience Group	190	169	171
Light Group, remote fuel door and decklid releases, front armrest.			
Power Lock Group, 2-door	295	263	266
2-door with Comfort/ Convenience Group	200	178	180
4-door	335	298	302
4-door with Comfort/ Convenience Group	240	213	216
Includes power door locks, remote fuel door and decklid releases.			
Max Edition Option Group, 4-door with Pkg. 353A	290	258	261
Includes alloy wheels, black luggage rack, black antenna, 2-tone paint.			
Cruise control	215	191	194
Cassette player	150	134	135
Decklid luggage rack	110	96	99
Clearcoat paint	85	76	77
2-tone paint, 4-door	150	134	135
Polycast wheels	185	165	167
Alloy wheels	265	236	239
185/70R14 performance whitewall tires	80	71	72

Prices are accurate at time of publication; subject to manufacturer's change.

Ford Tempo

	Retail Price	Dealer Invoice	Fair Price
GL 2-door notchback (Central States)	$9615	$8849	$9049
GL 2-door notchback	10885	10006	10206
GL 4-door notchback	10885	10006	10206
LX 4-door notchback	12710	11666	11866
Destination charge	495	495	495

Standard Equipment:

GL: 2.3-liter 4-cylinder engine, 5-speed manual transmission, power steering, motorized front shoulder belts, cloth reclining front bucket seats, tinted glass, consolette, visor mirrors, intermittent wipers, coolant temperature gauge, AM/FM radio, 185/70R14 tires, wheel covers. **LX** adds to GL: touring suspension, illuminated entry, power locks, remote fuel door and decklid releases, tilt steering wheel, power mirrors, front armrest, upgraded upholstery, cargo tiedown net, seatback pockets, Light Group, tachometer and trip odometer, floormats, performance tires, polycast wheels.

Optional Equipment:

	Retail Price	Dealer Invoice	Fair Price
3.0-liter V-6 engine	655	583	590
Requires air conditioning.			
3-speed automatic transmission	535	476	482
Air conditioning	780	694	702
Sport Instrument Cluster, GL	85	76	77
Tachometer and trip odometer.			
Driver-side air bag, GL	465	414	419
LX	325	290	293
Includes passenger-side motorized shoulder belt. Not available with tilt steering wheel (deleted from LX with credit), cruise control, 5-speed manual transmission or 3.0-liter V-6 engine.			
Preferred Pkg. 225A, GL	310	277	279
Air conditioning, Light Group, power mirrors, rear defogger.			
Preferred Pkg. 226A, GL 2-door	1255	1118	1130
GL 4-door	1295	1153	1166
Pkg. 225A plus 3-speed automatic transmission (may be deleted without loss of package discount when ordered with 3.0-liter V-6 engine), cassette player, tilt steering wheel, front armrest, rear defogger, power locks, remote fuel door and decklid releases, cassette player, polycast wheels, floormats.			
SRS Pkg. 227A, GL 2-door	1150	1025	1035
GL 4-door	1190	1060	1071
Driver-side air bag, 3-speed automatic transmission, air conditioning, Light Group, power mirrors, front armrest, rear defogger, power locks, remote fuel door and decklid releases, floormats.			

	Retail Price	Dealer Invoice	Fair Price
Preferred Pkg. 233A, LX	$960	$855	$864
Air conditioning, rear defogger, cassette player, 3-speed automatic transmission (may be deleted without loss of package discount when ordered with 3.0-liter V-6 engine), decklid luggage rack, 3.0-liter V-6 engine.			
Front armrest, GL	55	49	50
Rear defogger	160	143	144
Light Group, GL	35	31	32
Power Lock Group, GL			
2-door	295	263	266
4-door	335	298	302
Power door locks, remote fuel door and decklid releases.			
Power mirrors, GL	115	102	104
Cassette player, GL	150	134	135
Premium sound system	130	116	117
Upgraded speakers and amplifier.			
AM/FM radio delete (credit)	(235)	(209)	(209)
Power driver's seat	290	258	261
Requires power mirrors.			
Cruise control	215	191	194
Not available with air bag.			
Decklid luggage rack	110	98	99
Tilt steering wheel	140	124	126
Not available with air bag.			
Polycast wheels, GL	185	165	167
Power windows, 4-doors	315	280	284
Decklid luggage rack	110	98	99
Front floormats, GL	25	23	24
Rear floormats, GL	20	17	18
Clearcoat paint	85	76	77

MERCURY VILLAGER/ NISSAN QUEST

Specifications

Specifications	4-door van
Wheelbase, in.	112.2
Overall length, in.	189.9
Overall width, in.	73.7
Overall height, in.	67.6
Curb weight, lbs.	4015
Cargo vol., cu. ft.	114.8

Mercury Villager LS

	4-door van
Fuel capacity, gals.	20.0
Seating capacity	7
Front head room, in.	39.4
Max. front leg room, in.	39.9
Rear head room, in.	39.7
Min. rear leg room, in.	34.8

Powertrain layout: transverse front engine/front-wheel drive.

Engines	ohc V-6
Size, liters/cu. in.	3.0/181
Horsepower @ rpm	151 @ 4800
Torque (lbs./ft.) @ rpm	174 @ 4400
Availability	S

EPA city/highway mpg

4-speed OD automatic	17/23

Built in Avon Lake, Ohio.

PRICES

Mercury Villager	Retail Price	Dealer Invoice	Fair Price
GS 4-door van	$18375	$16355	$17575
LS 4-door van	23155	20562	22355
Nautica 4-door van	24635	21864	23835
Destination charge	540	540	540

Standard Equipment:

GS: 3.0-liter V-6 engine, 4-speed automatic transmission, driver-side air bag, anti-lock brakes, power steering, cloth reclining front bucket seats, 3-passenger bench seat, cloth upholstery, AM/FM cassette player, tachometer, coolant temperature gauge, trip odometer, dual outside mirrors, visor mirrors, tinted glass, variable-intermittent wipers, rear wiper/washer, remote fuel door release, black bodyside moldings, color-keyed bumpers, cornering lamps, front door map pockets, floormats, 205/75R15 all-season tires, wheel covers. **LS** adds: front air conditioning, 2-passenger middle and 3-passenger rear bench seats, tilt steering column, cruise control, power windows and locks, Light Group, privacy glass, rear defogger, lighted visor mirrors, luggage rack, lighted visor mirrors, leather-wrapped steering wheel, seatback map pockets, rear cargo net, lockable underseat storage bin, 2-tone paint, color-keyed bodyside molding, striping. **Nautica** adds to LS: two middle bucket seats, leather upholstery, unique exterior paint, yellow striping, white alloy wheels, duffle bag.

Optional Equipment:

	Retail Price	Dealer Invoice	Fair Price
Front air conditioning, GS	$855	$727	$787
Auxiliary rear air conditioning with rear heater, GS	465	395	428
Includes rear seat fan and temperature controls. Requires Preferred Equipment Pkg. 692A.			
Preferred Equipment Pkg. 691A, GS	1505	1279	1385
Front Air conditioning, 7-passenger seating, power windows and door locks, tilt steering column, cruise control, rear defogger, power mirrors.			
Preferred Equipment Pkg. 692A, GS	2310	1964	2125
Pkg. 691A plus power driver's seat, player, luggage rack, underseat storage bin, alloy wheels.			
Preferred Equipment Pkg. 695A, LS	345	294	317
Power driver's seat, rear air conditioning with rear heater, premium AM/FM cassette player, flip open liftgate window, alloy wheels.			
Preferred Equipment Pkg. 696A, LS	1750	1489	1610
Pkg. 695A plus power passenger seat, quad bucket seats, keyless entry system, headlamp delay system, electronic instrumentation.			
Preferred Equipment Pkg. 697A, Nautica	1750	1489	1610
Power driver's seat, power passenger seat, rear air conditioning with rear heater, premium AM/FM cassette player, flip open liftgate window, keyless entry system, headlamp delay system, electronic instrumentation, locking alloy wheels..			
Power windows and locks, GS	530	451	488
Requires 7-passenger seating.			

	Retail Price	Dealer Invoice	Fair Price
Light Group, GS	$155	$132	$143
Overhead dual map lights, dual liftgate lights, front door step lights, power rear vent windows, under instrument panel lights with time delay. Requires rear defogger.			
Handling Suspension, LS	87	74	80
Includes 215/70R15 performance tires, firm ride suspension, rear stabilizer bar. Requires alloy wheels.			
Trailer Towing Pkg.	250	213	230
Includes heavy duty battery, conventional spare tire, 3500 pound trailert rating.			
Power mirrors, GS	100	85	92
Power moonroof, LS and Nautica	776	659	714
7-passenger seating, GS	330	281	304
Quad captains chairs, LS	600	510	552
8-way power driver's seat	395	336	363
4-way power front passenger's seat	195	166	179
Requires 8-way power driver seat.			
Leather upholstery, LS	865	735	796
Requires quad captains chairs, power driver and passenger seats.			
Electronic instrumentation, LS	244	207	224
Keyless entry and headlamp delay systems, LS	300	255	276
Tilt steering column and cruise control, GS	370	314	340
Rear defogger, GS	170	144	156
Flip open liftgate window	90	77	83
Requires rear defogger.			
Pivacy glass, GS	415	352	382
Requires rear defogger.			
Premium AM/FM cassette player, LS	330	281	304
Includes rear radio controls with front seat lockout, dual mini headphone jacks, cassette/CD storage console, diversity antenna. GS requires Preferred Equipment Pkg. 629A.			
Premium AM/FM cassette and CD player,			
GS with Pkg. 629A	660	561	607
LS with Pkg. 695A or 696A, and Nautica with Pkg. 697A	330	281	304
Includes rear radio controls with front seat lockout, dual mini headphone jacks, cassette/CD storage console, diversity antenna.			
Supersound AM/FM cassette and CD player, LS and Nautica	900	765	828
Includes rear radio controls with front seat lockout, dual mini headphone jacks, cassette/CD storage console, power diversity antenna, subwoofer speaker.			

	Retail Price	Dealer Invoice	Fair Price
Luggage rack, GS	$145	$123	$133
Underseat storage bin, GS	35	30	32
Bodyside striping, GS	45	38	41
Locking alloy wheels	380	323	350

Nissan Quest

	Retail Price	Dealer Invoice	Fair Price
XE 4-door van	$19079	$16541	$18279
GXE 4-door van	23589	20452	22789
Destination charge	380	380	380

Standard Equipment:

XE: 3.0-liter V-6 engine, 4-speed automatic transmission, driver-side air bag, motorized front shoulder belts, front air conditioning, power steering, cloth reclining front bucket seats, 2-passenger middle bench seat and 3-passenger rear bench seat, Quest Trac flexible seating, remote fuel door release, rear defogger, tilt steering column, dual mirrors, tachometer, trip odometer, variable intermittent wipers, rear intermittent wiper/washer, color-keyed bodyside moldings, visor mirrors, cornering lamps, door map pockets, AM/FM cassette, tinted glass, carpeted front and rear floormats, console with cassette/CD storage, tilt-out middle and rear quarter windows, cargo area net, cargo area mat, full wheel covers, 205/75R15 all-season tires. **GXE** adds: anti-lock brakes, rear air conditioning, rear heater controls, cruise control, power driver's seat, power locks and windows, power rear quarter windows, upgraded upholstery and door trim panels, power mirrors, illuminated visor mirrors, upgraded radio with rear controls, leather-wrapped steering wheel, power antenna, dual liftgate with opening window, side and rear privacy glass, map light, lockable underseat storage, alloy wheels.

Optional Equipment:

	Retail Price	Dealer Invoice	Fair Price
Extra Performance Pkg., XE	950	805	903
GXE	525	445	499
Heavy duty battery and radiator, tuned springs, shock absorbers and rear stabilizer bar, full-size spare tire, 215/70HR15 tires, alloy wheels (XE), 3500 lb. towing capacity.			
Power Pkg., XE	825	699	784
Power windows, locks, and mirrors.			
Convenience Pkg., XE	800	677	760
Cruise control, upgraded radio with power antenna, leather-wrapped steering wheel, privacy rear glass, lighted right visor mirror, luggage rack, lockable underseat storage. Requires Power Pkg.			

	Retail Price	Dealer Invoice	Fair Price
Rear air conditioning, XE	$625	$529	$594
Requires Power Pkg.			
Anti-lock brakes, XE	700	593	665
2-tone paint, GXE	300	254	285
Premium Audio Pkg., GXE	1015	859	864
AM/FM cassette/CD player, subwoofer, eight speakers.			
Leather Trim Pkg., GXE	1000	847	950
Leather uphostery. Requires Luxury Pkg.			
Luxury Pkg., GXE	800	677	760
Power passenger seat, middle row captain's chairs, illuminated Digital Touch System, automatic headlamp control.			
Power sunroof, GXE	825	699	784
GXE Extra Performance Pkg. is required when power sunroof and Leather Trim Pkg. are combined.			

MITSUBISHI DIAMANTE

Mitsubishi Diamante LS

Specifications

Specifications	4-door notchback	5-door wagon
Wheelbase, in.	107.1	107.1
Overall length, in.	190.2	192.4
Overall width, in.	69.9	69.9
Overall height, in.	52.6	57.9
Curb weight, lbs.	3483	3610
Cargo vol., cu. ft.	13.6	72.1
Fuel capacity, gals.	19.0	18.8
Seating capacity	5	5
Front head room, in.	38.6	39.7

	4-door notchback	5-door wagon
Max. front leg room, in.	43.9	43.9
Rear head room, in.	36.9	38.4
Min. rear leg room, in.	34.2	36.0

Powertrain layout: transverse front engine/front-wheel drive.

Engines

	ohc V-6	dohc V-6
Size, liters/cu. in.	3.0/182	3.0/182
Horsepower @ rpm	175 @ 5500	202 @ 6000
Torque (lbs./ft.) @ rpm	185 @ 3000	201 @ 3500
Availability	S[1]	S[2]
EPA city/highway mpg		
4-speed OD automatic	18/24	18/24

1. ES, wagon. 2. LS.

Built in Japan and Australia.

PRICES

Mitsubishi Diamante	Retail Price	Dealer Invoice	Fair Price
ES 4-door notchback	$25525	$21431	$21931
5-door wagon	—	—	—
LS 4-door notchback	32500	26006	26506
Destination charge	470	470	470

Wagon prices and options not available at time of publication.

Standard Equipment:

ES: 3.0-liter V-6, 4-speed automatic transmission, 4-wheel disc brakes, power steering, driver- and passenger-side air bags, 7-way adjustable cloth front bucket seats, automatic climate control, power windows, power locks, power mirrors, cruise control, alarm system, automatic shut-off headlamps, rear defogger, console with armrest, tilt steering column, folding rear armrest, dual cup holders, tinted glass, front and rear map lights, remote fuel door and decklid releases, tachometer, coolant temperature gauge, trip odometer, variable intermittent wipers, AM/FM cassette with equalizer and power diversity antenna, steering wheel mounted radio controls, floormats, 205/65VR15 tires, full-size spare tire. **Wagon** adds: rear wiper/washer, 60/40 folding split rear seatback, luggage tiedown hooks, woodgrain interior accents. **LS** adds to ES:

3.0-liter DOHC engine, anti-lock 4-wheel disc brakes, speed-sensitive power steering, leather seats and interior trim, dual power front seats with driver-side memory, Mitsubishi/Infinity audio system with equalizer and eight speakers, heated power mirrors, remote keyless entry system, alloy wheels.

Optional Equipment:	Retail Price	Dealer Invoice	Fair Price
Anti-lock brakes, ES	$1100	$880	$965
Mitsubishi/Infinity audio system, ES	429	300	355
Includes steering wheel controls, equalizer, and eight speakers.			
CD auto changer	699	488	579
Power sunroof	863	690	757
Leather Seat Pkg., ES	1888	1548	1676
Includes power memory driver's seat, leather seat, door, and console trim.			
Traction control, LS	678	556	601
Power passenger seat with memory, LS	369	295	323
Keyless entry system, ES	242	157	194
Sunroof wind reflector	57	37	45
Trunk mat, ES	71	46	57

MITSUBISHI ECLIPSE/ EAGLE TALON/ PLYMOUTH LASER

Specifications	3-door hatchback
Wheelbase, in.	97.2
Overall length, in.	172.8
Overall width, in.	66.7
Overall height, in.	51.4
Curb weight, lbs.	2542
Cargo vol., cu. ft.	10.2
Fuel capacity, gals.	15.9
Seating capacity	4
Front head room, in.	37.9
Max. front leg room, in.	43.9
Rear head room, in.	34.1
Min. rear leg room, in.	28.5

Powertrain layout: transverse front engine/front-wheel drive or permanent 4WD.

Mitsubishi Eclipse GSX

Engines	ohc I-4	dohc I-4	Turbo dohc I-4
Size, liters/cu. in.	1.8/107	2.0/122	2.0/122
Horsepower @ rpm	92 @ 5000	135 @ 6000	195 @ 6000
Torque (lbs./ft.) @ rpm	105 @ 3500	125 @ 3000	203 @ 3000
Availability	S[1]	S[2]	S[3]
EPA city/highway mpg			
5-speed OD manual	23/32	22/29	21/28
4-speed OD automatic	23/30	22/27	19/23

1. Base and GS Eclipse; Talon DL; base Laser. 2. Eclipse GS DOHC; Talon ES; Laser RS. 3. Eclipse GS Tubro and GSX; Talon TSi and AWD; Laser RS Turbo and AWD.

Built in Normal, Ill.

PRICES

Mitsubishi Eclipse	Retail Price	Dealer Invoice	Fair Price
3-door hatchback, 5-speed	$11979	$10482	$10782
3-door hatchback, automatic	12659	11075	11375
GS 1.8 3-door hatchback, 5-speed	14089	12256	12556
GS 1.8 3-door hatchback, automatic	14769	12849	13149
GS DOHC 3-door hatchback, 5-speed	15819	13764	14164
GS DOHC 3-door hatchback, automatic	16499	14357	14757
GS Turbo 3-door hatchback, 5-speed	18529	16117	16617
GS Turbo 3-door hatchback, automatic	19339	16827	17327
GSX 3-door hatchback, 5-speed	21269	18504	19004
GSX 3-door hatchback, automatic	22089	19214	19714
Destination charge	420	420	420

Prices are accurate at time of publication; subject to manufacturer's change.

Standard Equipment:

1.8-liter 4-cylinder engine, 5-speed manual or 4-speed automatic transmission, 4-wheel disc brakes, motorized front shoulder belts, cloth reclining front bucket seats, split folding rear seat, tilt steering column, map lights, remote fuel door and hatch releases, visor mirrors, tachometer, coolant temperature gauge, trip odometer, AM/FM radio, tinted glass, rear defogger, fog lamps, digital clock, remote mirrors, 185/70R14 tires. **GS** adds: power steering, driver-side lumbar support, power mirrors, cargo cover, center storage console with coin and cup holders, AM/FM cassette, rear spoiler, lower body-side cladding, upgraded door trim, alloy wheels. **GS DOHC** adds: 2.0-liter DOHC engine, air conditioning, sport suspension, cruise control, automatic power antenna, intermittent wipers, rear wiper/washer, rear spoiler, wraparound rear spoiler, 205/55HR16 all-season tires, full wheel covers. **GS Turbo** adds: turbocharged intercooled engine, gas-charged shock absorbers, air conditioning, engine oil cooler, 6-way adjustable driver's seat, power windows and door locks, turbo boost gauge, leather-wrapped steering wheel, AM/FM cassette/CD player with equalizer and diversity antenna, alloy wheels. **GSX** adds: permanent 4-wheel drive, anti-lock brakes, limited-slip rear differential.

Optional Equipment:	Retail Price	Dealer Invoice	Fair Price
Anti-lock brakes, GS Turbo	$952	$781	$866
Power steering, base	274	225	249
Air conditioning, base, GS	835	685	760
AM/FM cassette, base	178	146	162
AM/FM cassette with equalizer and diversity antenna, GS DOHC	250	205	227
AM/FM cassette with CD player, GS DOHC	740	607	673
CD player (NA Turbo)	642	417	529
Requires AM/FM cassette.			
Power Pkg., GS, GS DOHC	472	387	429
Power windows and locks.			
Keyless entry system, (NA base)	242	157	199
Requires Power Pkg.			
Leather Pkg., GS Turbo, GSX	448	368	408
Leather front seats.			
Lower body paint and graphic accent, GS DOHC	125	105	115
Alloy wheels, GS DOHC	330	271	300
Rear wiper/washer, GS	135	111	123
Cruise control, GS	221	181	201
Sunroof (NA base)	377	309	343

	Retail Price	Dealer Invoice	Fair Price
Wheel covers, base	$106	$87	$96
Wheel locks, GS DOHC	33	21	27
Floormats	58	38	48
Mud guards	123	80	101

Eagle Talon

	Retail Price	Dealer Invoice	Fair Price
DL 3-door hatchback	$11892	$11083	$11383
ES 3-door hatchback	14362	13331	13731
TSi 3-door hatchback	15885	14717	15217
TSi AWD 3-door hatchback	17978	16620	17120
Destination charge	430	430	430

Standard Equipment:

DL: 1.8-liter 4-cylinder engine, 5-speed manual transmission, 4-wheel disc brakes, motorized front shoulder belts, cloth reclining front bucket seats, split folding rear seat, front console, tinted glass, tachometer, coolant temperature and oil pressure gauges, trip odometer, map lights, dual remote mirrors, visor mirrors, AM/FM radio, remote fuel door and hatch releases, tilt steering column, intermittent wipers, rear spoiler, 185/70R14 tires, wheel covers. **ES** adds: 2.0-liter 4-cylinder engine, power steering, driver's seat lumbar support adjustment, console with storage and armrest, power mirrors, AM/FM cassette, rear defogger, floormats, tonneau cover, fog lamps, 205/55R16 tires. **TSi** adds: turbocharged engine, performance seats, turbo boost gauge, leather-wrapped steering wheel, 205/55VR16 tires. **TSi AWD** adds: permanent 4-wheel drive, limited-slip differential, firmer suspension, alloy wheels.

Optional Equipment:

	Retail Price	Dealer Invoice	Fair Price
4-speed automatic transmission,			
base and ES	716	609	630
TSi and TSi AWD	857	728	754
Anti-lock brakes, ES and TSi	699	594	615
Pkg. 21T/22T, DL	1099	934	967
Air conditioning, power steering. Pkg. 22T requires automatic transmission.			
Pkg. 21L/22L, DL	515	438	453
Power steering, rear defogger, cupholder console, cargo area cover, front floormats. Pkg. 22L requires automatic transmission.			
Pkg. 21M/22M, DL	1758	1494	1547
Pkg. 21L plus air conditioning, cruise control, cassette player. Pkg. 22M requires automatic transmission.			

	Retail Price	Dealer Invoice	Fair Price
Pkg. 23B/24B, ES	$1045	$888	$920
Air conditioning, cruise control. Pkg. 24B requires automatic transmission.			
Pkg. 23C/24C, ES	1646	1399	1448
Pkg. 23B plus power windows and locks, rear wiper/washer. Pkg. 24C requires automatic transmission.			
Pkg. 23D/24D, ES	2164	1839	1904
Pkg. 23C plus cassette player with equalizer, alloy wheels. Pkg. 24D requires automatic transmission.			
Pkg. 25G/26G, TSi	2164	1839	1904
Air conditioning, cruise control, rear wiper/washer, power windows and locks, cassette player with equalizer, alloy wheels. Pkg. 26G requires automatic transmission.			
Pkg. 25J/26J, TSi AWD	1862	1583	1639
Air conditioning, cruise control, rear wiper/washer, power windows and locks, cassette player with equalizer. Pkg. 26J requires automatic transmission.			
Rear defogger, DL	130	111	114
AM/FM cassette with CD player, ES and TSi	517	439	455
AM/FM cassette, DL	198	168	174
Removable sunroof	373	317	328
Leather seats, TSi	444	377	391
Alloy wheels, ES w/Pkg. 23C/24C	302	257	266

Plymouth Laser

	Retail Price	Dealer Invoice	Fair Price
3-door hatchback	$11542	$10811	$11111
RS 3-door hatchback	13910	12884	13284
RS Turbo 3-door hatchback	15444	14265	14765
RS Turbo AWD 3-door hatchback	17572	16220	16720
Destination charge	430	430	430

Standard Equipment:

1.8-liter 4-cylinder engine, 5-speed manual transmission, motorized front shoulder belts, 4-wheel disc brakes, cloth reclining front bucket seats, split folding rear seatback, center console, tachometer, coolant temperature and oil pressure gauges, trip odometer, tinted glass, remote fuel door and hatch releases, dual remote mirrors, visor mirrors, map lights, AM/FM radio, tilt steering column, intermittent wipers, 185/70R14 tires. **RS** adds: 2.0-liter DOHC 4-cylinder engine, power steering, driver-seat lumbar support adjustment, rear defogger, power mirrors, cassette player, tonneau cover, rear spoiler, 205/55R16 tires, wheel covers. **RS Turbo** adds: turbocharged, intercooled engine, turbo boost gauge, leather-wrapped steering wheel, 205/55VR16 tires. **RS Turbo AWD** adds: sport suspension, alloy wheels.

Optional Equipment:

	Retail Price	Dealer Invoice	Fair Price
Pkg. 21T/22T, base	$1099	$934	$989
Air conditioning, power steering. Pkg. 22T requires automatic transmission.			
Pkg. 21B/22B, base	827	703	744
Power steering, cup holder console, rear defogger, rear spoiler, cargo area cover, striping, floormats. Pkg. 22B requires automatic transmission.			
Pkg. 21C/22C, base	1654	1406	1489
Pkg. 21B plus air conditioning. Pkg. 22C requires automatic transmission.			
Pkg. 21D/22D, base	2070	1760	1863
Pkg. 21C plus cruise control, cassette player. Pkg. 22D requires automatic transmission.			
Pkg. 23F/24F, RS	921	783	829
Air conditioning, console cup holder, striping, floormats. Pkg. 24F requires automatic transmission.			
Pkg. 23G/24G, RS	1489	1265	1340
Pkg. 23F plus cruise control, cassette player with equalizer, rear wiper/washer. Pkg. 24G requires automatic transmission.			
Pkg. 23H/24H, RS	2013	1711	1812
Pkg. 23G plus power windows and locks, fog lamps. Pkg. 24H requires automatic transmission.			
Pkg. 25H/26H, RS Turbo	2013	1711	1812
Air conditioning, power windows and locks, cruise control, cassette player with equalizer, console cup holder, rear wiper/washer, fog lamps, striping, floormats. Pkg. 26H requires automatic transmission.			
Pkg. 25Q, RS Turbo AWD	2013	1711	1812
Pkg. 26Q, RS Turbo AWD	1956	1622	1760
Air conditioning, power windows and locks, cruise control, cassette player with equalizer, console cup holder, rear wiper/washer, fog lamps (Pkg. 25Q), striping, floormats. Pkg. 26Q requires automatic transmission.			
4-speed automatic transmission	716	609	630
Anti-lock brakes (Not available on base)	699	594	615
Cassette player	198	168	174
CD player (Not available on base)	517	439	455
Rear defogger, base	130	111	114
Sunroof	373	317	328
Gold Decor Pkg. (Not available on base)	NC	NC	NC
Gold striping and badging. Requires alloy wheels.			
Alloy wheels, RS and RS Turbo	302	257	266

MITSUBISHI EXPO/ EAGLE SUMMIT WAGON/ PLYMOUTH COLT VISTA

Mitsubishi Expo LRV

Specifications	4-door wagon	Expo 5-door wagon
Wheelbase, in.	99.2	107.1
Overall length, in.	168.6	177.4
Overall width, in.	66.7	66.7
Overall height, in.	62.1	62.6
Curb weight, lbs.	2745	3020
Cargo vol., cu. ft.	67.8	75.0
Fuel capacity, gals.	14.5	15.8
Seating capacity	5	7
Front head room, in.	40.0	39.3
Max. front leg room, in.	40.8	40.5
Rear head room, in.	38.6	39.3
Min. rear leg room, in.	36.1	37.7

Powertrain layout: transverse front engine/front-wheel drive or permanent 4WD.

Engines	ohc I-4	ohc I-4
Size, liters/cu. in.	1.8/112	2.4/143
Horsepower @ rpm	113 @ 6000	136 @ 5500

	ohc I-4	ohc I-4
Torque (lbs./ft.) @ rpm	116 @ 4500	145 @ 4250
Availability	S[1]	S[2]
EPA city/highway mpg		
5-speed OD manual	24/29	22/27
4-speed OD automatic	24/29	20/26

1. Base Expo LRV; Summit DL; base Vista. 2. Expo and LRV Sport; Summit LX and AWD; Vista SE and AWD.

Built in Japan.

PRICES

Mitsubishi Expo	Retail Price	Dealer Invoice	Fair Price
Base LRV 4-door wagon, 5-speed	$13019	$11716	$12216
Base LRV 4-door wagon, automatic	13859	12474	12974
LRV Sport 4-door wagon, 5-speed	16799	14619	15119
LRV Sport 4-door wagon, automatic	17489	15219	15719
Base 5-door wagon, 5-speed	15689	13648	14148
Base 5-door wagon, automatic	16379	14248	14748
Base AWD 5-door wagon, 5-speed	17129	14900	15400
Base AWD 5-door wagon, automatic	17819	15500	16000
Destination charge	445	445	445

Standard Equipment:

Base LRV: 1.8-liter 4-cylinder engine and 5-speed manual transmission, or 2.4-liter 4-cylinder engine and 4-speed automatic transmission, driver-side air bag, power steering, tilt steering column, cloth reclining front bucket seats, 50/50 folding rear bench seat, coolant temperature gauge, trip odometer, remote fuel door release, front air dam, color-keyed bumpers and bodyside molding, 2-tone paint, dual outside mirrors, rear window defogger, variable intermittent wipers, wheel covers, 185/75R14 tires. **LRV Sport** adds: 2.4-liter 4-cylinder engine, air conditioning, rear heater ducts, power windows and locks, power mirrors and tailgate lock/release, remote keyless entry, rear intermittent wiper/washer, cruise control, tachometer, digital clock, center armrest, map pockets, cargo cover, AM/FM cassette, 205/70R14 all-season tires, alloy wheels. **Base Expo** adds to base LRV: 2.4-liter 4-cylinder engine, 7-passenger seating with split folding middle and rear reclining bench seats, power mirrors, power tailgate lock/release, tachometer, digital clock, cargo cover, front storage tray, rear intermittent wiper/washer, 205/70R14 all-season tires. **Expo AWD** adds permanent 4-wheel drive.

Optional Equipment:	Retail Price	Dealer Invoice	Fair Price
Anti-lock brakes, (NA LRV base)	$976	$800	$866
Air conditioning	829	680	736
Power Pkg., Expo	894	715	784
LRV base	719	575	631
Power windows and locks, cruise control, remote keyless entry. LRV base adds: power mirrors and requires automatic transmission.			
Convenience Pkg., LRV base	596	477	523
Rear cargo cover, digital clock, center armrest, upgraded door trim, power door locks, power tailgate release, rear intermittent wiper/washer.			
Luggage rack	274	178	220
CD player, Expo	626	407	503
Power sunroof (NA LRV Sport or Expo AWD)	685	548	601
Cargo Kit, LRV	99	70	82
Cargo tray and net.			
AM/FM stereo, LRV base	334	217	268
AM/FM cassette	466	312	379
Floormats, LRV	73	47	58
Expo	85	55	68
Mud guards (front and rear)	84	54	67
Wheel locks, Expo	37	24	29
Alloy wheels, Expo	291	233	255

Eagle Summit Wagon	Retail Price	Dealer Invoice	Fair Price
DL 4-door wagon	$13114	$12158	$12614
LX 4-door wagon	14340	13261	13840
AWD 4-door wagon	15018	13871	14518
Destination charge	430	430	430

Standard Equipment:

DL: 1.8-liter 4-cylinder engine, 5-speed manual transmission, driver-side air bag, motorized front passenger, shoulder belt, power steering, cloth/vinyl reclining front bucket seats with center console, folding and removable rear seat, coolant temperature gauge, trip odometer, remote fuel door release, dual outside mirrors, intermittent wipers, passenger-side visor mirrors, 185/75R14 tires. **LX** adds: 2.4-liter 4-cylinder engine, cloth seats, split folding and removable rear seat with reclining back, tilt steering column, power mirrors, tinted glass, driver-side visor mirror, power locks, remote tailgate lock, rear wiper/washer, rear seat heater ducts, two-tone paint, rear stabilizer bar, wheel covers. **AWD** adds to DL: full-time 4-wheel drive, 2.4-liter 4-cylinder engine, remote tailgate lock, power mirrors, rear wiper/washer, driver-side visor mirror, rear stabilizer bar, 205/70R14 tires, wheel covers.

Optional Equipment:	Retail Price	Dealer Invoice	Fair Price
Pkg. 21C/22C, DL	$1156	$994	$1017
Air conditioning, tinted glass, rear defogger, rear wiper/washer, power mirrors, AM/FM radio, power tailgate lock, rear stabilizer bar, wheel covers. Pkg. 22C requires automatic transmission.			
Pkg. 21D/22D/24D, DL	1796	1545	1580
Pkg. 21C plus power locks, cruise control, cassette player, floormats. Pkg. 22D requires automatic transmission. Pkg. 24D requires 2.4-liter engine, automatic transmission.			
Pkg. 23K/24K, LX	1609	1384	1416
Air conditioning, rear defogger, power windows, cruise control, remote keyless entry, cassette player, cargo area cover, floormats. Pkg. 24K requires automatic transmission.			
Pkg. 23S/24S, AWD	673	579	592
Tinted glass, rear defogger, remote keyless entry, AM/FM radio, floormats, full cloth seats, split back reclining rear seat, upgraded interior trim. Pkg. 24S requires automatic transmission.			
Pkg. 23W/24W, AWD	2138	1839	1881
Pkg. 23S plus air conditioning, power windows, cruise control, cassette player, tachometer. Pkg. 24W requires automatic transmission.			
2.4-liter 4-cylinder engine, DL	181	156	159
4-speed automatic transmission	723	622	636
Anti-lock brakes	699	601	615
Includes rear disc brakes.			
Air conditioning, AWD	790	679	695
Rear defogger	66	57	58
Roof rack	151	130	133
AM/FM radio, DL and AWD	288	248	253
AM/FM cassette, DL and AWD	181	156	159
2-tone paint, LX and AWD	193	166	170
Floormats, DL and AWD	55	47	48

Plymouth Colt Vista	Retail Price	Dealer Invoice	Fair Price
Base 4-door wagon	$13114	$12158	$12614
SE 4-door wagon	14340	13261	13840
AWD 4-door wagon	15018	13871	14518
Destination charge	430	430	430

Standard Equipment:

Base: 1.8-liter 4-cylinder engine, 5-speed manual transmission, driver-side air bag, motorized front passenger shoulder belt, power steering, cloth/vinyl reclining front bucket seats with center console, folding and removable rear seat, rear seat heater ducts, coolant temperature gauge, trip odometer, tilt steering column, remote fuel door release, dual outside mirrors, intermittent wipers, passenger-side visor mirror, 185/75R14 tires. **SE** adds: 2.4-liter 4-cylinder engine, cloth seats with armrests, split folding and removable rear seat with reclining back, power mirrors, tinted glass, driver-side visor mirror, power locks, remote tailgate lock, rear wiper/washer, 2-tone paint, wheel covers. **AWD** adds to base: 2.4-liter 4-cylinder engine, full-time 4-wheel drive, power mirrors, driver-side visor mirror, rear wiper/washer, 205/70R14 tires, wheel covers.

Optional Equipment:	Retail Price	Dealer Invoice	Fair Price
Pkg. 21C/22C, base	$1156	$994	$1017
Air conditioning, tinted glass, rear defogger, rear wiper/washer, power mirrors, AM/FM radio, power tailgate lock, rear stabilizer bar, wheel covers. Pkg. 22C requires automatic transmission.			
Pkg. 21D/22D/24D, base	1796	1545	1580
Pkg. 21C plus power locks, cruise control, cassette player, floormats. Pkg. 22D requires automatic transmission. Pkg. 24D requires 2.4-liter engine, automatic transmission.			
Pkg. 23K/24K, SE	1609	1384	1416
Air conditioning, rear defogger, power windows, cruise control, remote keyless entry, cassette player, cargo area cover, floormats. Pkg. 24K requires automatic transmission.			
Pkg. 23S/24S, AWD	673	579	592
Tinted glass, rear defogger, remote keyless entry, AM/FM radio, floormats, full cloth seats, split back reclining rear seat, upgraded interior trim. Pkg. 24S requires automatic transmission.			
Pkg. 23W/24W	2138	1839	1881
Pkg. 23S plus air conditioning, power windows, cruise control, AM/FM cassette, tachometer. Pkg. 24W requires automatic transmission.			
2.4-liter 4-cylinder engine, base	181	156	159
4-speed automatic transmission	723	622	636
Anti-lock brakes	699	601	615
Includes rear disc brakes.			
Air conditioning, AWD	790	679	695
Rear defogger	66	57	58
Roof rack	151	130	133
AM/FM radio, base and AWD	288	248	253
AM/FM cassette, base and AWD	181	156	159
2-tone paint, SE and AWD	193	166	170
Floormats, base and AWD	55	47	48

MITSUBISHI GALANT

Mitsubishi Galant ES

Specifications

	4-door notchback
Wheelbase, in.	103.7
Overall length, in.	187.0
Overall width, in.	68.1
Overall height, in.	53.1
Curb weight, lbs.	2755
Cargo vol., cu. ft.	12.5
Fuel capacity, gals.	16.9
Seating capacity	5
Front head room, in.	39.4
Max. front leg room, in.	43.3
Rear head room, in.	37.5
Min. rear leg room, in.	35.0

Powertrain layout: transverse front engine/front-wheel drive.

Engines

	ohc I-4	dohc I-4
Size, liters/cu. in.	2.4/144	2.4/144
Horsepower @ rpm	141 @ 5500	160 @ 6000
Torque (lbs./ft.) @ rpm	148 @ 3000	160 @ 4250
Availability	S[1]	S[2]

EPA city/highway mpg

5-speed OD manual	23/30	22/29

	ohc I-4	dohc I-4
4-speed OD automatic	22/28	20/26

1. S, ES, LS. 2. GS.

Built in Normal, Ill.

PRICES

Mitsubishi Galant	Retail Price	Dealer Invoice	Fair Price
S 4-door notchback, 5-speed	$13600	$12104	—
S 4-door notchback, automatic	14500	12905	—
ES 4-door notchback, automatic	17195	14615	—
LS 4-door notchback, automatic	18670	15870	—
GS 4-door notchback, 5-speed	20494	17420	—
GS 4-door notchback, automatic	21277	18086	—
Destination charge	393	393	393

Fair price not available at time of publication.

Standard Equipment:

S: 2.4-liter 4-cylinder engine, 5-speed manual or 4-speed automatic transmission, driver- and passenger-side air bags, power steering, 5-way adjustable driver's seat, tinted glass, cloth upholstery, rear defogger, tilt steering column, center console armrest with storage, driver-side door map pocket, cup holders, remote fuel door and decklid releases, driver-side visor mirror, intermittent wipers, tachometer, coolant temperature gauge, color-keyed bumpers and bodyside moldings, dual manual remote outside mirrors, day/night rearview mirror, digital clock, 185/70HR14 all-season tires, full wheel covers. **ES** adds: 4-speed automatic transmission, air conditioning, cruise control, power windows and door locks, AM/FM cassette with six speakers, automatic power diversity antenna, color-keyed dual power remote outside mirrors, folding rear seat with center armrest, full cloth upholstery and door trim, passenger-side visor mirror, door map pockets. **LS** adds: power glass sunroof with sun shade, variable intermittent wipers, 6-way adjustable front seats, fog lamps, ETACS-IV (includes ignition key illumination, seat belt warning timer/chime, headlight on warning chime, rear defogger timer, fade out dome light), lighted visor mirrors, front seatback map pockets, center sunvisor, floormats, 195/60HR15 all-season tires, alloy wheels. **GS** adds: 2.4-liter DOHC 4-cylinder engine, 5-speed manual or 4-speed automatic transmission, AM/FM cassette/CD player with six speakers, rear decklid spoiler, leather-wrapped steering wheel and shift knob, rear stabilzer bar.

Optional Equipment:	Retail Price	Dealer Invoice	Fair Price
Anti-lock brakes, ES, LS, and GS	$924	$758	—
Air conditioning, S	827	678	—
AM/FM cassette player, S	457	297	—
CD player, S, ES, and LS	641	449	—
S requires AM/FM cassette player.			
Keyless remote entry system, ES, LS, and GS	223	145	—
Mud guards	117	76	—
Floormats	73	47	—
Sunroof wind deflector, LS and GS	52	34	—

MITSUBISHI MIRAGE

Mitsubishi Mirage ES 4-door

Specifications	2-door notchback	4-door notchback
Wheelbase, in.	96.1	98.4
Overall length, in.	171.1	172.2
Overall width, in.	66.5	66.5
Overall height, in.	51.6	52.2
Curb weight, lbs.	2085	2195
Cargo vol., cu. ft.	10.7	10.5
Fuel capacity, gals.	13.2	13.2
Seating capacity	5	5
Front head room, in.	38.6	39.2
Max. front leg room, in.	42.9	42.9
Rear head room, in.	36.4	37.2
Min. rear leg room, in.	31.1	33.5

Powertrain layout: transverse front engine/front-wheel drive.

MITSUBISHI

Engines

	ohc I-4	ohc I-4
Size, liters/cu. in.	1.5/90	1.8/112
Horsepower @ rpm	92 @ 6000	113 @ 6000
Torque (lbs./ft.) @ rpm	93 @ 3000	116 @ 4500
Availability	S	S[1]
EPA city/highway mpg		
5-speed OD manual	32/39	26/33
3-speed automatic	28/32	
4-speed OD automatic		26/33

1. LS 2-door, ES and LS 4-door.

Built in Japan.

PRICES

Mitsubishi Mirage	Retail Price	Dealer Invoice	Fair Price
S 2-door notchback, 5-speed	$8989	$7433	$7633
ES 2-door notchback, 5-speed	10359	8317	8517
ES 2-door notchback, 3-speed automatic	10839	8747	8947
LS 2-door notchback, 5-speed	11879	9551	9751
LS 2-door notchback, 4-speed automatic	12459	9981	10181
S 4-door notchback, 5-speed	11369	8882	9082
S 4-door notchback, 3-speed automatic	11849	9312	9512
ES 4-door notchback, 5-speed	11929	9849	10049
ES 4-door notchback, 4-speed automatic	12579	10431	10631
LS 4-door notchback, 4-speed automatic	14529	11645	11845
Destination charge	420	420	420

Standard Equipment:

S 2-door: 1.5-liter 4-cylinder engine, 5-speed manual transmission, driver-side air bag, front bucket seats with vinyl and cloth upholstery, locking fuel-filler door, rear defogger, center console with storage, coolant temperature gauge, 145/80R13 tires. **ES 2-door** adds: 5-speed manual or 3-speed automatic transmission, power steering, height-adjustable driver's seat, cloth upholstery, day/night rearview mirror, front door map pockets, remote fuel filler and trunk release, trip odometer, radio accommodation package, color-keyed bumpers and grille, tinted glass, manual remote mirrors, wheel covers, 155/80R13 tires. **S 4-door** adds to S 2-door: 5-speed manual or 3-speed automatic transmission, power steering, day/night rearview mirror, door map pockets, color-keyed bumpers and grille, digital clock, cloth upholstery, child-proof rear door locks, low-fuel warning light, radio accommodation package, 175/70R13 all-season tires, wheel covers. **ES 4-door** adds to S 4-door: 1.8-liter engine, 5-speed manual or 4-speed automatic transmission, height-adjustable driver's seat, day/night rearview mirror, tinted glass, manual remote mirrors, upgraded door trim, remote fuel door and trunk release, trip odometer, intermittent wipers, 185/65R13 all-season tires. **LS 2-door** adds to ES 2-door: 1.8-liter engine, split folding rear seat, cloth upholstery, tachometer (with manual transmission), intermittent wipers, tilt steering column, full trunk trim, digital clock, trunk light, AM/FM cassette, rear spoiler, power mirrors, 185/65R13 all-season tires, alloy wheels. **LS 4-door** adds to ES 4-door: 4-speed automatic transmission, split folding rear seat with center armrest, cruise control, variable intermittent wipers, tilt steering column, power mirrors, windows and door locks, cloth upholstery, color-keyed bodyside molding, alloy wheels.

Optional Equipment:	Retail Price	Dealer Invoice	Fair Price
Air conditioning	$805	$660	$732
Cruise control, ES 4-door	225	180	202
Power Pkg., ES 4-door	531	425	478
Power windows and locks.			
Convenience Pkg., ES 4-door	169	135	152
Includes luxury front and rear seats, tilt steering column, upgraded upholstery, split folding rear seat with center armrest.			
Convenience Pkg., ES 2-door	215	172	193
Includes digital clock, intermittent wipers, cloth door trim, split folding rear seat, trunk trim, trunk courtesy light.			
CD player	626	407	516
Requires AM/FM cassette player.			
Radio accommodation pkg., S 2-door	76	53	64
AM/FM radio, S and ES	334	234	284
AM/FM cassette, S and ES	446	312	379
Rear spoiler, ES 2-door	213	170	191
Wheel locks, LS	33	21	27
Wheel trim rings, S	68	44	56
Mud guards, 2-doors (NA S)	99	67	83
4-doors	98	64	81
Floormats	64	41	52

Prices are accurate at time of publication; subject to manufacturer's change.

MITSUBISHI 3000GT/ DODGE STEALTH

Mitsubishi 3000GT VR-4

Specifications	3-door hatchback
Wheelbase, in.	97.2
Overall length, in.	178.9
Overall width, in.	72.4
Overall height, in.	49.1
Curb weight, lbs.	3064
Cargo vol., cu. ft.	11.1
Fuel capacity, gals.	19.8
Seating capacity	4
Front head room, in.	37.1
Max. front leg room, in.	44.2
Rear head room, in.	34.1
Min. rear leg room, in.	28.5

Powertrain layout: transverse front engine/front-wheel drive or permanent 4WD.

Engines	ohc V-6	dohc V-6	Turbo dohc V-6
Size, liters/cu. in.	3.0/181	3.0/181	3.0/181
Horsepower @ rpm	164 @ 5500	222 @ 6000	320 @ 6000
Torque (lbs./ft.) @ rpm	185 @ 4000	201 @ 4500	315 @ 2500
Availability	S[1]	S[2]	S[3]

EPA city/highway mpg	ohc V-6	dohc V-6	Turbo dohc V-6
5-speed OD manual	19/24	18/25	
6-speed OD manual			18/24
4-speed OD automatic	18/23	18/24	

1. Base Stealth. 2. Base and 3000GT SL; Stealth R/T. 3. 3000GT VR-4; Stealth R/T Turbo.

Built in Japan.

PRICES

Mitsubishi 3000GT	Retail Price	Dealer Invoice	Fair Price
3-door hatchback, 5-speed	$27175	$22286	$22786
3-door hatchback, automatic	28050	22998	23498
SL 3-door hatchback, 5-speed	31650	25955	26995
SL 3-door hatchback, automatic	32525	26667	27667
VR-4 3-door hatchback, 6-speed	40900	33529	35029
Destination charge	470	470	470

Standard Equipment:

3.0-liter DOHC V-6, 5-speed manual or 4-speed automatic transmission, 4-wheel disc brakes, power steering, driver- and passenger-side air bags, air conditioning, power windows, door locks and mirrors, ETACS alarm control system, cruise control, rear spoiler, 6-way adjustable cloth front bucket seats, split folding rear seat, center storage console with coin and cup holders, tachometer, coolant temperature and oil pressure gauges, voltmeter, trip odometer, remote fuel door and hatch releases, AM/FM cassette with equalizer and anti-theft circuitry, power antenna, tilt steering column, leather-wrapped steering wheel, fog lamps, variable intermittent wipers, rear intermittent wiper, visor mirrors, rear defogger, digital clock, tinted glass, cargo area cover, 225/55VR16 tires, alloy wheels. **SL** adds: anti-lock brakes, electronically controlled suspension, automatic climate control, 7-way adjustable driver's seat, rear wiper/washer, remote keyless entry, Mitsubishi/Infinity audio system with external amp, eight speakers and steering-wheel mounted radio controls, heated power mirrors, auxiliary power outlet. **VR-4** adds: turbocharged, intercooled engine, permanent 4-wheel drive, 4-wheel steering, limited-slip rear differential, Active Aero with retractable front air dam extension and motorized rear spoiler, Active Exhaust, leather seats, turbo boost gauge, 245/45ZR17 tires.

Optional Equipment:

CD auto changer	799	530	687
Sunroof, SL and VR-4	375	300	322

Prices are accurate at time of publication; subject to manufacturer's change.

	Retail Price	Dealer Invoice	Fair Price
Chrome wheels, VR-4	$500	$400	$430
Leather front seat trim, SL	1120	—	—
Yellow pearl paint, SL and VR-4	313	250	269
Mud guards	142	92	122

Dodge Stealth R/T Turbo

Dodge Stealth

	Retail Price	Dealer Invoice	Fair Price
3-door hatchback	$21145	$19223	$19723
R/T 3-door hatchback	23931	21674	22674
R/T Turbo 3-door hatchback	37894	33962	35462
Destination charge	430	430	430

Standard Equipment:

3.0-liter V-6 engine, 5-speed manual transmission, 4-wheel disc brakes, power steering, driver- and passenger-side air bags, cloth/vinyl reclining front bucket seats, driver's seat lumbar and height adjustment, split folding rear seat, console with armrest, tachometer, coolant temperature and oil pressure gauges, trip odometer, tinted glass, rear defogger, intermittent wipers, remote fuel door and hatch releases, power mirrors, AM/FM radio, tilt steering column, leather-wrapped steering wheel, visor mirrors, 205/65HR15 tires, wheel covers. **R/T** adds: 3.0-liter DOHC V-6 engine, 225/55VR16 tires, alloy wheels. **R/T Turbo** adds: turbocharged engine, 6-speed manual transmission, permanent 4-wheel drive, anti-lock brakes, 4-wheel steering, Electronic Variable Damping Suspension, automatic climate control, turbo boost gauge, heated power mirrors, power windows and locks, power driver's seat with power lumbar adjustment, AM/FM cassette with equalizer, power antenna, cruise control, remote keyless entry system, security alarm, lighted visor mirrors, rear spoiler, rear wiper/washer, floormats, 245/45ZR17 tires.

Optional Equipment:	Retail Price	Dealer Invoice	Fair Price
Pkg. 21C/22C, base and Pkg. 23H/24H, R/T	$2294	$1973	$2065
Air conditioning, power windows and locks, cruise control, remote keyless entry system, cassette player with equalizer, rear wiper/washer, rear spoiler, floormats. Pkgs. 22C and 24H require automatic transmission.			
Pkg. 23M/24M, R/T	3197	2749	2877
Pkg. 23H plus trunk-mounted CD changer, eight Infinity speakers. Pkg. 24M requires automatic transmission.			
Pkg. 23P/24P, R/T	7980	6863	7182
Pkg. 23M Luxury Equipment Group (Electronic Variable Damping Suspension, power driver's seat, heated power mirrors, steering wheel radio controls, power antenna), sunroof. Pkg. 24P requires automatic transmission.			
Pkg. 25W, R/T Turbo AWD	903	777	813
Trunk-mounted CD changer, eight Infinity speakers.			
Pkg. 25Y, R/T Turbo AWD	1264	1087	1138
Pkg. 25W plus sunroof.			
4-speed automatic transmission, base, R/T	863	742	777
Leather seats, R/T	843	724	759
Security Pkg.	1225	1054	1103
Base w/Pkgs. 21C, 22C	960	826	864
R/T w/Pkgs. 23H, 24H, 23M, 24M	960	826	864
Anti-lock brakes, security alarm, remote keyless entry system, power locks.			
Trunk-mounted CD changer	542	466	488
Requires Option Pkg.			
Sunroof	361	310	325
Requires Option Pkg.			
Chrome wheels, R/T Turbo AWD	482	415	434
Extra cost paint	181	156	163

NISSAN ALTIMA

Specifications	4-door notchback
Wheelbase, in.	103.1
Overall length, in.	180.5

Nissan Altima GLE

	4-door notchback
Overall width, in.	67.1
Overall height, in.	55.9
Curb weight, lbs.	2829
Cargo vol., cu. ft.	14.0
Fuel capacity, gals.	15.9
Seating capacity	5
Front head room, in.	39.3
Front leg room, max., in.	42.6
Rear head room, in.	37.6
Rear leg room, min. , in.	34.7

Powertrain layout: transverse front engine/front-wheel drive.

Engines	dohc I-4
Size, liters/cu. in.	2.4/146
Horsepower @ rpm	150 @ 5600
Torque (lbs/ft) @ rpm	154 @ 4400
Availability	S

EPA city/highway mpg

5-speed OD manual	24/30
4-speed OD automatic	21/29

Built in Smyrna, Tenn.

PRICES

Nissan Altima	Retail Price	Dealer Invoice	Fair Price
XE 4-door notchback, 5-speed	$13999	$12351	$13199

	Retail Price	Dealer Invoice	Fair Price
XE 4-door notchback, automatic	$14889	$13137	$14089
GXE 4-door notchback, 5-speed	15154	13216	14354
GXE 4-door notchback, automatic	15979	13935	15179
SE 4-door notchback, 5-speed	18179	15761	17379
SE 4-door notchback, automatic	19004	16476	18204
GLE 4-door notchback, automatic	19179	16628	18379
Destination charge	380	380	380

Standard Equipment:

XE: 2.4-liter DOHC 4-cylinder engine, 5-speed manual or 4-speed automatic transmission, driver- and passenger-side air bags, power steering, tilt steering column, rear window defroster, dual cup holders, remote trunk and fuel door releases, cloth seats, center front console, tachometer, coolant temperature gauge, low fuel warning light, digital clock, child safety rear door locks, tinted glass, dual power mirrors, front map pockets, 205/60R15 tires, styled steel wheels. **GXE** adds: power windows with auto down driver's window, power locks, rear seat center armrest with trunk pass-through. **SE** adds: 4-wheel disc brakes, air conditioning, cruise control, front sport seats, AM/FM cassette, power diversity antenna, variable intermittent wipers, alloy wheels, fog lights, front cornering lights, bodyside cladding and rear spoiler, power sunroof, front sport seats, leather-wrapped steering wheel and shift knob. **GLE** adds to GXE: automatic transmission, automatic temperature control, cruise control, variable intermittent wipers, front cornering lights, theft deterrent system, head-up display, AM/FM cassette and CD player, power diversity antenna, power sunroof, adjustable lumbar support, alloy wheels.

Optional Equipment:

	Retail Price	Dealer Invoice	Fair Price
Anti-lock 4-wheel disc brakes, XE *Requires XE Option Pkg.*	995	843	897
Anti-lock brakes with limited-slip differential *Not available XE; GXE requires GXE Value Opt. Pkg.*	1195	1012	1077
Cruise control, XE *Requires automatic transmission.*	230	195	207
Leather Trim Pkg., SE and GLE *Not available with sport seats.*	1000	847	901
XE Opt. Pkg. *Air conditioning, AM/FM cassette, cruise control.*	1825	1545	1644

Prices are accurate at time of publication; subject to manufacturer's change.

	Retail Price	Dealer Invoice	Fair Price
Power sunroof, GXE	$825	$699	$743
Requires GXE Value Option Pkg. with automatic transmission.			
GXE Value Opt. Pkg.	1200	1016	1081
AM/FM cassette, air conditioning, cruise control, power antenna.			

NISSAN MAXIMA

Nissan Maxima GXE

Specifications

Specifications	4-door notchback
Wheelbase, in.	104.3
Overall length, in.	187.6
Overall width, in.	69.3
Overall height, in.	55.1
Curb weight, lbs.	3129
Cargo vol., cu. ft.	14.5
Fuel capacity, gals.	18.5
Seating capacity	5
Front head room, in.	39.5
Max. front leg room, in.	43.7
Rear head room, in.	36.9
Min. rear leg room, in.	33.2

Powertrain layout: transverse front engine/front-wheel drive.

Engines

Engines	ohc V-6	dohc V-6
Size, liters/cu. in.	3.0/181	3.0/181
Horsepower @ rpm	160 @ 5200	190 @ 5600

	ohc V-6	dohc V-6
Torque (lbs./ft.) @ rpm	182 @ 2800	190 @ 4000
Availability	S[1]	S[2]
EPA city/highway mpg		
5-speed OD manual		21/26
4-speed OD automatic	19/26	19/25

1. GXE. 2. SE.

Built in Japan.

PRICES

Nissan Maxima	Retail Price	Dealer Invoice	Fair Price
GXE 4-door notchback, automatic	$22429	$19446	$19946
SE 4-door notchback, 5-speed	23529	20400	20900
SE 4-door notchback, automatic	24464	21210	21710
Destination charge	380	380	380

Standard Equipment:

GXE: 3.0-liter V-6, 4-speed automatic transmission, driver-side air bag, motorized front shoulder belts, power steering, air conditioning, cruise control with steering mounted controls, power windows with auto-down driver's window, power locks with keyless entry, cloth reclining front bucket seats, driver's seat height and lumbar adjustments, fold down rear armrest, door map pockets, heated power mirrors, cruise control, tinted glass, AM/FM cassette with automatic power diversity antenna, theft deterrent system, tilt steering column, variable-intermittent wipers, dual cup holders, rear defogger, remote fuel door and decklid releases, illuminated entry, visor mirrors, dual overhead map lights, tachometer, trip odometer, coolant temperature gauge, digital clock, 205/65R15 tires, alloy wheels. **SE** deletes keyless entry and adds: 3.0-liter DOHC V-6 engine, 5-speed manual or 4-speed automatic transmission, 4-wheel disc brakes, limited-slip differential, Bose audio system, rear spoiler, leather-wrapped steering wheel and shifter, fog lamps.

Optional Equipment:

Anti-lock brakes *SE requires sunroof.*	995	843	897
CD player, SE *Requires sunroof; deletes cup holders.*	400	339	360

	Retail Price	Dealer Invoice	Fair Price
Luxury Pkg., GXE	$2595	$2197	$2338
Power sunroof, 4-way power front seats, Nissan-Bose AM/FM cassette/ CD audio system, automatic climate control, leather-wrapped steering wheel, shift lever, and parking brake handle.			
Leather Trim Pkg., GXE	1025	868	923
SE	1425	1207	1284
SE includes 4-way power front seats and requires sunroof; GXE requires Luxury Pkg.			
Pearlglow paint	350	297	316
Power sunroof, SE	875	741	788

NISSAN PATHFINDER

Nissan Pathfinder SE

Specifications	5-door wagon
Wheelbase, in.	104.3
Overall length, in.	171.9
Overall width, in.	66.5
Overall height, in.	65.7
Curb weight, lbs.	3885
Cargo vol., cu. ft.	80.2
Fuel capacity, gals.	20.4
Seating capacity	5
Front head room, in.	39.3
Max. front leg room, in.	42.6
Rear head room, in.	36.8
Min. rear leg room, in.	33.1

Powertrain layout: longitudinal front engine/rear-wheel drive or on-demand 4WD.

Engines	ohc V-6
Size, liters/cu. in.	3.0/181
Horsepower @ rpm	153 @ 4800
Torque (lbs./ft.) @ rpm	180 @ 4000
Availability	S
EPA city/highway mpg	
5-speed OD manual	15/18
4-speed OD automatic	15/18

Built in Japan.

PRICES

Nissan Pathfinder	Retail Price	Dealer Invoice	Fair Price
XE 2WD 5-door wagon, 5-speed	$19669	$17253	$17653
XE 2WD 5-door wagon, automatic	20889	18324	18724
XE 4WD 5-door wagon, 5-speed	21339	18719	19119
XE 4WD 5-door wagon, automatic	22708	19921	20321
SE 4WD 5-door wagon, 5-speed	25249	22148	22548
SE 4WD 5-door wagon, automatic	26349	23113	23513
LE 4WD 5-door wagon, automatic	29239	25649	26049
Destination charge	380	380	380

Standard Equipment:

XE: 3.0-liter V-6, 5-speed manual or 4-speed automatic transmission, anti-lock rear brakes, power steering, part-time 4WD with automatic locking front hubs (4WD), cloth reclining front bucket seats, split folding and reclining rear seat, tachometer, coolant temperature gauge, trip odometer, digital clock, rear wiper/washer, tinted glass, dual outside mirrors, front tow hooks, AM/FM cassette with diversity antenna, tilt steering column, rear defogger, front door map pockets, remote fuel door release, cargo tiedown hooks, skid plates, fender flares and mud guards (4WD), 235/75R15 tires, chrome wheels. **SE** adds: power windows and locks, cruise control, variable-intermittent wipers, heated power mirrors, remote rear window release, voltmeter, rear quarter privacy glass, upgraded upholstery, flip-up removable sunroof, lighted

Prices are accurate at time of publication; subject to manufacturer's change.

visor mirrors, map lights, driver's seat height and lumbar support adjustments, folding rear armrests, step rail, fog lamps, rear wind deflector, alloy wheels, remote security system, outside spare tire carrier, 31x10.5 tires. **LE** adds: 4-speed automatic transmission, 4-wheel disc brakes, air conditioning, limited-slip differential, running board and splash guards, heated front seats, leather upholstery, leather-wrapped steering wheel, CD player.

Options not available at time of publication.

NISSAN SENTRA

Nissan Sentra GXE

Specifications	2-door notchback	4-door notchback
Wheelbase, in.	95.7	95.7
Overall length, in.	170.3	170.3
Overall width, in.	65.6	65.6
Overall height, in.	53.9	53.9
Curb weight, lbs.	2324	2346
Cargo vol., cu. ft.	11.7	11.7
Fuel capacity, gals.	13.2	13.2
Seating capacity	5	5
Front head room, in.	38.5	38.5
Max. front leg room, in.	41.9	41.9
Rear head room, in.	36.6	36.6
Min. rear leg room, in.	30.9	30.9

Powertrain layout: transverse front engine/front-wheel drive.

Engines	dohc I-4	dohc I-4
Size, liters/cu. in.	1.6/97	2.0/122

	dohc I-4	dohc I-4
Horsepower @ rpm	110 @ 6000	140 @ 6400
Torque (lbs./ft.) @ rpm	108 @ 4000	132 @ 4800
Availability	S	S[1]
EPA city/highway mpg		
5-speed OD manual	29/38	23/31
4-speed OD automatic	26/35	23/30

1. SE-R.

Built in Smyrna, Tenn., and Japan.

PRICES

Nissan Sentra	Retail Price	Dealer Invoice	Fair Price
E 2-door notchback, 5-speed	$10199	$9571	$9771
E 2-door notchback, automatic	12149	11401	11601
XE 2-door notchback, 5-speed	12549	11136	11336
XE 2-door notchback, automatic	13349	11846	12046
SE 2-door notchback, 5-speed	13049	11513	11713
SE 2-door notchback, automatic	13849	12219	12419
SE-R 2-door notchback, 5-speed	14249	12572	12872
SE-R 2-door notchback, automatic	15049	13277	13577
E 4-door notchback, 5-speed	11049	10368	10568
E 4-door notchback, automatic	12349	11588	11788
XE 4-door notchback, 5-speed	12749	11314	11514
XE 4-door notchback, automatic	13549	12024	12224
GXE 4-door notchback, 5-speed	14819	13074	13374
GXE 4-door notchback, automatic	15619	13780	14080
Destination charge	380	380	380

Standard Equipment:

E 2-door: 1.6-liter DOHC 4-cylinder engine, 5-speed manual or 4-speed automatic transmission, door-mounted automatic front shoulder belts, cloth reclining front bucket seats, rear defogger, tinted glass, coolant temperature gauge, dual cup holders, door map pockets, trip odometer, 155/80R13 tires (models with automatic transmission have 175/70R13 tires, power steering and tilt steering column); **4-door** has motorized front shoulder belts, child-safety rear door locks. **XE** adds: air conditioning, cruise control, AM/FM cassette with diversity antenna, power steering, tilt steering column, power mirrors, body-color bumpers, deluxe door trim, intermittent wipers, locking glovebox, remote trunk and fuel-door releases, digital clock, wheel covers, 175/70R13 tires. **GXE** adds to XE: driver-side air bag, power windows and locks, velour upholstery, split folding rear seat, tachometer, alloy wheels. **SE** deletes air conditioning and adds to XE: front air dam, rear spoiler, sport bucket seats, velour uoholstery, leather-wrapped steering wheel, leather-wrapped shift knob (5-speed), rear spoiler, tachometer. **SE-R** adds to SE: 2.0-liter DOHC engine, 4-wheel disc brakes, limited-slip differential, sport suspension, fog lights, 185/60R14 tires, alloy wheels.

Optional Equipment:	Retail Price	Dealer Invoice	Fair Price
Driver-side air bag (std., GXE)	$575	$487	$531
Anti-lock brakes, GXE and SE-R	700	593	647
Not available with sunroof on GXE. GXE includes rear discs.			
Air conditioning (std. XE and GXE)	995	843	919
Power sunroof, GXE and SE-R	825	699	762
Not available with anti-lock brakes on GXE.			
Power Steering Pkg., E with manual transmission	500	423	462
Power steering, tilt steering column, front and rear stabilizer bars, 175/70R13 all-season tires, wheel covers.			
Value Option Pkg., SE and SE-R	1300	1101	1201
Air conditioning, AM/FM cassette with diversity antenna, cruise control.			
Cruise control, SE and SE-R	230	195	213
AM/FM cassette with diversity antenna, SE and SE-R	600	508	554

1995 OLDSMOBILE AURORA

Specifications	4-door notchback
Wheelbase, in.	113.8
Overall length, in.	205.4
Overall width, in.	74.4
Overall height, in.	55.4
Curb weight, lbs.	4000
Cargo vol., cu. ft.	16.1
Fuel capacity, gals.	20.0
Seating capacity	5
Front head room, in.	38.4

1995 Oldsmobile Aurora

	4-door notchback
Max. front leg room, in.	42.6
Rear head room, in.	36.9
Min. rear leg room, in.	38.4

Powertrain layout: transverse front engine/front-wheel drive.

Engines	dohc V-8
Size, liters/cu. in.	4.0/244
Horsepower @ rpm	250 @ 5600
Torque (lbs./ft.) @ rpm	260 @ 4400
Availability	S
EPA city/highway mpg	
4-speed OD automatic	16/25

Built in Orion, Mich.

PRICES

1995 Oldsmobile Aurora	Retail Price	Dealer Invoice	Fair Price
4-door notchback	$31370	$29017	—
Destination charge	625	625	625

Fair price not available at time of publication.

Standard Equipment:

4.0-liter DOHC V-8 engine, 4-speed automatic transmission, anti-

Prices are accurate at time of publication; subject to manufacturer's change.

lock 4-wheel disc brakes, driver- and passenger-side air bags, traction control, variable-assist power steering, automatic climate control system, tinted glass, AM/FM radio with cassette player, power antenna, steering wheel touch controls, leather-wrapped steering wheel, leather upholstery, power front buckets seats with 2-position memory for driver's side, power windows and door locks, power mirrors, intermittent wipers, Pass-Key theft deterrent system, remote keyless entry system, tachometer, temperature, voltage, and oil pressure gauges, trip odometer, oil level sensor, cruise control, rear defogger, folding rear armrest with trunk pass-through, 235/60R16 tires, alloy wheels.

Optional Equipment:	Retail Price	Dealer Invoice	Fair Price
Power sunroof	$995	$856	—
Bose Acoustimass Sound System	671	577	—
Heated driver and front passenger seats	295	254	—
235/60VR16 tires	395	340	—
Includes 3.71 axle ratio.			
Engine block heater	18	15	—

OLDSMOBILE CUTLASS CIERA/BUICK CENTURY

Specifications	4-door notchback	5-door wagon
Wheelbase, in.	104.9	104.9
Overall length, in.	190.3	194.4
Overall width, in.	69.5	69.5
Overall height, in.	54.1	54.5
Curb weight, lbs.	2833	3086
Cargo vol., cu. ft.	15.8	74.4
Fuel capacity, gals.	16.5	16.5
Seating capacity	6	8
Front head room, in.	38.6	38.6
Max. front leg room, in.	42.1	42.1
Rear head room, in.	38.3	38.9
Min. rear leg room, in.	35.8	34.7

Powertrain layout: transverse front engine/front-wheel drive.

Engines	ohv I-4	ohv V-6
Size, liters/cu. in.	2.2/133	3.1/191

Oldsmobile Cutlass Ciera S

	ohv I-4	ohv V-6
Horsepower @ rpm	120 @ 5200	160 @ 5200
Torque (lbs./ft.) @ rpm	130 @ 4000	185 @ 4000
Availability	S	O
EPA city/highway mpg		
3-speed automatic	25/31	
4-speed OD automatic		19/29

Built in Oklahoma City, Okla.

PRICES

Oldsmobile Cutlass Ciera	Retail Price	Dealer Invoice	Fair Price
S 4-door notchback	$16070	$14383	$14883
S Special Edition 4-door notchback, Pkg. R7B	14195	13850	—
S Special Edition 4-door notchback, Pkg. R7C	16195	15333	—
Cruiser S 5-door wagon	17570	15725	16225
Crusier S Special Edition wagon, Pkg. R7D	17195	16278	—
Destination charge	525	525	525

S Special Edition fair price not available at time of publication. S Special Edition models include destination charge. Additional "value-priced" models may be available in California.

Standard Equipment:

S: 2.2-liter 4-cylinder engine, 3-speed automatic transmission, anti-lock brakes, driver-side air bag, door-mounted automatic front seatbelts, power steering, air conditioning, 55/45 bench seat with armrest and power seatback recliners, automatic power locks, tilt steering wheel, AM/FM radio, tinted glass, left remote and right manual mirrors, rear defogger, intermittent wipers, illuminated entry system, reading lights, 185/75R14 whitewall tires, wheel covers. **S Special Edition Pkg. R7B** adds to S: floormats. **S Special Edition Pkg. R7C** adds to S: 3.1-liter V-6 engine, 4-speed automatic transmission, power windows, cruise control, power mirrors, cassette player, front storage armrest. **Cruiser S Special Edition** adds to Cruiser S wagon: rear-facing third seat, roof luggage carrier, rear air deflector.

Optional Equipment:	Retail Price	Dealer Invoice	Fair Price
3.1-liter V-6 engine, S 4-door	$810	$697	$713
Includes 4-speed automatic transmission.			
Option Pkg. 1SB, S 4-door	562	483	495
S wagon	717	617	631
Cruise control, power mirrors, cassette player, front storage armrest, floormats. Wagon adds: roof luggage carrier, rear air deflector.			
Option Pkg. 1SC, S 4-door	1232	1060	1084
S wagon	1327	1141	1168
Pkg. 1SB plus power windows, Remote Lock Control Pkg., 6-speaker radio, power antenna.			
Variable-assist power steering, S	62	53	55
Requires V-6 and Pkg. 1SC.			
Power driver's seat, S	305	262	268
Requires Pkg. 1SC.			
Custom leather trim, S	425	366	374
Requires Pkg. 1SC.			
Wagon Pkg., S wagon	328	282	289
Rear-facing third seat, rear vent windows and cargo area cover. Requires Pkg. 1SB or 1SC.			
Power windows, S	340	292	299
Requires Pkg. 1SB.			
Remote Lock Control Pkg. S 4-door	185	159	163
S wagon	125	108	110
Includes door and decklid/tailgate lock releases, illuminated entry and key-chain transmitter. Requires Pkg. 1SB.			
Wire wheel covers, S	240	206	211
Not available with 195/75R14 tires.			
Cassette player, Special Edition	140	120	123
Cassette player with equalizer, S	150	129	132
S requires Pkg. 1SC.			
High-capacity cooling	40	34	35
Requires V-6.			
Engine block heater	18	15	16

	Retail Price	Dealer Invoice	Fair Price
Decklid luggage rack, S 4-door	$115	$99	$101
Requires Pkg. 1SB or 1SC.			
Woodgrain exterior trim, S wagon	325	280	286
Requires Molding Pkg.			
Floormats, S	45	39	40
Molding Pkg., S	151	130	133
Lower bodyside moldings, rocker panel and wheel opening moldings, door edge guards.			
Trunk net, S	30	26	27
Striping, S	45	39	40
195/75R14 whitewall tires, S	40	34	35
with alloy wheels	295	254	260

Buick Century

	Retail Price	Dealer Invoice	Fair Price
Special 4-door notchback	$15800	$14141	$14641
National Marketing Edition 4-door notchback	14995	14214	—
Special 5-door wagon	16650	14902	15402
National Marketing Edition 5-door wagon	15995	15191	—
Custom 4-door notchback	17000	14875	15375
Destination charge	525	525	525

National Marketing Edition models' fair price not available at time of publication. National Marketing Edition models include destination charge and are available with limited optional equipment. Additional "value-priced" models may be available in California.

Standard Equipment:

Special: 2.2-liter 4-cylinder engine, 3-speed automatic transmission, anti-lock brakes, driver-side air bag, door-mounted automatic front seatbelts, power steering, air conditioning, automatic power door locks, tilt steering wheel, intermittent wipers, left remote and right manual mirrors, tinted glass, battery voltage and engine temperature gauges, trip odometer, map lights, instrument panel courtesy lights, 55/45 cloth seats with armrest, power front seatback recliners, AM/FM radio with digital clock with seek and scan, body-color bodyside molding, 185/75R14 tires, wheel covers. **Wagon** has: remote tailgate release, split-folding rear seatback, cargo area light, cargo area storage compartments, black bodyside moldings. **National Marketing Edition** models add: cruise control, power windows, rear defogger, rear facing third seat (wagon), front storage armrest, remote decklid release (4-door), roof luggage carrier (wagon), air deflector (wagon), cargo area cover (wagon), swingout rear vent windows (wagon), visor mirrors, floormats, 185/75R14 whitewall tires. **Custom** adds: front storage armrest with cup holders, covered visor mirrors, bright wheel opening moldings, door courtesy lights, whitewall tires, styled wheel covers.

Optional Equipment:	Retail Price	Dealer Invoice	Fair Price
3.1-liter V-6 engine	$610	$525	$555
4-speed automatic transmission	200	172	182
Requires 3.1-liter V-6 engine.			
Luxury Pkg. SD, Special 4-door	582	501	530
Special wagon	737	634	671
Cruise control, rear defogger, covered visor mirrors, front storage armrest, 185/75R14 whitewall tires, front and rear floormats. Wagon also includes roof luggage carrier and air deflector.			
Prestige Pkg. SE, Special 4-door	1244	1070	1132
Special wagon	1593	1370	1450
Pkg. SD plus power windows and mirrors, remote trunk release, cassette player, mirror reading lights, trunk net. Wagon also includes rear-facing third seat and swing-out vent window, and cargo area security cover.			
Luxury Pkg. SD, Custom 4-door	1254	1078	1141
Includes cruise control, rear defogger, power windows and mirrors, cassette player, automatic power antenna, remote trunk release, mirror reading lights, trunk net, front and rear floormats, accent stripes, 195/75R14 whitewall tires.			
Prestige Pkg. SE, Custom 4-door	1856	1596	1689
Custom 4-door Pkg. SD plus 6-way power driver's seat, remote keyless entry, lighted visor mirrors, premium speaker system.			
Remote keyless entry	135	116	123
Decklid luggage rack, notchbacks	115	99	105
Cassette player, Special, Special w/Pkg. SD and National Marketing Edition models	140	120	127
CD player, Special and Special w/Pkg.	414	356	377
Special w/Pkg. SE, Custom w/Pkg. SD/SE	274	236	249
Premium speakers, notchbacks	70	60	64
Wagon	35	30	32
Power antenna, Special	85	73	77
Requires power windows.			
Power windows, Special	330	284	300
6-way power driver's seat, Special w/Pkg. SD or SE, Custom w/Pkg. SD and National Marketing models	305	262	278

	Retail Price	Dealer Invoice	Fair Price
Bodyside stripes, Special	$45	$39	$41
Bodyside woodgrain trim, wagon	350	301	319
Leather and vinyl 55/45 seat w/storage armrest, notchbacks	500	430	455
Rear wiper, wagon	85	73	77
Lighted visor mirrors, Special, Special w/Pkg. SE.	92	79	84
Requires mirror reading lights.			
Mirror reading lights, Special, Special w/Pkg. SE	6	5	5
Remote decklid release, notchbacks	60	52	55
Door edge guards	25	22	23
Heavy duty engine and transmission cooling	40	34	36
Requires 3.1-liter V-6 engine.			
Locking wire wheel covers	240	206	218
Styled steel wheels, Special	115	99	105
Alloy wheels	295	254	268
185/75R14 tires, Special w/Pkg. SD/SE (credit)	(68)	(58)	(58)
National Marketing Edition models	NC	NC	NC
185/75R14 whitewall tires, Special	68	58	62
195/75R14 tires, Special	40	34	36
195/75R14 tires, Special w/Pkg. SD/SE (credit)	(28)	(24)	(24)
Custom, Custom w/Pkg. SD/SE (credit)	(68)	(58)	(58)
195/75R14 whitewall tires, Special	108	93	98
Special w/Pkg. SD/SE	40	34	36

OLDSMOBILE CUTLASS SUPREME/BUICK REGAL

Specifications	2-door notchback	4-door notchback	Cutlass 2-door conv.
Wheelbase, in.	107.5	107.5	107.5
Overall length, in.	193.9	193.7	193.9
Overall width, in.	71.0	71.0	71.0
Overall height, in.	53.3	54.8	54.3

Prices are accurate at time of publication; subject to manufacturer's change.

Oldsmobile Cutlass Supreme convertible

	2-door notchback	4-door notchback	Cutlass 2-door conv.
Curb weight, lbs.	3307	3405	3651
Cargo vol., cu. ft.	15.5	15.5	12.1
Fuel capacity, gals.	16.5	16.5	16.5
Seating capacity	6	6	5
Front head room, in.	37.8	38.7	38.5
Max. front leg room, in.	42.3	42.4	42.3
Rear head room, in.	37.0	38.3	38.9
Min. rear leg room, in.	34.8	36.2	34.8

Powertrain layout: transverse front engine/front-wheel drive.

Engines	ohv V-6	dohc V-6	ohv V-6
Size, liters/cu. in.	3.1/191	3.4/207	3.8/231
Horsepower @ rpm	160 @ 5200	210 @ 5200	170 @ 4800
Torque (lbs./ft.) @ rpm	185 @ 4000	215 @ 4000	225 @ 3200
Availability	S	O[1]	O[2]
EPA city/highway mpg			
4-speed OD automatic	19/29	17/26	19/28

1. Cutlass Supreme. 2. Regal.

Built in Doraville, Ga., and Canada.

PRICES

Oldsmobile Cutlass Supreme	Retail Price	Dealer Invoice	Fair Price
S 2-door notchback	$17670	$15461	$15961

	Retail Price	Dealer Invoice	Fair Price
S 4-door notchback	$17770	$15549	$16049
Special Edition 2-door and 4-door notchback, Pkg. R7B	17195	16278	—
Special Edition 2-door and 4-door notchback, Pkg. R7C	18195	17223	—
2-door convertible	25470	22286	22786
Destination charge	525	525	525

Special Edition fair price not available at time of publication. Special Edition prices include destination charge. Additional "value-priced" models may be available in California.

Standard Equipment:

S: 3.1-liter V-6 engine, 4-speed automatic transmission, anti-lock 4-wheel disc brakes, driver-side air bag, door-mounted automatic front shoulder belts, power steering, air conditioning, cloth reclining front bucket seats, 4-way manual driver's seat, tilt steering wheel, analog temperature gauges, center console with cup holder, automatic power door locks, AM/FM radio, left remote and right manual mirrors, tinted glass, rear defogger, intermittent wipers, illuminated entry system, reading lights, Pass-Key theft-deterrent system, visor mirrors, 205/70R15 tires, wheel covers. **Special Edition Pkg. R7B** adds to S: Sport Luxury Pkg., Option Pkg. 1SB. **Special Edition Pkg. R7C** adds to S: Option Pkg. 1SC, Sport Luxury Pkg., leather seats, power driver's seat, Custom Trim Pkg. **Convertible** adds to S: leather seats, power driver's seat, 4-way manual passenger's seat, cruise control, leather-wrapped steering wheel, front console with armrest, power windows, power mirrors, power decklid release, fog lamps, floormats, 225/60R16 tires, alloy wheels.

Optional Equipment:

	Retail Price	Dealer Invoice	Fair Price
3.4-liter DOHC V-6, S	1520	1307	1322
S with BYP Sport Luxury Pkg., Special Edition	1123	966	977
Conv.	1085	856	944
3.4-liter DOHC V-6 engine, sport suspension, rear spoiler, dual exhausts, special alloy wheels.			
Option Pkg. 1SB, S	487	419	424
Cruise control, power mirrors, cassette player, floormats.			
Option Pkg. 1SC, S 2-door	1203	1035	1047
S 4-door	1268	1090	1103
Pkg. 1SB plus power windows, Remote Lock Control Pkg., power antenna, lighted visor mirrors, 6-speaker radio.			

	Retail Price	Dealer Invoice	Fair Price
Option Pkg. 1SD, S 2-door	$2053	$1766	$1786
S 4-door	2118	1821	1843
Pkg. 1SC plus automatic air conditioning, power driver's seat, Custom Trim Pkg., steering wheel touch controls.			
BYP Sport Luxury (SL) Pkg., S	913	785	794
S with leather seats or Pkg. 1SD	823	708	716
Special front and rear fascias, rocker moldings, body-color wheel opening moldings, fog lamps, leather-wrapped steering wheel, "Cutlass Supreme SL" lettering on doors, 215/60R16 tires, alloy wheels. Requires Option Pkg. 1SB, 1SC, or 1SD.			
Option Pkg. 1SB, conv.	296	255	258
Remote Lock Control Pkg., lighted visor mirrors, power antenna.			
Option Pkg. 1SC, conv.	691	594	601
Pkg. 1SB plus automatic air conditioning, leather-wrapped steering wheel, steering wheel touch controls.			
55/45 front seats, S	NC	NC	NC
Includes storage armrest and seatback recliners. Not available with 3.4-liter V-6, leather seats, or head-up instrument display.			
Custom Trim Pkg., S	150	129	131
Includes split folding rear seat back. Requires Option Pkg. 1SB, 1SC, or 1SD.			
Power driver's seat, S	305	262	265
Requires Pkg. 1SC.			
Astroroof	695	598	605
Requires power driver's seat, Pkg. 1SC or 1SD.			
Power windows, S 2-door	275	237	239
S 4-door	340	292	296
Requires Pkg. 1SB.			
Remote Lock Control Pkg., Special Edition	185	159	161
Alloy wheels, S	285	245	248
Not available with BYP Sport Luxury Pkg. or 3.4-liter V-6.			
Cassette player with equalizer, S with Pkg. 1SC, conv.	130	112	113
S with Pkg. 1SD, conv. with Pkg. 1SC	100	86	87
AM/FM radio with CD player, S with Pkg. 1SC , conv.	256	220	223
S with Pkg. 1SD, conv. with Pkg. 1SC	226	194	197
Custom leather trim, S	665	572	579
S requires Pkg. 1SD or power driver's seat.			
Floormats, S	45	39	40
Head-up instrument display, S, conv.	250	215	218
S requires Pkg. 1SD. Conv. requires Pkg. 1SC.			

	Retail Price	Dealer Invoice	Fair Price
Decklid luggage carrier, S	$115	$99	$100

Requires Option Pkg. 1SB, 1SC, or 1SD. Not available with 3.4-liter V-6.

	Retail Price	Dealer Invoice	Fair Price
Bodyside moldings, S, conv.	60	52	53
Engine block heater	18	15	16
Trunk cargo net, S, conv.	30	26	27

Buick Regal

	Retail Price	Dealer Invoice	Fair Price
Custom 2-door notchback	$18324	$16033	$16533
National Marketing Edition Custom 2-door notchback	17795	16932	—
Custom 4-door notchback	18624	16296	16796
National Marketing Edition Custom 4-door notchback	18795	17827	—
Limited 4-door notchback	20124	17609	18109
Gran Sport 2-door notchback	20324	17783	18283
National Marketing Edition Gran Sport 2-door notchback	19295	18413	—
Gran Sport 4-door notchback	20624	18046	18546
Destination charge	525	525	525

National Marketing Edition models' fair price not available at time of publication. National Marketing Edition models include destination charge and are available with limited optional equipment.

Standard Equipment:

Custom: 3.1-liter V-6 engine, 4-speed automatic transmission, driver-side air bag, anti-lock 4-wheel disc brakes, power steering, air conditioning, door-mounted automatic front seatbelts, automatic power door locks, power windows with driver-side express down and passenger lockout, tilt steering wheel, cloth reclining 55/45 front seat with storage armrest and cup holders, front seatback recliners, tinted glass, intermittent wipers, Pass-Key theft-deterrent system, left remote and right manual mirrors, visor mirrors, AM/FM radio with clock, 205/70R15 tires. **National Marketing Edition Custom** adds: 3.8-liter V-6 engine (4-door), automatic air conditioning with dual climate controls, cruise control, 6-way power driver's seat, power mirrors, AM/FM cassette with Concert Sound II speakers, power antenna, overhead console with courtesy lights, power decklid release, rear defogger, remote keyless entry system, dome reading light (4-door), convenience net, body-color grille, front and rear floormats, alloy wheels (4-door). **Limited** adds to Custom: 3.8-liter V-6 engine, 4-way manual driver's seat and 2-

way manual passenger's seat, seatback map pockets, front overhead courtesy/reading lights. **Gran Sport** adds: Gran Touring suspension, leather-wrapped steering wheel, cloth reclining bucket seats, console with armrest, storage, and cup holders, fog lamps (2-door), body-color grille, 225/60R16 all-season tires, alloy wheels. **National Marketing Edition Gran Sport** adds to Gran Sport 2-door: automatic air conditioning with dual climate controls, cruise control, 6-way power driver's seat, power mirrors, remote keyless entry system, AM/FM cassette with Concert Sound II speakers, power antenna, power decklid release, rear defogger, convenience net, front and rear floormats.

Optional Equipment:

	Retail Price	Dealer Invoice	Fair Price
3.8-liter V-6	$395	$340	$359
Luxury Pkg. SD, Custom	848	729	772
Power mirrors, power antenna, cruise control, rear defogger, remote decklid release, cassette tape player, trunk net, floormats.			
Prestige Pkg. SE, Custom 2-door	1432	1232	1303
Custom 4-door	1443	1241	1313
Pkg. SD plus remote keyless entry, front and rear courtesy/reading lights, 6-way power driver's seat, Concert Sound II speakers, trunk net.			
Luxury Pkg. SD, Limited 4-door	918	789	835
Power mirrors, power antenna, cruise control, rear defogger, remote decklid release, cassette player, dual climate controls, Concert Sound II speakers, floormats.			
Prestige Pkg. SE, Limited 4-door	1640	1410	1492
Pkg. SD plus 6-way power driver's seat, remote keyless entry, steering-wheel-mounted radio and temperature controls, lighted visor mirrors, door courtesy lights, trunk net.			
Luxury Pkg. SD, Gran Sport	918	789	835
Power mirrors, power antenna, cruise control, rear defogger, remote decklid release, dual climate controls, cassette player, Concert Sound II speakers, floormats.			
Prestige Pkg. SE, Gran Sport 2-door	1570	1350	1429
4-door	1640	1410	1492
Pkg. SD plus 6-way power driver's seat, remote keyless entry, steering wheel radio and temperature controls, lighted visor mirrors, trunk net. 4-door includes door courtesy lights.			
Gran Touring Pkg., Custom and Limited	675	581	614
Gran Touring suspension, leather-wrapped steering wheel, 225/60R16 tires, alloy wheels.			
UX1 audio system, Custom w/SD/SE, Limited w/SD/SE, Gran Sport w/SD/SE, National Marketing Edition 2-doors	150	129	137
Includes AM stereo, search and repeat, and equalizer.			

	Retail Price	Dealer Invoice	Fair Price
CD player, Custom w/SD/SE, Limited w/SD/SE, Gran Sport w/SD/SE, National Marketing Edition 2-doors	$274	$236	$249
Steering wheel radio and temperature controls, Custom w/SD/SE, National Marketing Edition 2-doors	125	108	114
Concert Sound II speakers, Custom w/SD	70	60	64
Power antenna, Custom	85	73	77
Remote keyless entry, Limited w/SD, Gran Sport w/SD	135	116	123
Power sunroof, Custom w/SE, Limited w/SE, Gran Sport w/SE	695	598	632
Gran Sport also requires 6-way power driver's seat.			
6-way power driver's seat, Custom w/SD	305	262	278
Limited w/SD, Gran Sport w/SD	270	232	246
Dual 6-way power front seats, Limited w/SE, Gran Sport w/SE, National Marketing Edition Gran Sport	305	262	278
Leather/vinyl 55/45 front seat, Limited	500	430	455
Leather/vinyl bucket seats, Limited and Gran Sport	500	430	455
Leather bucket seats with console, National Marketing Edition	500	430	455
Lighted visor mirrors, Custom w/SE	92	79	84
Rear defogger delete, (credit)	(170)	(146)	(146)
Heavy duty cooling	150	129	137
Includes engine oil cooler. Requires 3.8-liter V-6 engine.			
Decklid luggage rack	115	99	105
Chrome bodyside/fascia molding, Custom 2-door w/SE	150	129	137
Wire wheel covers, Custom, Limited, National Marketing Edition Custom 2-door	240	206	218
15-inch alloy wheels, Custom, Limited, National Marketing Edition Custom 2-door	325	280	296

PLYMOUTH ACCLAIM/ DODGE SPIRIT

Specifications

	4-door notchback
Wheelbase, in.	103.5

Prices are accurate at time of publication; subject to manufacturer's change.

PLYMOUTH

Plymouth Acclaim

	4-door notchback
Overall length, in.	181.2
Overall width, in.	68.1
Overall height, in.	53.5
Curb weight, lbs.	2831
Cargo vol., cu. ft.	14.4
Fuel capacity, gals.	16.0
Seating capacity	6
Front head room, in.	38.4
Max. front leg room, in.	41.9
Rear head room, in.	37.9
Min. rear leg room, in.	38.3

Powertrain layout: transverse front engine/front-wheel drive.

Engines	ohc I-4	ohc V-6
Size, liters/cu. in.	2.5/153	3.0/181
Horsepower @ rpm	101 @ 4400	142 @ 5000
Torque (lbs./ft.) @ rpm	140 @ 2400	171 @ 2400
Availability	S	O
EPA city/highway mpg		
5-speed OD manual	24/29	
3-speed automatic	22/27	21/27
4-speed OD automatic		19/24

Built in Newark, Del.

PRICES

Plymouth Acclaim/Dodge Spirit	Retail Price	Dealer Invoice	Fair Price
4-door notchback	$12470	$11339	$11539

	Retail Price	Dealer Invoice	Fair Price
Destination charge	$505	$505	$505

Standard Equipment:

2.5-liter 4-cylinder engine, 5-speed manual transmission, power steering, driver-side air bag, motorized front passenger shoulder belt, cloth reclining front bucket seats, coolant temperature gauge, voltmeter, trip odometer, center console, tinted glass, dual remote mirrors, visor mirrors, bodyside moldings, AM/FM radio with two speakers, intermittent wipers, floormats, striping, 185/70R14 tires, wheel covers.

Optional Equipment:

	Retail Price	Dealer Invoice	Fair Price
Pkg. 22D/24D	1179	1038	1096
Pkg. 26D	1977	1716	1839
3-speed automatic transmission, air conditioning, 50/50 split front bench seat, rear defogger, tilt steering wheel, cruise control, floormats. Pkg. 24D includes 2.5-liter flexible fuel engine. Pkg. 26D includes 3.0-liter V-6 engine.			
Pkg. 24E/28E	883	751	777
Power windows and locks, heated power mirrors, split folding rear seat, remote decklid release. Requires Pkg. 24D or 26D. Pkg. 28E (V-6 engine) also requires 4-speed automatic transmission.			
4-speed automatic transmission	173	147	152
Requires Pkg. 28E.			
Anti-lock 4-wheel disc brakes	699	594	615
Not available with Pkg. 26D.			
Argent Special Equipment Group	200	170	176
Luggage rack, 195/70R14 tires, argent alloy wheels. Requires option package (NA with 5-speed manual transmission).			
Gold Decor Special Equipment Group	200	170	176
Luggage rack, gold badging and trim, 195/70R14 tires, alloy wheels with gold accents. Requires option package.			
Rear defogger	173	147	152
Cassette player and four speakers	170	145	150
Requires option package.			
Power driver's seat, w/Pkg. 24E or 28E	306	260	269
Power locks, w/Pkg. 22D, 24D, or 26D	250	213	220
Mini trip computer/Message Center	93	79	82
Requires option package.			
195/70R14 whitewall tires,			
w/Pkg. 22D, 24D, or 24E	104	88	92
w/Pkg. 26D or 28E	73	62	64
Conventional spare tire	95	81	84
Extra-cost paint	97	82	85

PLYMOUTH SUNDANCE/ DODGE SHADOW

Plymouth Sundance Duster 3-door

Specifications	3-door hatchback	5-door hatchback
Wheelbase, in.	97.2	97.2
Overall length, in.	171.9	171.9
Overall width, in.	67.3	67.3
Overall height, in.	53.1	53.1
Curb weight, lbs.	2608	2643
Cargo vol., cu. ft.	33.3	33.3
Fuel capacity, gals.	14.0	14.0
Seating capacity	5	5
Front head room, in.	38.3	38.3
Max. front leg room, in.	41.5	41.5
Rear head room, in.	37.4	37.4
Min. rear leg room, in.	34.0	34.0

Powertrain layout: transverse front engine/front-wheel drive.

Engines	ohc I-4	ohc I-4	ohc V-6
Size, liters/cu. in.	2.2/135	2.5/153	3.0/181
Horsepower @ rpm	93 @ 4800	100 @ 4800	141 @ 5000
Torque (lbs./ft.) @ rpm	122 @ 3200	135 @ 2800	171 @ 2400
Availability	S[1]	O[2]	S[3]
EPA city/highway mpg			
5-speed OD manual	26/33	24/29	17/25

	ohc I-4	ohc I-4	ohc V-6
3-speed automatic	23/30	22/27	
4-speed OD automatic			19/24

1. Base models. 2. Base models and Sundance Duster; standard, Shadow ES. 3. Sundance Duster; optional, Shadow ES.

Built in Sterling Heights, Mich.

PRICES

Plymouth Sundance	Retail Price	Dealer Invoice	Fair Price
3-door hatchback	$8806	$8263	$8453
5-door hatchback	9206	8631	8821
Duster 3-door hatchback	11046	10246	10436
Duster 5-door hatchback	11446	10606	10796
Destination charge	505	505	505

Standard Equipment:

Base: 2.2-liter 4-cylinder engine, 5-speed manual transmission, power steering, driver-side air bag, cloth reclining front bucket seats, mini console with storage, tinted rear window, trip odometer, coolant temperature gauge, voltmeter, left remote mirror, bodyside moldings, removable shelf panel, 185/70R14 tires. **Duster** adds: 3.0-liter V-6 engine, sport suspension, dual outside mirrors, AM/FM radio, rear spoiler, body-color bumpers and bodyside cladding, 195/60R15 tires, wheel covers.

Optional Equipment:

	Retail Price	Dealer Invoice	Fair Price
Pkgs. 21Y, 22Y, 23Y, 24Y, base	1545	1313	1336
Air conditioning, tinted glass, rear defogger, dual remote mirrors, AM/FM radio, visor mirrors, intermittent wipers, Light Group, floormats, wheel covers, body-color fascias, color-keyed instrument panel bezels, body-side moldings, striping. Pkg. 22Y requires 3-speed automatic transmission; Pkg. 23Y requires 2.5-liter engine; Pkg. 24Y requires 2.5-liter engine and 3-speed automatic transmission.			
Pkg. 23H, 24H, 27H, 28H, Duster	978	831	846
Air conditioning, tinted glass, rear defogger, cassette player, remote hatch release, Light Group, tachometer, intermittent wipers, console with storage armrest and cup holders, fog lamps, floormats, visor mirrors.			
2.5-liter 4-cylinder engine, base	286	243	247
Duster (credit)	(794)	(675)	(675)
3-speed automatic transmission, base	557	473	482
4-speed automatic transmission, Duster	730	621	631
Air conditioning and tinted glass	900	765	779
Light Group	77	65	67

Prices are accurate at time of publication; subject to manufacturer's change.

	Retail Price	Dealer Invoice	Fair Price
Anti-lock brakes	$699	$594	$605
Requires automatic transmission.			
Overhead console,			
Duster w/Pkgs. 23-28H	265	225	229
Includes temperature readout and compass. Requires power windows and locks, power mirrors.			
Rear defogger	173	147	150
Power locks, Base 3-door w/Pkgs. 21-24Y,			
Duster 3-door	199	169	172
Base 5-door w/Pkgs. 21-24Y,			
Duster 5-door	240	204	208
Dual remote mirrors, Base	69	59	60
Power mirrors, Duster w/Pkgs. 23-28H	57	48	49
Power driver's seat,			
Duster w/Pkgs. 23-28H	306	260	265
Requires power windows, locks, and mirrors.			
Power windows, Duster			
3-door w/Pkgs. 23-28H	265	225	229
Duster 5-door w/Pkgs. 23-28H	331	281	286
Requires power locks and mirrors.			
AM/FM radio, Base	284	241	246
AM/FM cassette, Base w/Pkgs. 21-24W	504	428	436
Base w/Pkgs. 21-24Y	170	145	147
Duster	220	187	190
Infinity cassette system with equalizer,			
Duster w/Pkgs. 23-28G	520	442	450
Duster w/Pkgs. 23-28H	300	255	260
Requires power door locks, intermittent wipers.			
Infinity CD system with equalizer,			
Duster w/Pkgs. 23-28G	690	587	597
Duster w/Pkgs. 23-28H	470	400	407
Requires tilt steering wheel, intermittent wipers.			
Intermittent wipers	66	56	57
Cruise control	224	190	194
Requires tilt steering wheel.			
Light Group	77	65	67
Sunroof	379	322	328
Not available with overhead console.			
Tilt steering wheel	148	126	128
Requires intermittent wipers.			
Remote liftgate release,			
Base w/Pkgs. 21Y-24Y	24	20	21
Alloy wheels, Base	376	320	325
Base w/Pkgs. 21Y-24Y, Duster	328	279	284

	Retail Price	Dealer Invoice	Fair Price
Conventional spare tire with steel wheel	$85	$72	$74
with alloy wheel, Duster	213	181	184
Extra-cost paint	97	82	84
Floormats	46	39	40

Dodge Shadow

	Retail Price	Dealer Invoice	Fair Price
3-door hatchback	$8806	$8263	$8453
5-door hatchback	9206	8631	8821
ES 3-door hatchback	10252	9532	9722
ES 5-door hatchback	10652	9892	10082
Destination charge	505	505	505

Standard Equipment:

2.2-liter 4-cylinder engine, 5-speed manual transmission, power steering, driver-side air bag, motorized front passenger shoulder belt, cloth/vinyl reclining front bucket seats, mini console with storage, trip odometer, coolant temperature gauge, voltmeter, left remote mirror, tinted rear window, removable shelf panel, 185/70R14 tires. **ES** adds: 2.5-liter 4-cylinder engine, dual remote mirrors, AM/FM radio, color-keyed bumpers, rear spoiler, striping, sport suspension, 195/60HR15 tires, wheel covers.

Optional Equipment:

	Retail Price	Dealer Invoice	Fair Price
3-speed automatic transmission	557	473	482
3.0-liter engine, ES	794	675	687
2.5-liter engine, base	286	243	247
Pkgs. 21Y/22Y/23Y/24Y, base	1545	1313	1336
Air conditioning, tinted glass, rear defogger, dual remote mirrors, AM/FM radio, visor mirrors, intermittent wipers, Light Group, floormats, wheel covers, body-color fascias, color-keyed instrument panel bezels, bodyside moldings, striping. Pkg. 22Y requires 3-speed automatic transmission; Pkg. 23Y requires 2.5-liter engine; Pkg. 24Y requires 2.5-liter engine and 3-speed automatic transmission.			
Pkg. 28G, ES	1424	1211	1232
Adds 3.0-liter engine and 4-speed automatic transmission.			
Pkg. 23H, 24H, 27H, 28H, ES	978	831	846
Air conditioning, tinted glass, rear defogger, cassette player, remote hatch release, Light Group, tachometer, intermittent wipers, console with storage armrest and cup holders, fog lamps, floormats, visor mirrors.			
4-speed automatic transmission, ES	730	621	631
Requires 3.0-liter engine.			
Air conditioning and tinted glass	900	765	779

	Retail Price	Dealer Invoice	Fair Price
Anti-lock brakes	$699	$594	$605
Requires automatic transmission			
Light Group	77	65	67
Overhead console, ES w/Pkgs. 23-28H	265	225	229
Includes thermometer and compass. Requires power windows and locks, power mirrors.			
Rear defogger	173	147	150
Power locks, 3-door	199	169	172
5-door	240	204	208
Base requires Option Pkg.			
Dual remote mirrors, base	69	59	60
Power mirrors, ES w/Pkgs. 23-28H	57	48	49
Requires power door locks.			
Power driver's seat, ES w/Pkgs. 23-28H.	306	260	265
Requires power windows, locks, and mirrors.			
Power windows, ES 3-door w/Pkgs. 23-28H	265	225	229
ES 5-door w/Pkgs. 23-28H	331	281	286
Requires power locks and mirrors.			
AM/FM radio, base	284	241	246
AM/FM cassette, base w/Pkgs. 21-24W	504	428	436
Base w/Pkgs. 21-24Y	170	145	147
ES	220	187	190
AM/FM cassette with Infinity speakers and equalizer, ES w/Pkgs. 23-28G	520	442	450
ES w/Pkgs. 23-28H	300	255	260
Requires power door locks, intermittent wipers.			
Intermittent wipers	66	56	57
AM/FM CD with Infinity speakers and equalizer, ES w/Pkgs. 23G-28G	690	587	597
ES w/Pkgs. 23-28H	470	400	407
Cruise control	224	190	194
Requires tilt steering wheel.			
Sunroof	379	322	328
Tilt steering wheel	148	126	128
Requires intermittent wipers.			
Remote liftgate release, base w/Pkgs. 21-24Y	24	20	21
Conventional spare tire	85	72	74
ES with alloy wheel	213	181	184
205/60R14 tires, ES (credit)	(107)	(91)	(91)
Requires 14-inch alloy wheels.			
14-inch alloy wheels, base w/Pkgs. 21-24W	376	320	325

	Retail Price	Dealer Invoice	Fair Price
Base w/Pkgs. 21-24Y, ES	$328	$279	$284
15-inch alloy wheels, ES	328	279	284
Floormats	46	39	40
Extra-cost paint	97	82	84

PONTIAC GRAND AM

Pontiac Grand Am SE 4-door

Specifications

	2-door notchback	4-door notchback
Wheelbase, in.	103.4	103.4
Overall length, in.	186.9	186.9
Overall width, in.	67.5	67.5
Overall height, in.	53.2	53.2
Curb weight, lbs.	2736	2793
Cargo vol., cu. ft.	13.2	13.2
Fuel capacity, gals.	15.2	15.2
Seating capacity	5	5
Front head room, in.	37.8	37.8
Max. front leg room, in.	43.3	43.3
Rear head room, in.	36.5	37.0
Min. rear leg room, in.	33.9	34.9

Powertrain layout: transverse front engine/front-wheel drive.

Engines

	ohc I-4	dohc I-4	dohc I-4	ohv V-6
Size, liters/cu. in.	2.3/138	2.3/138	2.3/138	3.1/191
Horsepower @ rpm	115 @ 5200	155 @ 6000	175 @ 6200	155 @ 5200

	ohc I-4	dohc I-4	dohc I-4	ohv V-6
Torque (lbs./ft.) @ rpm	140 @ 3200	150 @ 4800	150 @ 5200	185 @ 4000
Availability	S[1]	O	S[2]	O
EPA city/highway mpg				
5-speed OD manual	23/35		21/30	
3-speed automatic	22/32			
4-speed OD automatic	22/31	21/30		20/29

1. SE. 2. GT.

Built in Lansing, Mich.

PRICES

Pontiac Grand Am	Retail Price	Dealer Invoice	Fair Price
SE 2-door notchback	$12514	$11450	$11850
SE 4-door notchback	12614	11542	11942
GT 2-door notchback	15014	13738	14138
GT 4-door notchback	15114	13829	14229
Destination charge	485	485	485

Additional "value-priced" models may be available in California.

Standard Equipment:

SE: 2.3-liter 4-cylinder engine, 5-speed manual transmission, anti-lock brakes, driver-side air bag, power steering, cloth reclining front bucket seats, center console with armrest, storage and coin holder, overhead compartment, left remote and right manual mirrors, front door map pockets, AM/FM radio, tinted glass, automatic power locks, decklid release, fog lamps, trip odometer, illuminated entry, visor mirrors, rear seat headrests, 185/75R14 tires, wheel covers. **GT** adds to SE: 2.3-liter DOHC Quad 4 engine (175 horsepower), air conditioning, rally gauge cluster (includes tachometer, voltmeter, oil pressure and coolant temperature gauges), intermittent wipers, rear decklid spoiler, 205/55R16 tires, alloy wheels.

Optional Equipment:

	Retail Price	Dealer Invoice	Fair Price
2.3-liter DOHC (155 horsepower) 4-cylinder engine, GT (credit)	(140)	(120)	(120)
Requires 4-speed automatic transmission.			
3.1-liter V-6 engine, SE	410	353	373
GT (credit)	(140)	(120)	(120)
Requires 4-speed automatic transmission. SE also requires air conditioning and 15- or 16-inch tires.			
3-speed automatic transmission	555	477	505

	Retail Price	Dealer Invoice	Fair Price
4-speed automatic transmission	$755	$649	$687
Air conditioning, SE	830	714	755
Option Group 1SB, SE	1575	1355	1433
Air conditioning, cruise control, cassette player, intermittent wipers, rear defogger, tilt steering wheel.			
Option Group 1SC, SE 2-door	2086	1794	1898
SE 4-door	2151	1850	1957
Group 1SB plus power windows with driver-side express down, power mirrors, split folding rear seat.			
Option Group 1SB, GT	535	460	487
Cruise control, cassette player.			
Option Group 1SC, GT 2-door	1046	900	952
GT 4-door	1111	955	1011
Group 1SB plus power windows with driver-side express down, power mirrors, split folding rear seat.			
Sport Interior Group, SE and GT	432	372	393
with Group 1SC	282	243	257
with leather upholstery	907	780	825
with leather upholstery and Group 1SC	757	651	689
Driver-seat lumbar adjuster, articulated front headrests, 4-way manual seat adjuster, leather-wrapped steering wheel and shift knob, reading and courtesy lamps, sunvisor extensions, split folding rear seat, passenger assist grips.			
Rally gauge cluster, SE	111	95	101
Cruise control	225	194	205
Rear defogger	170	146	155
Power mirrors	86	74	78
Power driver's seat	340	292	309
with Sport Interior Group	305	262	278
Power windows with driver-side express down, 2-door	275	237	250
4-door	340	292	309
Power sunroof	595	512	541
Split folding rear seat	150	129	137
Tilt steering wheel, SE	145	125	132
Intermittent wipers, SE	65	56	59
Remote keyless entry system	135	116	123
AM/FM cassette player	140	120	127
AM/FM cassette player with equalizer	375	323	341
with group 1SB or 1SC	235	202	214
AM/FM CD player w/equalizer	580	499	528
with Group 1SB or 1SC	440	378	400

	Retail Price	Dealer Invoice	Fair Price
Rear decklid spoiler, SE	$110	$95	$100
Rear decklid spoiler delete, GT (credit)	(110)	(95)	(95)
195/65R15 tires, SE	158	136	144
205/55R16 tires, SE	223	192	203
Crosslace wheel covers, SE	55	47	50
16-inch alloy wheels, SE	300	258	273

SAAB 900

Saab 900S 5-door

Specifications

	3-door hatchback	5-door hatchback	2-door conv.
Wheelbase, in.	102.4	102.4	99.1
Overall length, in.	182.6	182.6	184.3
Overall width, in.	67.4	67.4	66.5
Overall height, in.	56.5	56.5	55.1
Curb weight, lbs.	2990	2950	2950
Cargo vol., cu. ft.	49.8	49.8	10.7
Fuel capacity, gals.	18.0	18.0	18.0
Seating capacity	5	5	4
Front head room, in.	38.0	38.0	36.8
Max. front leg room, in.	42.3	42.3	41.7
Rear head room, in.	37.6	37.6	NA
Min. rear leg room, in.	36.0	36.0	NA

Powertrain layout: transverse front engine/front-wheel drive (hatchbacks); longitudinal front engine/front-wheel drive (convertible).

Engines

	dohc I-4	Turbo dohc I-4	dohc I-4	dohc V-6
Size, liters/cu. in.	2.1/129	2.0/129	2.3/140	2.5/152
Horsepower @ rpm	140 @ 6000	185 @ 5500	150 @ 5700	170 @ 5900
Torque (lbs./ft.) @ rpm	133 @ 2900	195 @ 2100	155 @ 4300	167 @ 4200
Availability	S[1]	S[2]	S[3]	S[4]
EPA city/highway mpg				
5-speed OD manual	20/26	20/26	20/28	18/25
3-speed automatic	18/21	18/21		
4-speed OD automatic			19/26	19/25

1. 900S conv. 2. 900 SE 3-door, Turbo conv. 3. 900S hatchbacks. 4. 900SE 5-door.

Built in Sweden and Finland.

PRICES

Saab 900	Retail Price	Dealer Invoice	Fair Price
S 3-door hatchback	$22290	—	—
S 5-door hatchback	21990	—	—
SE 3-door hatchback	27280	—	—
SE 5-door hatchback	26990	—	—
S 2-door convertible	33275	28750	29550
Turbo 2-door convertible	38415	32730	33530
Commemorative Edition Turbo 2-door convertible	40415	35646	36446
Destination charge	460	460	460

Dealer invoice and fair price for hatchbacks not available at time of publication.

Standard Equipment:

S hatchbacks: 2.3-liter 4-cylinder engine, 5-speed manual transmission, anti-lock 4-wheel disc brakes, driver- and passenger-side air bags, front seatbelt pretensioners, power steering, air conditioning, cruise control, power door and trunk locks, theft alarm system, power windows, automatic power antenna, telescopic steering wheel, front fog lamps, rear fog lamp, dual heated power mirrors, rear defogger, intermittent wipers, solar-control tinted glass, AM/FM cassette, trip computer, cellular phone and CD pre-wiring, cloth heated reclining front bucket seats, folding rear seat, front console with storage, headlamp wipers/washers, rear wiper/washer, tachometer, analog clock, front spoiler, front and rear stabilizer bars, tool kit, bodyside moldings, floormats, 195/60VR15 tires, full wheel covers. **SE 3-door** adds: 2.0-liter turbocharged 4-cylinder engine, leather upholstery, power front seats, automatic climate control, premium sound system, power glass sunroof, Saab Car Computer, sport suspension, 205/50ZR16 tires, alloy wheels. **SE 5-door** adds: 2.5-liter V-6, traction control, 195/60VR15 tires. **S convertible** deletes passenger-side air bag and adds: 2.1-liter 4-cylinder engine, power top, power heated front seats, leather upholstery, leather-wrapped steering wheel, 185/65TR15 tires. **Turbo convertible** adds: 2.0-liter turbocharged 4-cylinder engine, engine oil cooler, turbo boost gauge, AM/FM cassette/CD player with equalizer, 195/60VR15 tires. **Commemorative Edition convertible** adds: wood dashboard fascia, tan leather upholstery, black metallic paint, unique alloy wheels.

Optional Equipment:	Retail Price	Dealer Invoice	Fair Price
4-speed automatic transmission, hatchbacks	$895	$759	—
Not available SE 3-door			
3-speed automatic transmission, convertibles	705	576	620
Power glass sunroof, S hatchbacks	980	901	—
Child booster seat, 5-door models	250	—	—
Wood dashboard fascia, Turbo convertible	650	540	572

SAAB 9000

Specifications	4-door notchback	5-door hatchback
Wheelbase, in.	105.2	105.2
Overall length, in.	188.2	187.4
Overall width, in.	69.4	69.4
Overall height, in.	55.9	55.9
Curb weight, lbs.	3210	3110
Cargo vol., cu. ft.	17.8	56.5
Fuel capacity, gals.	17.4	17.4
Seating capacity	5	5
Front head room, in.	38.5	38.5
Max. front leg room, in.	41.5	41.5
Rear head room, in.	37.4	37.4
Min. rear leg room, in.	38.7	38.7

Powertrain layout: transverse front engine/front-wheel drive.

Saab 9000 Aero

Engines	dohc I-4	Turbo dohc I-4
Size, liters/cu. in.	2.3/140	2.3/140
Horsepower @ rpm	146 @ 5600	200 @ 5500
Torque (lbs./ft.) @ rpm	151 @ 3800	238 @ 1800
Availability	S	S[1]
EPA city/highway mpg		
5-speed OD manual	19/27	20/28
4-speed OD automatic	17/27	18/26

1. Turbo models, Aero.

Built in Sweden.

PRICES

Saab 9000	Retail Price	Dealer Invoice	Fair Price
CS 5-door hatchback	$28725	$25925	$26725
CS Turbo 5-door hatchback	31780	28514	29314
CSE 5-door hatchback	33045	28980	29780
CSE Turbo 5-door hatchback	36100	31569	32369
CDE Turbo 4-door notchback	36685	32055	32855
9000 Aero, 5-door notchback	38690	33815	34615
Destination charge	460	460	460

Standard Equipment:

CS: 2.3-liter DOHC 4-cylinder engine, 5-speed manual transmission, anti-lock 4-wheel disc brakes, driver- and passenger-side air bags, power steering, automatic climate control, removable

AM/FM cassette player, cruise control, power glass sunroof, cloth reclining heated bucket seats, folding rear seat, power door locks and windows, dual heated power mirrors, automatic power antenna, remote decklid release, tachometer, trip odometer, intermittent wipers, headlamp wipers/washers, rear wiper/washer, solar-control tinted glass, dual visor mirrors, rear defogger, locking center console with storage, overhead console with swivel map light, front and rear fog lamps, courtesy lights, dual rear reading lights, lighted visor mirrors, front spoiler, analog clock, floormats, 195/65TR15 tires, alloy wheels. **CS Turbo** adds: 200-horsepower 2.3-liter turbocharged engine with intercooler, turbo boost gauge. **CSE** adds to CS: power front seats with driver-side memory, leather upholstery, leather-wrapped steering wheel and shift boot cover, Saab Car Computer with digital clock, removable CD player and equalizer, CD changer pre-wiring, 195/65VR15 tires. **CSE Turbo** adds to CSE: 200-horsepower 2.3-liter turbocharged engine with intercooler, turbo boost gauge. **CDE Turbo** deletes rear fog lamp, adds to CSE Turbo: 5-speed manual or 4-speed automatic transmission, wood interior trim, rear seat pass-through, 205/60ZR15 tires. **Aero** adds: 225-horsepower 2.3-liter turbocharged engine, aerodynamic body trim, sport suspension, rear spoiler, 205/55ZR16 tires.

Optional Equipment:	Retail Price	Dealer Invoice	Fair Price
4-speed automatic transmission, CS, CS Turbo, CSE and CSE Turbo	$945	$801	$851
Leather interior, CS and CS Turbo	1520	1289	1368

Includes leather upholstery, leather-wrapped steering wheel, leather shift boot (5-speed).

SATURN

Specifications	2-door notchback	4-door notchback	5-door wagon
Wheelbase, in.	99.2	102.4	102.4
Overall length, in.	173.2	176.3	176.3
Overall width, in.	67.5	67.6	67.6
Overall height, in.	50.6	52.5	53.7
Curb weight, lbs.	2280	2314	2362
Cargo vol., cu. ft.	10.9	11.9	56.3
Fuel capacity, gals.	12.8	12.8	12.8
Seating capacity	4	5	5
Front head room, in.	37.5	38.5	38.8
Max. front leg room, in.	42.6	42.5	42.5

Saturn SL1

	2-door notchback	4-door notchback	5-door wagon
Rear head room, in.	35.0	36.3	37.4
Min. rear leg room, in.	26.5	32.6	32.6

Powertrain layout: transverse front engine/front-wheel drive.

Engines

	ohc I-4	dohc I-4
Size, liters/cu. in.	1.9/116	1.9/116
Horsepower @ rpm	85 @ 5000	124 @ 5600
Torque (lbs./ft.) @ rpm	107 @ 2400	122 @ 4800
Availability	S[1]	S[2]
EPA city/highway mpg		
5-speed OD manual	28/37	25/34
4-speed OD automatic	26/35	23/32

1. SL, SL1, SW1, SC1. 2. SL2, SW2, SC2.

Built in Spring Hill, Tenn.

PRICES

Saturn Sedan/Wagon	Retail Price	Dealer Invoice	Fair Price
SL 4-door notchback, 5-speed	$9995	$8696	—
SL1 4-door notchback, 5-speed	10795	9392	—
SL1 4-door notchback, automatic	11595	10088	—
SL2 4-door notchback, 5-speed	11795	10262	—
SL2 4-door notchback, automatic	12595	10958	—
SW1 5-door wagon, 5-speed	11695	10175	—
SW1 5-door wagon, automatic	12495	10871	—

Prices are accurate at time of publication; subject to manufacturer's change.

	Retail Price	Dealer Invoice	Fair Price
SW2 5-door wagon, 5-speed	$12595	$10958	—
SW2 5-door wagon, automatic	13395	11654	—
Destination charge	330	330	330

Fair price not available at time of publication.

Standard Equipment:

SL: 1.9-liter 4-cylinder engine, 5-speed manual transmission, driver-side air bag, cloth/vinyl reclining front bucket seats, 60/40 folding rear seatback, tachometer, trip odometer, tilt steering column, intermittent wipers, rear defogger, AM/FM radio, remote fuel door and decklid releases, door pockets, digital clock, right visor mirror, front console, child-safety rear door locks, wheel covers, 175/70R14 tires. **SL1** adds: 5-speed manual or 4-speed automatic transmission, power steering, upgraded interior trim. **SL2** adds: 1.9-liter DOHC engine, driver's seat height and lumbar support adjustments, dual outside mirrors, sport suspension, upgraded upholstery, color-keyed bumpers, 195/60R15 tires. **SW1** adds to SL1: dual mirrors, cargo area net. **SW2** adds to SW1: 1.9-liter DOHC engine, color-keyed bumpers, driver's seat height and lumbar support adjustments, sport suspension, upgraded upholstery, 195/60R15 tires.

Optional Equipment:

	Retail Price	Dealer Invoice	Fair Price
Anti-lock brakes (includes rear discs), 5-speed	675	587	—
Anti-lock brakes (includes rear disc brakes and traction control), automatic	725	631	—
Air conditioning	885	770	—
Option Pkg. 1, SL1	1800	1566	—
SW1, SW2	1765	1536	—
Air conditioning, cruise control, power windows and locks, right outside mirror (SL1).			
Option Pkg. 2, SL2	2065	1797	—
Option Pkg. 1 plus sawtooth alloy wheels.			
Power sunroof, SL1, SL2	650	566	—
AM/FM cassette radio	195	170	—
AM/FM cassette w/equalizer	355	309	—
AM/FM w/CD player and equalizer	600	522	—
Power door locks, SL1, SW1	245	213	—
Coaxial speakers	70	61	—
Cruise control (NA on SL)	240	209	—
Right outside mirror, SL1	35	30	—
Fog lamps, SL2, SW2	150	131	—
Leather upholstery, SL2, SW2	660	574	—

	Retail Price	Dealer Invoice	Fair Price
Rear spoiler, SL2	$175	$152	—
Sawtooth alloy wheels, SL2, SW2	300	261	—

Saturn SC1/SC2

	Retail Price	Dealer Invoice	Fair Price
SC1 2-door notchback, 5-speed	$11695	$10175	—
SC1 2-door notchback, automatic	12495	10871	—
SC2 2-door notchback, 5-speed	12895	11219	—
SC2 2-door notchback, automatic	13695	11915	—
Destination charge	330	330	330

Fair price not available at time of publication.

Standard Equipment:

SC1: 1.9-liter 4-cylinder engine, 5-speed manual or 4-speed automatic transmission, driver-side air bag, motorized front shoulder belts, power steering, cloth/vinyl reclining front bucket seats, 60/40 rear seatback, tachometer, trip odometer, tilt steering column, intermittent wipers, rear defogger, AM/FM radio, remote fuel door and decklid releases, door pockets, digital clock, right visor mirror, front and rear consoles, dual remote outside mirrors, color-keyed bumpers, wheel covers, 175/70R14 tires. **SC2** adds: 1.9-liter DOHC engine, driver's seat height and lumbar support adjustments, sport suspension, upgraded upholstery, retractable headlamps, 195/60R15 tires.

Optional Equipment:

	Retail Price	Dealer Invoice	Fair Price
Anti-lock brakes (includes rear discs), 5-speed	675	587	—
Anti-lock brakes (includes rear disc brakes and traction control), automatic	725	631	—
Air conditioning	885	770	—
Option Pkg. 1, SC1	1640	1427	—
Air conditioning, cruise control, power windows and locks.			
Option Pkg. 2, SC2	1840	1601	—
Option Pkg. 1 plus sawtooth alloy wheels.			
Power sunroof	650	566	—
AM/FM cassette radio	195	170	—
AM/FM cassette with equalizer	355	309	—
AM/FM with CD player and equalizer	600	522	—
Coaxial speakers	70	61	—
Cruise control	240	209	—
Leather upholstery, SC2	660	574	—

	Retail Price	Dealer Invoice	Fair Price
Rear spoiler	$175	$152	—
Sawtooth alloy wheels, SC1	400	348	—
Includes 195/60R15 tires.			
Teardrop alloy wheels, SC2	200	174	—

SUBARU LEGACY

Subaru Legacy GT

Specifications

	4-door notchback	5-door wagon
Wheelbase, in.	101.6	101.6
Overall length, in.	178.9	181.9
Overall width, in.	66.5	66.5
Overall height, in.	53.5	54.7
Curb weight, lbs.	2730	2825
Cargo vol., cu. ft.	14.3	71.0
Fuel capacity, gals.	15.9	15.9
Seating capacity	5	5
Front head room, in.	38.0	38.4
Max. front leg room, in.	43.1	43.1
Rear head room, in.	36.0	37.8
Min. rear leg room, in.	34.8	35.6

Powertrain layout: longitudinal front engine/front-wheel drive or permanent 4WD.

Engines

	ohc flat-4	Turbo ohc flat-4
Size, liters/cu. in.	2.2/135	2.2/135
Horsepower @ rpm	130 @ 5600	160 @ 5600

	ohc flat-4	Turbo ohc flat-4
Torque (lbs./ft.) @ rpm	137 @ 4400	181 @ 2800
Availability	S	S[1]
EPA city/highway mpg		
5-speed OD manual	23/31	19/25
4-speed OD automatic	22/29	18/23

1. Sport Sedan and Touring Wagon.

Built in Lafayette, Ind., and Japan.

PRICES

Subaru Legacy	Retail Price	Dealer Invoice	Fair Price
L 4-door notchback, 5-speed w/SW equipment	$13999	$12693	$12893
L 5-door wagon, 5-speed w/SW equipment	14999	13599	13799
L 4-door notchback, 4-speed automatic w/YW equipment	16450	14605	14805
L 5-door wagon, 4-speeed automatic w/YW equipment	17150	15225	15425
L 4-door notchback, 5-speed w/HW equipment	16450	14605	14805
L 5-door wagon, 5-speed w/HW equipment	17150	15225	15425
L 4-door notchback, 4-speed automatic w/HW equipment	17250	15326	15526
L 5-door wagon, 4-speed automatic w/HW equipment	17950	15946	16146
L 4-door notchback, 4-speed automatic w/RW equipment	18245	16199	16399
L 5-door wagon, 4-speed automatic w/RW equipment	18945	16819	17019
L AWD 4-door notchback, 5-speed w/HW equipment	18050	16024	16224
L AWD 5-door wagon, 5-speed w/SW equipment	16499	14959	15159
L AWD 4-door notchback, 4-speed automatic w/HW equipment	18850	16745	16945
L AWD 5-door wagon, 4-speed automatic w/YW equipment	18750	16644	16844
L AWD 4-door notchback, 4-speed automatic w/RW equipment	19845	17618	17818

Prices are accurate at time of publication; subject to manufacturer's change.

	Retail Price	Dealer Invoice	Fair Price
L AWD 5-door wagon, 5-speed, w/HW equipment	$18750	$16644	$16844
L AWD 5-door wagon, 4-speed automatic w/HW equipment	19550	17365	17565
L AWD 5-door wagon, 5-speed, w/RW equipment	19745	17517	17717
L AWD 5-door wagon, 4-speed automatic w/RW equipment	20545	18238	18438
LS 4-door notchback, 4-speed automatic	19700	17379	17579
LS 5-door wagon, 4-speed automatic	20400	17994	18194
LS AWD 4-door notchback, 4-speed automatic	21300	18784	18984
LS AWD 5-door wagon, 4-speed automatic	22000	19400	19600
LSi AWD 4-door notchback, 4-speed automatic	21850	19226	19426
LSi AWD 5-door wagon, 4-speed automatic	22850	20104	20304
Sport Sedan 4-door notchback, 5-speed	21400	18873	19073
Sport Sedan 4-door notchback, 4-speed automatic	22200	19594	19794
Sun Sport 5-door wagon, 5-speed	18400	16475	16675
Sun Sport 5-door wagon, 4-speed automatic	19200	17196	17396
Outdoor AWD 5-door wagon, 5-speed	19000	16894	17094
Outdoor AWD 5-door wagon, 4-speed automatic	19800	17615	17815
GT AWD 5-door wagon, 5-speed	19700	17594	17794
GT AWD 5-door wagon, 4-speed automatic	20500	18315	18515
Alpine Sport AWD 5-door wagon, 5-speed	19900	17794	17994
Alpine Sport AWD 5-door wagon, 4-speed automatic	20700	18515	18715
Touring Wagon AWD 5-door, 4-speed	23200	20454	20654
Destination charge	445	445	445

Prices are for vehicles distributed by Subaru of America. Prices may be higher in areas served by independent distributors.

Standard Equipment:

L with SW equipment: 2.2-liter 4-cylinder engine, 5-speed manual transmission, front wheel drive or permanent 4-wheel drive, 4-wheel disc brakes, driver-side air bag, power steering, power mirrors, cloth reclining front bucket seats, 60/40 split folding rear seat with trunk pass-through, tilt steering column with memory, intermittent wipers, rear wiper washer (wagon), tachometer, tinted glass, remote fuel door release, rear defogger, bodyside moldings, 185/70HR14 all-season tires. **L with YW equipment** adds: 4-speed automatic transmission, air conditioning, AM/FM radio. **L with HW equipment** adds to L with YW equipment: 5-speed manual or 4-speed automatic transmission, cruise control, power windows and door locks, digital clock, AM/FM cassette player with graphic equalizer. **L with RW equipment** adds to L with HW equipment: anti-lock 4-wheel disc brakes. **LS** add to L with RW equipment: power moonroof with sunshade, variable intermittent wipers, rear center armrest (notchback), cloth headliner, leather-wrapped steering wheel, AM/FM cassette and CD player, power antenna, door courtesy lights, air suspension (wagon), lighted visor mirrors, alloy wheels. **LSi** adds to LS: leather upholstery and door trim panels. **Sport Sedan and Touring Wagon** add to L with RW equipment: 2.2-liter turbocharged 4-cylinder engine, sport reclining front bucket seats with driver-side height adjustment, suede upholstery, sport suspension, functional hood scoop, front air dam, rear spoiler (Sport Sedan), leather-wrapped steering wheel, power moonroof with sunshade, AM/FM cassette and CD player, power antenna, lighted visor mirrors, 195/60HR15 all-season tires, alloy wheels. **Sun Sport wagon** adds to L front wheel drive wagon with HW equipment: power moonroof, AM/FM cassette and CD player, power antenna, woven cloth upholstery, front air dam, aero side and rear effects, exterior graphics, color-keyed grille, luggage rack with bicycle attachment, polished 7-spoke alloy wheels. **Outdoor wagon** adds to L AWD wagon with HW equipment: air suspension, engine block skid plate, passenger-side underseat storage tray, woven cloth upholstery, luggage rack with bicycle attachment, rear cargo area mat, cargo net, exterior graphics, color-keyed grille, front and rear mud guards, mag-type wheel covers. **GT wagon** adds to L AWD wagon with HW equipment: anti-lock 4-wheel disc brakes, raised roof design, AM/FM cassette and CD player, aero side and rear effects, roof rails, front air dam, mesh alloy wheels, woven cloth upholstery, **Alpine Sport Wagon** adds to L AWD wagon with HW equipment: anti-lock 4-wheel disc brakes, power engine block skid plate, engine block heater, luggage rack with ski attachment, AM/FM cassette and CD player, rear cargo area mat, exterior graphics, color-keyed grille, front and rear mud guards, polished 7-spoke alloy wheels.

Optional Equipment:	Retail Price	Dealer Invoice	Fair Price
Metallic paint	$120	$100	$107

Prices are accurate at time of publication; subject to manufacturer's change.

TOYOTA CAMRY

Toyota Camry SE 2-door

Specifications

Specifications	2-door notchback	4-door notchback	5-door wagon
Wheelbase, in.	103.1	103.1	103.1
Overall length, in.	187.8	187.8	189.4
Overall width, in.	69.7	69.7	69.7
Overall height, in.	54.9	55.1	56.3
Curb weight, lbs.	2910	2932	3175
Cargo vol., cu. ft.	14.9	14.9	74.8
Fuel capacity, gals.	18.5	18.5	18.5
Seating capacity	5	5	7
Front head room, in.	38.4	38.4	39.2
Max. front leg room, in.	43.5	43.5	43.5
Rear head room, in.	37.4	37.1	38.8
Min. rear leg room, in.	33.0	35.0	34.7

Powertrain layout: transverse front engine/front-wheel drive.

Engines

Engines	dohc I-4	dohc V-6
Size, liters/cu. in.	2.2/132	3.0/180
Horsepower @ rpm	130 @ 5400	188 @ 5200
Torque (lbs./ft.) @ rpm	145 @ 4400	203 @ 4400
Availability	S	O[1]
EPA city/highway mpg		
5-speed OD manual	23/30	
4-speed OD automatic	21/28	18/25

1. LE, XLE; standard, SE.

Built in Georgetown, Ky., and Japan.

PRICES

Toyota Camry	Retail Price	Dealer Invoice	Fair Price
DX 2-door notchback, 5-speed	$16428	$13882	$14928
DX 2-door notchback, automatic	17228	14558	15728
LE 2-door notchback, automatic	19268	16281	17768
LE V-6 2-door notchback, automatic	21588	18242	20088
SE V-6 2-door notchback, automatic	22618	19112	21118
DX 4-door notchback, 5-speed	16718	14127	15218
DX 4-door notchback, automatic	17518	14803	16018
DX 5-door wagon, automatic	18968	16028	17468
LE 4-door notchback, automatic	19558	16527	18058
LE 5-door wagon, automatic	20968	17718	19468
XLE 4-door notchback, automatic	21618	18159	20118
SE V-6 4-door notchback, automatic	22908	19357	21408
LE V-6 4-door notchback, automatic	21878	18487	20378
LE V-6 5-door wagon, automatic	23308	19695	21808
XLE V-6 4-door notchback, automatic	23978	20142	22478
Destination charge	385	385	385

Prices are for vehicles distributed by Toyota Motor Sales, U.S.A., Inc. The dealer invoice, fair price, and destination charge may be higher in areas served by independent distributors.

Standard Equipment:

DX: 2.2-liter DOHC 4-cylinder engine, 5-speed manual or 4-speed automatic transmission, driver- and passenger-side air bags, power steering, tachometer, coolant temperature gauge, trip odometer, cloth reclining front bucket seats, split folding rear seat with armrest, remote fuel door and trunk releases, rear defogger, dual remote outside mirrors, front door pockets, tilt steering column, cup holders, auto-off headlamps, intermittent wipers, rear wiper (wagon), AM/FM radio, tinted glass, 195/70HR14 all-season tires. **LE** adds: 2.2-liter DOHC 4-cylinder or 3.0-liter DOHC V-6 engine, 4-speed automatic transmission, 6-way manual driver's seat, air conditioning, cruise control, power windows, door locks, and mirrors, cassette player, power antenna, upgraded interior trim, door courtesy lights (2-door), 205/65HR15 all-season tires, alloy wheels (2-door). **SE** adds to DX: 3.0-liter DOHC V-6 engine, 4-speed automatic transmission, air conditioning, cruise control, 7-way power driver's seat, cassette player, power antenna, power windows, door locks and mirrors, sport suspension, rear spoiler, leather-wrapped steering wheel and parking brake handle, passenger-side visor mirror, 205/65VR15 all-season tires, alloy wheels. **XLE** adds to LE: power moonroof, 7-way power driver's seat, illuminated entry, map light, lighted visor mirrors, variable-intermittent wipers, alloy wheels. V-6 models have 4-wheel disc brakes.

Optional Equipment:	Retail Price	Dealer Invoice	Fair Price
Anti-lock brakes, 4-cyl. models	$1100	$902	$1045
Includes rear disc brakes.			
V-6 models	950	779	903
Anti-lock brakes and third seat, 4-cyl. wagon	1415	1154	1344
Includes rear disc brakes.			
V-6 wagon	1265	1031	1202
Air conditioning	975	780	926
Power Seat Pkg., LE 2-door	340	272	323
7-way power driver's seat.			
Folding third seat, 4-cyl. wagon	465	375	442
V-6 wagon	315	252	299
Leather trim, XLE and LE 2-door	1030	824	979
SE	975	780	926
Cruise control, DX	265	213	252
Power moonroof, SE and LE	960	760	903
Includes map lights and sunshade.			
Power door locks, DX 4-door and wagon	260	208	247
DX 2-door	220	176	209
AM/FM cassette, DX	170	127	162
Premium AM/FM cassette, (NA DX)	405	304	385
CD player, SE and XLE	1205	904	1145
Mud guards	50	40	48
Alloy wheels, LE	400	320	380
LE V-6	420	336	399

TOYOTA CELICA

Specifications	2-door notchback	3-door hatchback
Wheelbase, in.	99.9	99.9
Overall length, in.	177.0	174.0
Overall width, in.	68.9	68.9
Overall height, in.	51.0	50.8
Curb weight, lbs.	2560	2580
Cargo vol., cu. ft.	10.6	16.2
Fuel capacity, gals.	15.9	15.9
Seating capacity	4	4

Toyota Celica GT 2-door

	2-door notchback	3-door hatchback
Front head room, in.	38.3	38.3
Max. front leg room, in.	43.1	43.1
Rear head room, in.	34.9	34.9
Min. rear leg room, in.	26.6	26.6

Powertrain layout: transverse front engine/front-wheel drive.

Engines	dohc I-4	dohc I-4
Size, liters/cu. in.	1.8/108	2.2/132
Horsepower @ rpm	110 @ 5600	135 @ 5400
Torque (lbs./ft.) @ rpm	115 @ 2800	145 @ 4400
Availability	S[1]	S[2]
EPA city/highway mpg		
5-speed OD manual	27/34	23/29
4-speed OD automatic	26/32	23/30

1. ST. 2. GT.

Built in Japan.

PRICES

Toyota Celica	Retail Price	Dealer Invoice	Fair Price
ST 2-door notchback, 5-speed	$16168	$13824	—
ST 2-door notchback, automatic	16968	14508	—
GT 2-door notchback, 5-speed	18428	15664	—
GT 2-door notchback, automatic	19228	16344	—

Prices are accurate at time of publication; subject to manufacturer's change.

	Retail Price	Dealer Invoice	Fair Price
ST 3-door hatchback, 5-speed	$16508	$14114	—
ST 3-door hatchback, automatic	17308	14798	—
GT 3-door hatchback, 5-speed	18898	16063	—
GT 3-door hatchback, automatic	19698	16743	—
Destination charge	385	385	385

Fair price not available at time of publication. Prices are for vehicles distributed by Toyota Motor Sales, U.S.A., Inc. The dealer invoice, fair price, and destination charge may be higher in areas served by independent distributors.

Standard Equipment:

ST: 1.8-liter DOHC 4-cylinder engine, 5-speed manual or 4-speed automatic transmission, driver- and passenger-side air bags, power steering, cloth 4-way adjustable front sport seats, center console with armrest, split folding rear seat, dual cup holders, digital clock, rear defogger, remote fuel door and trunk/hatch releases, map lights, coolant temperature gauge, tachometer, trip odometer, intermittent wipers, auto-off headlamps, tinted glass, dual outside mirrors, AM/FM radio with four speakers, visor mirrors, cargo area cover (hatchback), 185/70R14 all-season tires. **GT** adds: 2.2-liter DOHC 4-cylinder engine, 4-wheel disc brakes, AM/FM cassette with six speakers, power antenna, power windows and door locks, tilt steering column, intermittent rear wiper (hatchback), upgraded door and interior trim, engine oil cooler (5-speed), 205/55VR15 all-season tires.

Optional Equipment:

	Retail Price	Dealer Invoice	Fair Price
Anti-lock brakes	825	676	—
Air conditioning	975	780	—
Power Pkg., ST	510	408	—
Power windows and locks.			
Leather trim, GT	1045	836	—
Includes power driver's seat, leather-wrapped steering wheel, shift knob and parking brake lever. Requires Power Pkg.			
Leather Sport Pkg., GT 3-door hatchback	1565	1252	—
Leather sport seats, leather-wrapped steering wheel, shift knob and parking brake lever, front sport suspension, alloy wheels.			
Fabric Sport Pkg., GT 3-door hatchback	905	724	—
Cloth sport seats, leather-wrapped steering wheel, shift knob and parking brake lever, front sport suspension, alloy wheels.			
Rear spoiler, hatchbacks	375	300	—

	Retail Price	Dealer Invoice	Fair Price
Intermittent rear wiper, ST hatchback	$155	$127	—
Tilt steering column, ST	155	133	—
Sunroof	740	592	—
Cruise control	265	212	—
Cassette player, ST	170	127	—
Premium cassette player with six speakers, GT	365	273	—
Premium audio system with CD player, GT	1205	903	—
Alloy wheels, GT	420	336	—

TOYOTA COROLLA

Toyota Corolla LE

Specifications	4-door notchback	5-door wagon
Wheelbase, in.	97.0	97.0
Overall length, in.	172.0	172.0
Overall width, in.	66.3	66.3
Overall height, in.	53.5	55.3
Curb weight, lbs.	2315	2403
Cargo vol., cu. ft.	12.7	64.8
Fuel capacity, gals.	13.2	13.2
Seating capacity	5	5
Front head room, in.	38.8	38.8
Max. front leg room, in.	42.4	42.4
Rear head room, in.	37.1	39.7
Min. rear leg room, in.	33.0	33.0

Powertrain layout: transverse front engine/front-wheel drive.

Engines

	dohc I-4	dohc I-4
Size, liters/cu. in.	1.6/97	1.8/110
Horsepower @ rpm	105 @ 5800	115 @ 5600
Torque (lbs./ft.) @ rpm	100 @ 4800	115 @ 4800
Availability	S[1]	S[2]
EPA city/highway mpg		
5-speed OD manual	27/34	27/34
3-speed automatic	26/29	
4-speed OD automatic		26/32

1. Base 4-door. 2. DX, LE.

Built in Fremont, Calif., Canada, and Japan.

PRICES

Toyota Corolla	Retail Price	Dealer Invoice	Fair Price
4-door notchback, 5-speed	$12098	$10767	$11267
4-door notchback, automatic	12598	11212	11712
DX 4-door notchback, 5-speed	13188	11340	11840
DX 4-door notchback, automatic	13988	12028	12528
LE 4-door notchback, automatic	16328	13993	14493
DX 5-door wagon, 5-speed	14298	12295	12795
DX 5-door wagon, automatic	15098	12984	13484
Destination charge	385	385	385

Standard Equipment:

1.6-liter DOHC 4-cylinder engine, 5-speed manual or 3-speed automatic transmission, driver- and passenger-side air bags, cloth reclining front bucket seats, console with storage, coolant temperature gauge, trip odometer, remote decklid and fuel door release, auto-off headlights, cup holders, color-keyed bumpers, wheel covers, tinted glass, 175/65R14 all-season tires. **DX** adds: 1.8-liter DOHC 4-cylinder engine, 5-speed manual or 4-speed automatic, power steering, dual remote mirrors, passenger visor mirror, cloth door trim with map pockets, full cloth seats with headrests, rear seat headrests, 60/40 split rear seat, bodyside moldings, rear luggage lamp, digital clock, intermittent wipers, rear cargo cover and power hatch lock (wagon), 185/65R14 all-season tires. **LE** adds: 4-speed automatic transmission, air conditioning, power windows and door locks, cruise control, 4-way adjustable driver's seat, power mirrors, dual visor mirrors, tachometer, variable intermittent wipers, AM/FM cassette radio with four speakers, tilt steering column.

Optional Equipment:

	Retail Price	Dealer Invoice	Fair Price
Anti-lock brakes	$825	$676	$743
Air conditioning, base and DX	920	736	828
Power steering, base	260	222	234
Alloy wheels, LE	400	320	360
Value Pkg., base	845	761	803
Air conditioning, power steering, floormats.			
Value Pkg., DX 4-door	1615	1454	1534
Air conditioning, tilt steering column, Power Pkg., deluxe AM/FM cassette player with four speakers, floormats.			
Value Pkg., LE	1640	1476	1558
Anti-lock brakes, sunroof, deluxe AM/FM cassette player with four speakers, alloy wheels, floormats.			
Convenience Pkg., base	1180	958	1062
Includes power steering, air conditioning.			
Tilt steering column, DX	155	133	140
Power sunroof, DX 4-door, LE	580	464	522
Includes map lights.			
Rear wiper, wagon	175	143	158
Radio Prep Pkg., base and DX	100	75	90
Includes two speakers, wiring harness, antenna.			
AM/FM radio with four speakers, base and DX	385	289	347
AM/FM cassette with four speakers, base and DX	555	416	500
LE	170	127	153
Power Pkg., DX	620	496	558
Power windows and locks.			
Tachometer, DX with 5-speed	65	52	59
Cruise control, DX	265	212	239
Includes variable intermittent wipers.			
All Weather Guard Pkg., base, 5-speed	235	191	212
Base, automatic	245	199	221
DX	65	55	59
Rear defogger, heavy duty battery, heater and wiper motor.			
Rear window defogger, base	170	136	153

TOYOTA PASEO

Specifications

	2-door notchback
Wheelbase, in.	93.7

Prices are accurate at time of publication; subject to manufacturer's change.

Toyota Paseo

	2-door notchback
Overall length, in.	163.2
Overall width, in.	65.2
Overall height, in.	50.2
Curb weight, lbs.	2070
Cargo vol., cu. ft.	7.7
Fuel capacity, gals.	11.9
Seating capacity	4
Front head room, in.	37.7
Max. front leg room, in.	41.1
Rear head room, in.	32.0
Min. rear leg room, in.	30.0

Powertrain layout: transverse front engine/front-wheel drive.

Engines	dohc I-4
Size, liters/cu. in.	1.5/90
Horsepower @ rpm	100 @ 6400
Torque (lbs./ft.) @ rpm	91 @ 3200
Availability	S
EPA city/highway mpg	
5-speed OD manual	28/34
4-speed OD automatic	26/32

Built in Japan.

PRICES

Toyota Paseo	Retail Price	Dealer Invoice	Fair Price
2-door notchback, 5-speed	$12838	$11169	$11569

	Retail Price	Dealer Invoice	Fair Price
2-door notchback, automatic	$13638	$11865	$12265
Destination charge	385	385	385

Prices are for vehicles distributed by Toyota Motor Sales, U.S.A., Inc. The dealer invoice, fair price, and destination charge may be higher in areas served by independent distributors.

Standard Equipment:

1.5-liter DOHC 4-cylinder engine, 5-speed manual or 4-speed automatic transmission, power steering, driver-side air bag, cloth reclining bucket seats, door map pockets, tinted glass, tachometer, trip odometer, digital clock, variable intermittent wipers, AM/FM radio, rear defogger, cup holders, remote trunk and fuel door releases, folding rear seat, 185/60R14 tires.

Optional Equipment:

	Retail Price	Dealer Invoice	Fair Price
Anti-lock brakes	825	676	784
Air conditioning	900	720	855
Cruise control	265	212	252
Pop-up glass moonroof	400	320	380
Includes sunshade and storage pouch.			
AM/FM cassette with four speakers	315	236	299
All Weather Guard Pkg.	65	54	62
Heavy duty battery, rear defogger with timer, heater.			
Alloy wheels	400	320	380
Rear spoiler	375	300	356

TOYOTA PREVIA

Specifications

	4-door van
Wheelbase, in.	112.8
Overall length, in.	187.0
Overall width, in.	70.8
Overall height, in.	68.7
Curb weight, lbs.	3535
Cargo vol., cu. ft.	157.8
Fuel capacity, gals.	19.8
Seating capacity	7
Front head room, in.	39.4
Max. front leg room, in.	40.1

Prices are accurate at time of publication; subject to manufacturer's change.

Toyota Previa LE

	4-door van
Rear head room, in.	38.5
Min. rear leg room, in.	36.6

Powertrain layout: longitudinal mid-engine/rear-wheel drive or permanent 4WD.

Engines

	dohc I-4	Supercharged dohc I-4
Size, liters/cu. in.	2.4/149	2.4/149
Horsepower @ rpm	138 @ 5000	161 @ 5000
Torque (lbs./ft.) @ rpm	154 @ 4000	201 @ 3600
Availability	S	S[1]
EPA city/highway mpg		
4-speed OD automatic	17/22	18/23

1. S/C models.

Built in Japan.

PRICES

Toyota Previa	Retail Price	Dealer Invoice	Fair Price
DX 2WD, automatic	$22818	$19509	$20009
LE 2WD, automatic	26578	22591	23091
LE S/C 2WD	28158	23934	24434
DX All-Trac, automatic	26148	22226	22726
LE All-Trac, automatic	29718	25260	25760